A Guide to
Co-Teaching

3 EDITION

A Guide to
Co-Teaching

New Lessons and Strategies to Facilitate Student Learning

3 EDITION

Richard A. Villa
Jacqueline S. Thousand
Ann I. Nevin

CORWIN

A SAGE Company

CORWIN
A SAGE Company

FOR INFORMATION:

Corwin

A SAGE Company

2455 Teller Road

Thousand Oaks, California 91320

(800) 233-9936

www.corwin.com

SAGE Publications Ltd.

1 Oliver's Yard

55 City Road

London EC1Y 1SP

United Kingdom

SAGE Publications India Pvt. Ltd.

B 1/I 1 Mohan Cooperative Industrial Area

Mathura Road, New Delhi 110 044

India

SAGE Publications Asia-Pacific Pte. Ltd.

3 Church Street

#10-04 Samsung Hub

Singapore 049483

Acquisitions Editor: Jessica Allan

Associate Editor: Julie Nemer

Editorial Assistant: Lisa Whitney

Production Editor: Cassandra Margaret Seibel

Copy Editor: Kim Husband

Typesetter: C&M Digitals (P) Ltd.

Proofreader: Caryne Brown

Indexer: Jean Casalegno

Cover Designer: Anupama Krishnan

Permissions Editor: Karen Ehrmann

Printed in the United States of America.

A catalog record of this book is available from the Library of Congress.

ISBN 978-1-4522-5778-5

This book is printed on acid-free paper.

SUSTAINABLE FORESTRY INITIATIVE

Certified Chain of Custody
Promoting Sustainable Forestry
www.sfiprogram.org
SFI-01268

SFI label applies to text stock

13 14 15 16 17 10 9 8 7 6 5 4 3 2 1

Contents

List of Tables and Figures

List of Tables

List of Figures

Letter to the Reader

Do you remember when you first knew that you were meant to be a teacher? Ann Nevin remembers being a first grader in a one-room schoolhouse on Troy Road in Schenectady, New York, when the teacher asked her to explain to an older classmate how to do a math problem. Richard Villa reflected daily on the teaching methods used by the nuns during his second-grade year, thinking that if his teachers taught in different ways, more of his classmates would be successful. Jacqueline Thousand similarly recalls playing teacher with her younger brother, who had to endure, from the time Jacqueline was in kindergarten, hours of her replicating what her teacher had done that day in school. We have in common the fact that we all fell in love with teaching at an early age, but we also share the fact that our sole model of teaching was the *lone arranger* model until well into our careers as educators.

Fortunately, we have learned a great deal about co-teaching through our co-teaching experiences with one another and with many other educators over the years. The most important thing that we have learned is that we greatly prefer co-teaching to teaching alone. Why? There are at least three reasons: IQ, CQ, and EQ. Our IQs (intelligence quotients) improve exponentially with a co-teaching partner's knowledge added to the experience, whereas our CQs (creativity quotients) increase because of the synergy that comes with problem solving with another person. Our EQs (emotional quotients) increase because of the interpersonal interactions that we have with our co-teaching partners. We have also noticed an increased appreciation and valuing of people who have different cultural heritages, knowledge bases, opinions, practices, and beliefs. We wrote this book so that you, too, might enjoy more fun, more creativity, more productivity, and more effective outcomes for your students. Each chapter is the result of our co-teaching with each other and collaborating to write this book. Aside from our own personal and professional experiences, there are many other reasons to prefer co-teaching and argue for the use of co-teaching arrangements in all schools. We hope you can add your own reasons as you explore better ways to teach.

New to This Edition

New to the third edition of *A Guide to Co-Teaching: New Lessons and Strategies to Facilitate Student Learning* are the following:

- a new title reflecting additions to lessons and strategies that facilitate student learning
- a new chapter on preparing co-teachers through co-teaching in clinical practice with examples of novice student teachers planning and co-teaching with their cooperating teachers (Chapter 11)
- updated chapters on the role of paraprofessionals as co-teachers (Chapter 8) and students as co-teachers (Chapter 9)
- an expanded discussion of the roles and responsibilities of administrators, including additional ideas for scheduling for co-teaching, and their role in instructional observation and coaching (Chapter 10)
- updated references throughout the book based on current collaborative and co-teaching research
- an expanded discussion on response to intervention (RTI)
- additional lesson plans in the Resources section linked to common core state standards and use of technology
- additional forms and tools to assist co-teaching teams in establishing trust, improving communication, and best utilizing planning time
- more detailed descriptions regarding the four approaches to co-teaching reflecting best-practice, teaching in a co-teaching environment, and observing co-taught classes
- an expanded Resources section

Acknowledgments

Corwin gratefully acknowledges the contributions of the following individuals:

Kevin Braney, Principal
Boulder High School
Boulder Valley School District
Boulder, CO

Elizabeth Garza, Associate
    Professor
School of Education
California State University San
    Marcos
San Marcos, CA

Rhonda Haniford, Principal
Centaurus High School
Boulder Valley School District
Boulder, CO

Ida Malian, Professor
Arizona State University
Phoenix, AZ

Julie Rich, Coordinator
Single Subject Credential Program
School of Education
California State University San
    Marcos
San Marcos, CA

Jodi Robledo, Assistant Professor
School of Education
California State University San
    Marcos
San Marcos, CA

Patricia Stall, Associate Professor
School of Education
California State University San
    Marcos
San Marcos, CA

Deborah Toups, Director of Special
    Education
Sequoia Union High School District
Redwood City, CA

About the Authors

Dr. Richard A. Villa is president of Bayridge Consortium, Inc., in San Diego, California. His primary field of expertise is the development of administrative and instructional support systems for educating all students within general education settings. Dr. Villa is recognized as an educational leader with the commitment and the conceptual, technical, and interpersonal skills to inspire and work collaboratively with others in order to implement current and emerging exemplary educational practices. This has resulted in the inclusion of children with intensive cognitive, physical, and emotional challenges as full members of the general education community in the school districts where he has worked and with which he has consulted. Dr. Villa has been a classroom teacher, special education administrator, pupil personnel services director, and director of instructional services. Dr. Villa provides training and coaching in co-teaching, differentiation of instruction, inclusive education, and systems change. He has presented at international, national, and state educational conferences and has provided technical assistance to departments of education in the United States, United Kingdom, Canada, Vietnam, Laos, and Honduras and to university personnel, public school systems, and parent and advocacy organizations. He has authored 15 books and more than 100 articles and book chapters. Dr. Villa is known for his enthusiastic, humorous style of presenting. Additional information about Dr. Villa can be found at www.ravillabayridge.com.

Dr. Jacqueline S. Thousand is a professor in the School of Education of the College of Education, Health and Human Services at California State University San Marcos, where she teaches special and general education professional preparation and master's-level courses and works with local school districts on school reform initiatives. Before moving to California, she taught at the University of Vermont, where she directed inclusion facilitator and early childhood–special education graduate and postgraduate professional preparation programs and coordinated federal grants, all concerned with the inclusion of students with disabilities in local schools. Dr. Thousand is a nationally known teacher, author, systems change consultant, and disability rights advocate. She has authored numerous books, research articles, and chapters on issues related to differentiated instruction and universal design, collaborative teaming and teaching, creative problem solving, cooperative group learning, organizational change, inclusive education, and positive behavioral supports. She is actively involved in international teacher education endeavors and serves on the editorial boards of several national and international journals.

Dr. Ann I. Nevin, professor emeritus at Arizona State University and faculty affiliate at Chapman University (Orange, CA), is a scholar and teacher educator who graduated magna cum laude from the University of Minnesota with a Ph.D. in educational psychology. As a hearing-impaired monolingual (English) female from a second-generation family of American Irish and German descent, Ann understands the importance of developing meaningful relationships with people who have been marginalized due to their cultural and linguistic heritages and whose voices have often been silenced or ignored. Her doctoral research focused on improving the effectiveness of educators and administrators who teach students with special learning needs. Ann's advocacy, research, and teaching include more than 40 years of working with a diverse array of people to help students with disabilities succeed. She co-developed various innovative teacher education programs in Vermont, Arizona, California, and Florida. She is actively involved in special-interest groups of the American Educational Research Association and is the author of books, research articles, and chapters.

PART I

Introduction to Co-Teaching

The first part of this third edition of *A Guide to Co-Teaching: New Lessons and Strategies to Facilitate Student Learning* comprises three chapters. Chapter 1 introduces you to the basics of co-teaching. It describes what co-teaching is and is not, presents the key elements of co-teaching, and describes the four approaches to co-teaching. Chapter 2 examines the historical origins of and the legal support for co-teaching. It shares the research and documented benefits of co-teaching for students and teachers. Chapter 3 introduces three co-teaching teams that are revisited throughout Part II of the book to illustrate the four approaches.

What Is Co-Teaching?

Topics Included in This Chapter:

❖ What co-teaching is not
❖ What is co-teaching?
❖ What does co-teaching look like?
❖ The elements of co-teaching
❖ Importance of systemic supports

1

We just found out that we are expected to co-teach. What is co-teaching? What is it not? What elements or variables need to be in place so that we know we are really co-teaching? Is there a process that will help us successfully co-teach? The answers to these questions are discussed in this chapter.

WHAT CO-TEACHING IS NOT ■

Although the concept of co-teaching is not new in education, there are many teaching arrangements that have been promoted in the history of American education that may look like co-teaching. If you are a person who learns from nonexemplars, then the following discussion may be helpful.

Using your own experience as a guide, can you think of nonexemplars for what co-teaching is not? We can think of several from our experience.

Co-teaching is not one person teaching one subject followed by another who teaches a different subject. Many teachers are familiar with this structure if their students travel in groups within a departmentalized administrative framework. In this case, however, the teachers often do not have time to plan or evaluate instruction. Instead, they are responsible for covering the subject matter individually within their curriculum areas (e.g., science), and then the math teachers are then replaced by the language arts teachers and so on.

Co-teaching is not one person teaching one subject while another person prepares instructional materials at the photocopier in the teachers' workroom or corrects papers in the teachers' lounge. This is a familiar arrangement for those teachers who have the luxury of working with a paraprofessional, a parent, or a community volunteer in the classroom.

Co-teaching is also not occurring when one teacher conducts a lesson and others stand or sit by and watch. This often happens when there are observers or volunteers who come into the classroom with no specific function or assignment.

Co-teaching is not happening when the ideas of one person prevail for what is to be taught or how it will be taught. This type of structure often occurs when a group of would-be co-teachers defer to the eldest, to the person with the most presumed authority, or to the person with the most convincing voice.

Finally, co-teaching is not simply the assignment of someone to act as a tutor. For example, the early schoolmistresses and schoolmasters in one-room schoolhouses were known to use older students to help teach younger students. It is not known to what extent the older student had input in the selection of the lesson, design, and delivery of the lesson, and so on. Many of those student helpers went on to normal schools to become teachers themselves. In this case, the student was an assistant teacher often assigned to teach individuals or groups of pupils while the schoolmistress taught another individual or group.

Instead, the 21st-century notion of co-teaching places it within the context of some of the most innovative practices in education. The reassignment of existing personnel to co-teaching teams results in a knowledge and skill exchange among team members and higher teacher-to-student ratios, outcomes that benefit more students than the individual student in need of intensive instructional support. Skrtic (1991) considers this a dynamic structure in which complex work is more likely to be accomplished and novel instruction is more likely to be crafted to meet individual student needs.

■ WHAT IS CO-TEACHING?

Co-teaching is two or more people sharing responsibility for teaching all of the students assigned to a classroom. It involves the distribution of responsibility among people for planning, differentiating instruction, and monitoring progress for a classroom of students. Co-teaching is a fun way for students to learn from two or more people who may have different ways of thinking or teaching. Some people say that co-teaching is a creative way to connect with and support others to help all children learn. Others say that co-teaching is a way to make schools more effective. Co-teaching can be likened to a healthy marriage or other committed partnership. Partners must establish trust, develop and work on communication, share the chores, celebrate, work together creatively to overcome the inevitable challenges and problems, and anticipate conflict and handle it in a constructive way.

■ WHAT DOES CO-TEACHING LOOK LIKE? FOUR APPROACHES

Co-teaching has many faces. In a national survey, teachers experienced in meeting the needs of students in a diverse classroom reported that they used four predominant approaches to co-teaching—supportive, parallel, complementary, and team teaching (Devecchi and Nevin 2010, Hehir and Katzman 2012, National Center for Educational Restructuring and Inclusion 1995).

Supportive Co-Teaching

Supportive co-teaching is when one teacher takes the lead instructional role and the other(s) rotates among the students to provide support. The co-teacher(s) taking the supportive role watches or listens as students work together, stepping in to provide one-to-one tutorial assistance when necessary, while the other co-teacher continues to direct the lesson. This is one of the two co-teaching approaches often favored by teachers who are new to co-teaching.

Parallel Co-Teaching

Parallel co-teaching is when two or more people work with different groups of students in different sections of the classroom. In parallel co-teaching, the co-teachers teach, monitor, or facilitate the learning of different groups of students, usually in the same room at the same time. Co-teachers rotate among the groups, and sometimes there may be one group of students that works without a co-teacher for at least part of the time. Teachers new to co-teaching often choose to begin with this approach.

Complementary Co-Teaching

Complementary co-teaching is when co-teachers do something to enhance the instruction provided by the other co-teacher(s). For example, one co-teacher might paraphrase the other's statements or model note-taking skills with a document projector. Sometimes, one of the complementary teaching partners preteaches the small-group social skill roles required for successful cooperative group learning and then monitors as students practice the roles during the lesson taught by the other co-teacher. As co-teachers gain confidence, complementary teaching and team teaching approaches are added to their repertoire.

Team Co-Teaching

Team co-teaching is when two or more people do what the traditional teacher has always done—plan, teach, assess, and assume responsibility for all of the students in the classroom. Team teachers share the leadership and the responsibilities. Co-teachers who team co-teach divide the lessons in ways that allow the students to experience each teacher's strengths and expertise. For example, for a lesson on inventions in science, one co-teacher whose interest is history will explain the impact on society. The other co-teacher, whose strengths are more focused on the mechanisms involved, explains how the particular inventions work.

The key to successful team co-teaching is that co-teachers simultaneously deliver the lessons. The bottom line and test of a successful team-teaching partnership is that the students view each teacher as knowledgeable and credible.

Under what circumstances can you envision using each of the four co-teaching approaches? Remember that while no one approach is better than another, ultimately, supportive co-teaching should be the least utilized approach. When deciding which to use, the goal always is to improve the educational outcomes of your students through the selected co-teaching approach. Each approach has value, and each approach has cautions associated with its use. In subsequent chapters of this book, we explain each of the four co-teaching approaches in detail. Many people who are beginning to co-teach start with supportive and parallel co-teaching because these approaches involve less structured coordination with members of the co-teaching team. Gradually, as co-teaching skills and relationships strengthen, co-teachers add complementary and team-teaching co-teaching, which require more time, coordination, and trust, to their repertoire.

■ THE ELEMENTS OF CO-TEACHING

Our definition represents an integration of our firsthand experiences with other school-based teams that actively support students in heterogeneous learning environments (Villa and Thousand 2004) and our reading of the literature on cooperative group learning (Johnson and Johnson 1999, 2009), collaboration and consultation (Fishbaugh 1997, 2000; Friend and Cook 2009; Hourcade and Bauwens 2002; Idol, Nevin, and Paolucci-Whitcomb 2000), and cooperation (Brandt 1987). Enhancing the initial definition presented in the previous paragraph, a co-teaching team may be defined as two or more people who agree to do the following:

1. Coordinate their work to achieve at least one *common, publicly agreed-on* goal (i.e., improved student outcomes). Effective coordination requires purposeful planning time.

2. Share a *belief system* that supports the idea that each of the co-teaching team members has unique and needed expertise

3. Demonstrate *parity* by alternatively engaging in the dual roles of teacher and learner, expert and novice, giver and recipient of knowledge or skills

4. Use a *distributed functions theory of leadership* in which the task and relationship functions of the traditional lone teacher are distributed among all co-teaching team members

5. Use a *cooperative process* that includes face-to-face interaction, positive interdependence, interpersonal skills, monitoring co-teacher progress, and individual accountability

Each of these factors is explained in more detail in the following sections.

Common, Agreed-On Goals

Some co-teachers begin with an agreement to collaborate in planning to differentiate for students who are struggling to learn. Their successes in planning together then lead them to agree to co-teach together for a longer period of time (e.g., instructional thematic units for a 6-week period of time). Other co-teachers may volunteer to co-teach together for a school year. And some co-teachers are assigned a partner and told that they will be co-teaching. The most successful co-teaching teams spend time, up front, discussing and agreeing upon shared goals or outcomes such as increasing student access to the curriculum and their ability to differentiate instruction for their diverse learners. These co-teachers learn that combining their unique expertise, skills, and resources results in the achievement of their goals, whether better outcomes for the students in the co-taught classrooms or the enhancement of their own effectiveness in instruction.

Shared Belief System

Co-teachers agree not only that they teach more effectively as a team but that their students also learn more effectively. The presence of two or more people with different knowledge, skills, and resources allows the co-teachers to learn from each other. Often individuals decide to become co-teachers as a result of taking inservice courses in specific instructional methods, such as cooperative group learning or differentiated instruction. Having a shared language to discuss teaching and learning is both an outcome and a necessary component of co-teaching.

Parity

Parity occurs when co-teachers perceive that their unique contributions and their presence on the team are valued. Treating each member of the co-teaching team with respect is a key to achieving parity. Co-teaching members develop the ability to exchange their ideas and concerns freely, regardless of differences in knowledge, skills, attitudes, or position. Soliciting opinions and being sensitive to the suggestions offered by each co-teacher are especially important when there is a perception of unequal status because of position, training, or experience. Parity between a teacher and a paraprofessional, for example, could be demonstrated when the paraprofessional uses his or her unique knowledge to enhance a lesson developed with the teacher. Reciprocally, the teacher is in an expert role when the paraprofessional imitates a teaching-learning procedure that the teacher has demonstrated. The outcome is that each member of the co-teaching team gives and takes direction for the co-teaching lesson so that the students can achieve the desired benefits.

Distributed Functions Theory of Leadership

Nancy Keller, an experienced co-teacher from Winooski, Vermont, states that as a member of a co-teaching team, "I do everything a normal teacher would do except that now there are two or more people doing it" (personal communication). What is important about this statement is the implicit recognition that co-teachers must agree to redistribute their classroom leadership and decision-making responsibilities among themselves. This phenomenon of role redistribution in which the functions of the traditional lone leader or lone teacher are divided among members of a team is known as the *distributed functions theory of leadership* (Johnson and Johnson 1999, 2009). There are functions or jobs that occur before, during, and after each lesson; co-teachers must decide how they will distribute these jobs from one lesson to the next. Some responsibilities must occur daily, others weekly or periodically, and still others once or twice a year. Teachers decide how the content will be presented—for example, one person may teach while the other(s) facilitates follow-up activities, or all members may share in the teaching of the lesson, with clear directions for when and how the teaching will occur. Another decision involves identifying the teacher who communicates with parents and administrators. Some co-teachers decide that co-teaching team members will rotate that responsibility. Still another decision involves describing how co-teaching team members will arrange to share their expertise; some decide to observe one another and practice peer coaching. Remember, when co-teachers make these decisions, they will experience more success if they use the cooperative process described in the next section.

Cooperative Process

There are five elements that facilitate cooperative processes: face-to-face interactions, positive interdependence, interpersonal skills, monitoring co-teacher progress, and individual accountability. Each of the five elements is now defined in more detail.

Face-to-Face Interactions

Face-to-face interaction is an important element for co-teachers as they make several important decisions. Co-teachers need to decide when and how often they will meet as well as how much time meetings will take during school hours. They need to decide when others (e.g., parents, specialists, paraprofessionals, psychologists) should be involved. They also need to develop a system for communicating information when formal meetings are not scheduled (e.g., a communication log book at the teachers' desk, Post-it notes on the bulletin board of the classroom). Face-to-face interactions are necessary for co-teachers to make these and other critical decisions.

Positive Interdependence

Positive interdependence is the heart of co-teaching. It involves the recognition that no one person can effectively respond to the diverse psychological and educational needs of the heterogeneous groups of students found in typical 21st-century classrooms. Co-teachers create the feeling that they are equally responsible for the learning of all students to whom they are now assigned and that they can best carry out their responsibilities by pooling their diverse knowledge, skills, and material resources. To establish positive interdependence, co-teachers can establish a common goal, create rewards for and celebrate their success, and divide the labor of the planning, delivery of instruction, and assessment.

Interpersonal Skills

Interpersonal skills include the verbal and nonverbal components of trust, trust building, conflict management, and creative problem solving. Such social interaction skills are needed for achieving the distribution of leadership functions and for ensuring that all students are making adequate progress. Individual co-teachers will find that they are functioning at different interpersonal skill levels, depending on their previous training, mastery of curriculum content, personality styles, communication preferences, and the number of colleagues with whom they are assigned to co-teach. Effective co-teacher partnerships encourage each member to improve his or her social skills by giving feedback and encouragement to each other.

Monitoring Co-Teacher Progress

Monitoring refers to the process of frequently debriefing about the successes and challenges of co-teaching lessons. Co-teachers check in with each other to determine whether (1) the students are achieving the lesson's learning goals, (2) the co-teachers are using good communication skills with each other, and (3) the learning activities need to be adjusted. Methods of monitoring can range from very simple to more complex. For example, some co-teachers use a checklist on which they each literally check off their agreed-on responsibilities. Some co-teachers set up a brief, 15-minute meeting each day while their students are at recess to discuss the three aspects of monitoring (goals, communication skills, adjusting the activities). Co-teaching team members also can take turns sharing accomplishments, reporting on what each one contributed to the success of the lesson, and making suggestions about what might need to be changed to improve the lesson.

Individual Accountability

Individual accountability is the engine of co-teaching. It is clear that co-teaching is effective based on the actual delivery of skills and knowledge by each co-teacher as well as each one's follow-through with respect to agreed-upon commitments such as preparing differentiated materials for a lesson. Individual accountability is a form of acknowledging the importance of the actions from each co-teacher. Individual accountability in co-teaching involves taking time to assess the individual performance of each partner for one or more of four purposes. One purpose is to increase partners' perceptions of their contributions to the co-teaching endeavor. A second purpose is to provide partners with recognition for their contributions. Yet another is to determine whether any adjustments need to be made in any of the partners' co-teaching roles and actions. A final purpose is to identify when one or more of the partners may need assistance (e.g., some modeling or coaching, access to additional resources or supports) to increase effectiveness in the performance of assigned roles and responsibilities.

You will see how the five elements of the cooperative process operate in varying degrees for each of four approaches to co-teaching—supportive, parallel, complementary, team teaching—that are defined in Chapter 3 and illustrated in Chapters 4 through 7.

■ IMPORTANCE OF SYSTEMIC SUPPORTS

Administrative support is another reason for the successful and beneficial outcomes of co-teaching. Beneficial outcomes increase when a school principal, assistant principal, or instructional coach works with the faculty to provide systematic professional development, establish coaching and mentoring opportunities for learning new ways of working together, and arrange master schedules so that co-teachers can plan together. An important aspect of administrative support is realizing that new roles and responsibilities emerge as a result of changing the way that teachers, paraprofessionals, related services personnel, and students work together. Parts II and III of this book illustrate the new roles and relationships that co-teaching affords adults and students. In Part IV, you learn about professional development and logistical and administrative supports that promote systematic development of co-teaching in schools (Chapter 10). Chapter 11 describes a paradigm shift in teacher preparation by detailing how some universities are preparing teaching candidates through a co-teaching clinical supervision model. Chapters 12 and 13 of Part IV offer guidelines for meshing planning with co-teaching activities and tips for communicating and managing conflict so that you thrive rather than merely survive with your co-teachers. In Chapter 14, you meet two middle-level teachers who show how they developed a shared voice through their individual and shared professional development activities. We hope you can agree that, although systemic support is important and valued, your individual action is even more important—you know that you can take action even in the absence of systemic supports. We are always inspired by Margaret Mead (an American anthropologist), who writes, "Never doubt that a small group of thoughtful, committed people can change the world; indeed it's the only thing that ever has." We hope you count yourself and your co-teacher among those people.

Why Co-Teach?

What History, Law, and Research Say

2

Topics Included in This Chapter:

❖ What are the origins of co-teaching?
❖ How does federal law support co-teaching?
❖ What are the benefits of co-teaching?
❖ What accounts for the benefits of co-teaching?
❖ Summary

Why do we devote the second chapter of this book to the tracing of the historical origins, the legal rationale, and the documented benefits of co-teaching? As you begin to co-teach, there will be those who ask you to explain or defend your co-teaching practice. This chapter offers you critical information to support your practice of co-teaching and your beliefs and experiences about the benefits of co-teaching. It is also an interesting account for those of you who enjoy knowing the historical context and the rationale for what you do.

WHAT ARE THE ORIGINS OF CO-TEACHING? ■

Do you wonder where the idea of co-teaching originated? The history and evolution of co-teaching in U.S. schools can be traced back to the 1960s, when it was popularized as an example of progressive education. In the 1970s, co-teaching was advanced by legislated school reforms and the need to modify instruction for a more diverse student population. By the 1990s, studies of the effectiveness of school-based collaborative activities, with co-teaching as one example, appeared in the research and practice literature. School personnel began to trust that co-teaching led to results that were valued by students, their teachers, parents, the larger community, and boards of education. For example, in an early synthesis of collaborative consultation research, the emerging data for preschool through high school levels indicated that students with disabilities at all grade levels could be educated effectively in general education environments, making both academic and social gains, when teachers, support personnel, and families collaborated (Villa et al. 1996). Another comprehensive study by Walther-Thomas (1997) evaluated co-teaching models in 23 schools across eight school districts. Outcomes included improved academic and social skills of low-achieving students, improved attitudes and self-concepts reported by students with disabilities, and more positive peer relationships. Students perceived that these improvements were the result of more teacher time and attention. The co-teachers themselves (general and special education teachers) reported professional growth, personal support, and an enhanced sense of community within the general education classrooms. The most frequently mentioned drawback was the lack of staff development to learn how to be more effective co-teachers. They might have benefited from a book like this!

■ HOW DOES FEDERAL LAW SUPPORT CO-TEACHING?

Federal legislative changes, such as those required by the Individuals with Disabilities Education Improvement Act (IDEIA) of 2004 (Pub. L. No. 108–446) and the 2001 reauthorization of the Elementary and Secondary Education Act (ESEA; Pub. L. No. No. 107–110) commonly referred to as the No Child Left Behind Act (NCLB), have focused attention on students with increasingly diverse learning characteristics achieving high academic performance in general education. To illustrate the recent increase in student diversity, data from the U.S. Department of Education (2010) indicate that the proportion of students with disabilities with primary placements (80% of the school day or more) in general education increased from 45.73% in 1992 to 53.65% in 2006, an increase of nearly 8 percentage points. These proportions can be expected to increase given national trends over the past three decades and IDEIA's requirement to include students with disabilities as full participants in rigorous academic and general education curriculum and assessment. Changing legal requirements and student demographics combine to point to the need for increased collaborative planning and teaching among school personnel who are attempting to comply with legal mandates. Co-teaching is one cost-efficient, legally available supplementary aid and service that can be brought to general education to serve the needs of students with (and without) disabilities through IDEIA.

The stated goal of NCLB is "to close the achievement gap with accountability, flexibility, and choice, so that no child is left behind" (U.S. Department of Education 2007). As with IDEIA, NCLB's requirements for high standards and student performance are intended to foster conditions that lead to better instruction and learning, equality of opportunity to learn, and excellence in performance for all children. The specific conditions fostered by this comprehensive act are (1) the preparation, training, and recruitment of high-quality teachers; (2) language instruction for students with limited English proficiency and children of migrant workers; (3) schools equipped for the 21st century; (4) informed parental choice; (5) innovative and research-based instructional programs, particularly in literacy; and (6) accountability for educational outcomes.

A promising NCLB requirement is for all teachers to meet the standards that would certify them as highly qualified. According to NCLB, all teachers must demonstrate subject matter competence in every subject area they teach. Historically, special educators and teachers of students who are learning English often were responsible for teaching the core academic subjects (i.e., language arts, social studies, science, mathematics) to students with special needs or students learning English in separate classrooms. With the advent of NCLB and the 2004 IDEIA clarifications about the *highly qualified* requirements for special educators, it is now established that special educators must have an academic major or advanced degree and pass a competency exam or be deemed competent based on a *high objective uniform state standard of evaluation* (HOUSSE) in each academic subject they teach. In other words, for special educators to continue to teach core academic subjects only to children with disabilities, they now must obtain or demonstrate a rigorous background in each core academic subject taught.

The conference report accompanying the IDEIA amendments (H. Rep. No. 108–77) also clarifies that special educators could be considered highly qualified with their state credential or license without the additional subject matter requirements described in the last paragraph if their instruction was consultative in nature and included adjustments to the learning environment, modifications of instructional methods, and curricular adaptations. What this means is that a special educator co-teaching with a general educator can simultaneously address the *highly qualified* dilemma (i.e., by having the general educator be the highly qualified content teacher for students) and achieve the desired IDEIA outcome of increasing the time that students eligible for special education spend in general education core content area classes.

Creating co-teaching partnerships between highly qualified general educators, who have demonstrated subject area expertise, and special educators, who have complementary expertise in specialized content and strategies for adjusting curriculum, instruction, and the learning environment, also increases the probability of implementing the research-based curricular and instructional approaches required by NCLB and the general education early intervention—response to intervention (RTI)—approaches forwarded by IDEIA (Villa and Thousand 2011). It also should be noted here that experts have identified co-teaching as an important service-delivery approach for improving the conversational and instructional skills of students learning English (Bahamonde and Friend 1999; Mahoney 1997).

The inclusion of students with language and learning differences and their teachers in general education through co-teaching arrangements, combined with the practices required by NCLB and supported by the early intervention thrust of IDEIA, should actually help teachers in today's standards-based classrooms. All students need their teachers to learn and use the most effective teaching strategies, educational materials, and lesson formats currently known. Teachers can accomplish this by exchanging such information and expertise through their co-teaching partnerships.

In summary, at the heart of IDEIA and NCLB is the goal of increasing the achievement for all students—students with and without disabilities, students learning English, students who are considered disadvantaged. Legal trends, then, reinforce the notion that teachers and other school personnel (e.g., special educators, related services personnel such as speech and language therapists, teachers of students learning English, gifted and talented education educators) can no longer be most effective as isolated professionals. Moreover, as this book goes to press, nearly all states have adopted the national Common Core State Standards. Co-teaching partnerships are particularly important for educators across the nation to both implement new curriculum standards and differentiate instruction in order to provide students with learning and language differences access to these rigorous standards.

Parents, teachers, school administrators, and experts from across the country, together with state leaders, through their membership in the Council of Chief State School Officers (CCSSO) and the National Governors Association Center for Best Practices (NGA Center), lead the effort to develop a common core of state standards. Collaboration in planning and teaching provides a vehicle to assist educators in introducing and implementing these new standards for curriculum, assessment, and instruction. Given that many special educators and teachers of students who are English language learners do not have mastery of the grade-level curriculum standards and many general education teachers do not have skills to facilitate learning for diverse learners, a model for collaborative ESL and special education service delivery, including time and planning for teachers to work together to help students meet the standards, is essential.

■ WHAT ARE THE BENEFITS OF CO-TEACHING?

What are the documented benefits of co-teaching for teachers, students, and schools? The findings of a metasynthesis of qualitative research on co-teaching conducted by Scruggs, Mastropieri, and McDuffie (2007) revealed that collaboration between general and special educators enhanced the quality of instruction and supports for students with and without disabilities in a number of ways. For example, the students in co-taught classes were perceived to be more cooperative with one another. Students with disabilities were seen as benefitting from increased attention and access to positive peer models in general education co-taught classrooms. Co-teachers themselves identified an exchange of skills, resulting in increased competence in their colleague's respective areas of expertise (e.g., content mastery, classroom management, curricular adaptation). Schwab Learning (2003) studied the impact of collaborative partnerships and co-teaching. At 16 California schools, staff members and parents made a commitment that (1) every child would learn and be successful and (2) every teacher would be responsible for every learner. Teachers, administrators, and support staff creatively arranged for every student to receive blended services from Title I teachers, reading specialists, special educators, paraprofessionals, and so on. Results included decreased referrals to intensive special education services, increased overall student achievement, fewer disruptive problems, less paperwork, increased number of students qualifying for gifted and talented education, and decreased referrals for behavioral problems. In addition, teachers reported being happier and not feeling so isolated. New research on the impact of co-teaching and inclusion for students in secondary schools indicates similar results (e.g., Cramer, Lister, Nevin, and Thousand 2010; Dieker and Murawski 2003; Dove and Honigsfeld 2010; Villa et al. 2005).

Studies that document the impact of placement—where a student with disabilities is educated—are important because co-teaching is one method of providing an inclusive educational placement. Blackorby and colleagues (2005) reported on a comprehensive study of 11,000 students in the United States, which showed that students with disabilities who spend more time in general education classrooms are absent less, perform closer to grade level than their peers in pullout settings, and have higher achievement test scores. Although students with disabilities were found to perform overall more poorly than their same-grade peers without disabilities, overall, the study confirmed that students with disabilities in general education settings academically outperformed their peers who were educated in segregated settings when standards-based assessments were used.

What does the research say about students with a variety of instructional needs in co-teaching classrooms? Co-teaching is effective for students with a variety of instructional needs, including English language learners (Mahoney 1997; Pardini, 2006), those with hearing impairment (Compton et al. 1998; Kluwin 1999; Luckner 1999), those with learning disabilities (Rice and Zigmond 2000; Trent 1998; Welch 2000), high-risk students in a social studies class (Dieker 1998), general and special education students in a co-taught inquiry-based science class (Brisca-Vega, Brown, and Yasutake 2011), and students in a language remediation class (Miller, Valasky, and Molloy 1998). To illustrate, Welch showed that students with disabilities and their classmates all made academic gains in reading and spelling on curriculum-based assessments in the co-taught classrooms. Likewise, Caywood and Fordyce (2006) found that when general and special education co-teachers incorporated assistive technology into a restructured curriculum, peer assistance, one-on-one tutorials, cooperative group learning, activity-based instruction with supports through co-teaching, and systematic paraprofessional instruction in differentiated instruction so as to decrease student dependence on paraprofessionals (see Chapter 8), students with autism were successfully included in the co-taught high school language arts classrooms. Mahoney (1997) found that in addition to meeting educational needs, "for special education students, being part of the large class meant making new friends" (p. 59).

How is impact measured? According to research published since the first edition of this book, prevalent measures have included teacher grades and student scores on standardized achievement tests in math and reading (e.g., Garrigan and Thousand 2005; Magiera et al. 2005). As pointed out in a comprehensive critique of the literature on collaborative teaching (Thousand, Villa, and Nevin 2007), some researchers have examined the impact of co-teaching on the participating teachers through classroom observations and text analysis of teachers' verbatim responses to questionnaires, surveys, and interviews (e.g., Cramer and Nevin 2006; Magiera et al. 2005; Salazar and Nevin 2005; Santamaria and Thousand 2004). Rarely have researchers or practitioners analyzed the impact of co-teaching on other variables. However, in an earlier study by Vaughn and colleagues

(1998), measures were developed to account for friendships, self-concept, and peer acceptance. Students' perceptions of co-teaching in a secondary-level literacy class were studied by Wilson and Michaels (2006). Both general and special education students reported having positive experiences in the co-taught classroom.

Recent achievement results in school systems in which the authors have provided training and coaching show the impact of co-teaching. The schools have reported a variety of ways to measure the impact. For example, the principal of Boulder High School in Colorado was concerned with the high rate of D and F grades assigned to students in science, language arts, math, and world language classrooms. He assigned special educators to co-teach in those subject areas, resulting in a decrease in the percentage of D and F grades assigned to students in co-taught classrooms. The greatest gains occurred in Biology, Algebra 1, and Language Arts 9 and 10 (Villa et al., 2012). A principal in a second Boulder Valley high school, Centaurus, analyzed semester grade distribution data for students with and without disabilities in co-taught language arts, math, science, and social studies classrooms as compared to peers with and without disabilities placed in the same courses taught by a single teacher. Results indicated that the learning rate of both peers with and without disabilities was higher in all subject areas in the co-taught classrooms (Villa et al., 2012). In Gilroy, a northern California school district with two high schools composed of student populations with similar demographic profiles, one of the high schools implemented inclusive educational placements, co-teaching, and differentiated instruction while the other high school continued with traditional pullout resource room service delivery without a focus on differentiation in general education classrooms. After 1 year, students with disabilities in the inclusive co-taught and differentiated high school had a greater than 30% passing rate on the California High School Exit Exam in language arts and math than did students with disabilities in the high school implementing traditional practices (i.e., English/language arts 51% as compared to 21% and for math 55% as compared to 32% (Toups, D., personal communication, April 2012). Between 2003 and 2005, the gap in reading achievement for English language learners in the St. Paul Public Schools in Minnesota, where English language teachers and general education teachers co-teach at all grade levels, decreased from 13 to 6 percentage points, and in math, the gap decreased from 6.7 to 2.7 percentage points. When compared to students statewide, the district's students outscored their peers in reading and math for 3 years prior to the publication of the results as measured by the Test of Emerging Academic English (Pardini, 2006, p. 21).

Van Gardener, Sturmont, and Goel (2012) conducted a meta-analysis of research in which achievement gains were reported when general and special education teachers collaborated. Of the 23 studies they included, 7 showed both social and academic gains. Other researchers have documented the actions taken by general and special educators as they implement co-teaching (e.g., Garrigan and Thousand 2005; Magiera et al. 2005; Pugach and Winn 2011). The lack of agreement about what constitutes meaningful impact in co-teaching research may explain some discrepancies in results (e.g., Zigmond 2004). Research results could be improved and be more helpful to teachers if multiple measures were used to examine not only student achievement but also student social, self-esteem, and friendship development, as well as co-teachers' development of instructional competence, confidence, and self-efficacy (Thousand et al. 2007).

WHAT ACCOUNTS FOR THE ■ BENEFITS OF CO-TEACHING?

Modeling of Collaborative Skills and Increased Teacher Responsiveness

What can account for positive results such as those described here? First, co-teaching allows students to experience and imitate the cooperative and collaborative skills that teachers show when they co-teach. All students benefit when their teachers share ideas, work cooperatively, and contribute to one another's learning. There is a growing research base to support this claim. As previously suggested, with multiple instructors, there is increased flexibility in grouping and scheduling, thus making it possible for students to experience less wait time for teacher attention and increased time on task, an important factor documented to increase achievement.

Two Heads Are Better Than One

Second, co-teaching provides a greater opportunity to capitalize on the unique, diverse, and specialized knowledge, skills, and instructional approaches of the co-teachers (Bauwens, Hourcade, and Friend 1989; Hourcade and Bauwens 2002). For example, when content area teachers co-teach with education specialists such as special educators, reading specialists, or teachers of English learners, they meld their differing expertise. Stated otherwise, the expertise of the *masters of content*—the content area teachers—is blended with and supported by the expertise of the *masters of access*—the specialists in differentiating instruction. The result is a broader range of students having access to the core curriculum. Further, the higher teacher-to-student ratio that results allows for more immediate and accurate diagnoses of student needs and more active student participation in a variety of learning situations. Students and their teachers say they have more fun and feel better about the work they do while in co-taught classrooms, and principals and superintendents appreciate the increased community spirit at schools where co-teaching prevails.

Opportunities to Use Research-Based Interventions

Third, teachers who co-teach often find that they can structure their classes to more effectively use research-proven strategies required of both NCLB and the early intervention proposals of IDEIA. For example, Miller and colleagues (1998) described how a co-teacher team (a special educator, a general educator, and two paraprofessionals) integrated whole- and small-group instruction, peer teaching, and small cooperative learning groups to provide language-remediation activities within the general education curriculum. More recent research shows that differentiated instruction can be employed through co-teaching in classrooms with a wide variety of individual student differences and in multicultural and urban elementary, middle, and high schools (see, e.g., Cramer et al. 2006; Garrigan and Thousand 2005; Salazar and Nevin 2005).

Increased Capacity to Problem Solve and Individualize Learning

Fourth, co-teaching and other collaborative activities are vehicles for inventing solutions that traditional bureaucratic school structures have failed to conceptualize. Because team structures bring together people with diverse backgrounds and interests, their shared knowledge and skills often generate novel methods to individualize learning (Nevin et al. 1990; Skrtic 1987). In fact, collaborative co-teaching arrangements can be found in model schools in which all students (including students with severe disabilities) are educated in general education classrooms in their neighborhood schools (Villa and Thousand 2004). In interviews with 95 peer collaborators and 96 others who were not collaborating, Pugach and Johnson (1995) found that those in the peer-collaboration group had reduced referral rates to special services, increased confidence in handling classroom problems, increased positive attitudes toward the classroom, and more tolerance toward children with cognitive deficits. Powerful outcomes such as these encourage administrators, advocates, and even state departments of education (Arguelles, Hughes, and Schumm 2000) to adopt cooperative models such as co-teaching for the effective education of students with disabilities.

Empowerment of Co-Teaching Partners

Fifth, teachers view co-teaching as a way to become more empowered. There is evidence to suggest that teachers feel empowered when they can make decisions collaboratively (Duke, Showers, and Imber 1980). They report increases in their skills (Thousand, Nevin, and Fox 1987), and they experience increased higher-level thinking and generate more novel solutions (Thousand et al. 1995). Other valued outcomes include increased attendance and participation at team meetings, persistence in working on difficult tasks, and attainment of the overall team goals (Johnson and Johnson 2005).

Teacher satisfaction in co-teaching arrangements also has been linked to basic needs satisfaction. Glasser (1999) proposed that people choose to do what they do because it satisfies one or more of the five basic human needs: survival, power over or control of one's life, freedom and choice, a sense of belonging, and fun. Specifically, each teacher's potential for survival and power in educating a diverse student body creates opportunities for regular exchange of needed resources, expertise, technical assistance, and professional growth through reciprocal experiences. In co-teaching, teachers experience a sense of belonging and freedom from isolation by having others with whom to share the responsibility for accomplishing the challenging tasks of teaching in classrooms of diverse students. It is fun to problem solve creatively and to engage in stimulating adult dialogue and social interactions.

Based on interviews of co-teachers that we have conducted over the past two decades, co-teaching can help educators meet these five basic needs. For example, teachers report that co-teaching helps meet the need for survival and power because it promotes perspective taking, increases student–teacher direct contact time, and increases the number of students who get the help they need. Co-teaching helps meet the need for freedom and choice because it can facilitate a shared responsibility for all children, provide opportunities to work with a variety of students, and reduce the amount of direct support needed from administrators. Co-teaching helps meet the need for belonging because it can alleviate isolation, motivate a commitment to others, increase social support, and allow for integration of specialists' expertise into the classroom. Co-teaching helps meet the need for fun by enabling creativity, providing someone to laugh and talk with, creating a positive learning environment, and improving staff morale.

SUMMARY ■

In summary, co-teaching may offer the following beneficial outcomes:

1. Students develop better attitudes about themselves, academic improvement, and social skills.

2. Teacher-to-student ratio is increased, leading to better teaching and learning conditions.

3. Teachers are able to use research-proven teaching strategies effectively.

4. A greater sense of community is fostered in the classroom.

5. Co-teachers report professional growth, personal support, and enhanced motivation.

6. Increased job satisfaction can be experienced because needs for survival, power, freedom and choice, a sense of belonging, and fun are met.

Co-teaching provides a vehicle for teachers and students to move from feelings of isolation and alienation to feelings of community and collaboration. In other words, the lone arranger model of teaching is replaced with a co-teacher model. We hope you agree that the effort required by co-teaching is worth it because it results in happier and more successful children as well as more competent and confident faculty.

The Day-to-Day Workings of Co-Teaching Teams

3

Topics Included in This Chapter:

❖ Who co-teaches?
❖ Meet three co-teaching teams
❖ Roles and responsibilities of co-teaching partners
❖ Issues to resolve in planning co-teaching lessons
❖ Tracking the use of the four co-teaching approaches
❖ How do we know that we truly are co-teaching?

W ho co-teaches? Give us an example of an elementary, middle-level, and high school co-teaching team. How do we start? What are our roles and responsibilities when we co-teach? What are the roles and responsibilities of our partners? What are some of the issues that we will inevitably encounter? How does the co-teaching team resolve these issues? The answers to these questions are addressed in this chapter and elaborated upon in subsequent chapters.

WHO CO-TEACHES? ■

Practically anyone who has an instructional role in a school can co-teach: classroom teachers, paraprofessionals, special and bilingual educators, English language learning specialists, teacher librarians, content specialists such as reading teachers, support personnel such as speech and language therapists and school psychologists, volunteers, and students themselves. Returning to the marriage or committed partnership analogy introduced in Chapter 1, in our international and multicultural world, there are marriages in which partners may be very different or quite similar with regard to the culture, life history, or language that they bring to the marriage.

Which couples might have the more difficult time communicating? We have asked this question numerous times. The majority of people who respond suggest that people who come from different backgrounds or different cultures might have a more difficult time communicating, at least initially. Co-teachers with different content-area expertise, training backgrounds, or teaching experiences—essentially people who come from different cultures and speak different professional languages—may have a more difficult time communicating, at least initially.

As an old saying goes, however, although we get together on the basis of our similarity, we grow because of our differences. As in a successful marriage, once partners figure out and understand each other's perspectives, they are no longer just two individuals, but a union that is fundamentally different from each person alone. Furthermore, because of their differing perspectives, experiences, and skills, they create a synergy that is greater than either of their individual strengths.

Meet Three Co-Teaching Teams

How we co-teach is best explained by examples. In the following vignettes, you meet teachers who use the four co-teaching approaches explained in this book. Later, we peek into their classrooms to see how they implement supportive, parallel, complementary, and team-teaching approaches to co-teaching. Table 3.1 introduces you to the teachers at a glance, showing their names, their co-teaching partner(s), and the curriculum areas for which they are responsible.

Table 3.1 Meet the Co-Teaching Team Members

Meet the Partners	Co-Teaching Role(s)	Curriculum Area(s)
Elementary		
Ms. Gilpatrick	Combination first- and second-grade classroom teacher	All core areas
Ms. Hernandez	Paraprofessional	
Ms. Nugent	Speech and language therapist	
Middle Level		
Mr. Silva	Science, math, and English language learning teacher	Science, math, language arts, and social studies
Ms. Spaulding	Special educator	
Ms. Kurtz	Language arts and social studies teacher	
Ms. Olvina	Paraprofessional	
High School		
Mr. Woo	Social studies teacher	Social studies
Mr. Viana	Special educator	

An Elementary Co-Teaching Team

Ms. Gilpatrick is a veteran teacher of 27 years who currently teaches first grade but over the course of her career has taught all of the elementary grades, K through 6, and has had up to 40 students in a class. Currently, she has 24 students in her combination first- and second-grade classroom. Four of the 24 students are eligible for special education, and three are new to the United States and are learning English. Three additional students are eligible for Title I supplemental support in literacy. One student is eligible for district Gifted and Talented Education (GATE) services.

Ms. Nugent is the school's speech and language therapist who has a strong interest in the language and literacy development of young learners and emerging readers. She is new to the school district but has 7 years of experience in elementary school settings. As part of her interview, she was told that the school would be experimenting with a new model of collaboration and co-teaching and that, if she took the job, she would be expected to work closely with the general education teachers and other support personnel. She agreed that this was something she was interested in doing, although it would be a new experience for her. Ms. Nugent has traditionally pulled students out of the classroom to work individually and in small groups for speech and language services.

One of the students eligible for special education has autism and has a part-time paraprofessional, Ms. Hernandez, who spends 3 hours a day in the classroom during the literacy and mathematics blocks. Ms. Hernandez is a recent high school graduate and is attending the university part time in the evenings. She hopes one day to be a teacher.

A new school year is approaching. The staff had been alerted in the previous year that there were changes on the horizon. They received an article describing the benefits of in-class student supports and the effectiveness of co-teaching arrangements as part of the response to intervention (RTI) approach for providing early intervention instruction and reducing special education referral (see Chapter 2 for a more detailed description of RTI). At the annual district inservice and planning week that precedes the new term, details of the new plan are presented by the principal and the grade-level representatives, who attended a 3-day summer institute on inclusion, differentiated instruction, co-teaching, and RTI. Classroom teachers, none of whom have had previous training or experience co-teaching, are introduced to the three-tiered RTI concept of differentiating instruction for all students. They are told that the district is committed to the education of students of varying learning styles and abilities in general education classrooms through collaboration with and support from Title I, bilingual, GATE, special education, and related service (e.g., speech and language) personnel.

Ms. Gilpatrick and Ms. Nugent are paired as a teaching team, along with the paraprofessional, Ms. Hernandez. As already noted, neither of the professional educators has had experience in collaborative teaching. They admit to one another and Ms. Hernandez that they are looking forward to the year with trepidation. The two teachers have many questions. How will they work with one another on a day-to-day basis? What will the role of the paraprofessional be with the student with autism, other students in the classroom, and the teachers? How will the people who provide extra instruction coordinate their activities (e.g., programs for Title I, bilingual, and GATE)? What administrative support, training, and planning time will be provided?

Ms. Hernandez, too, has questions. What will her responsibilities be in the classroom, and to whom should she report? She learns that at this point, no time has been scheduled into her school day or week to meet with the professional educators to learn how to do her job. She wonders how she will ask questions or offer suggestions and ideas. Although she believes she has a lot to contribute, she feels timid about expressing her concerns because she is young and not yet a certified teacher.

A Middle-Level Co-Teaching Team

Mr. Silva is a seventh- and eighth-grade science and mathematics teacher who is bilingual in Spanish and English. He has an endorsement as a teacher of English language learners. He is starting his third year of teaching at the same new, relatively large suburban middle school at which he taught his first two years. Mr. Silva teaches five periods—three periods of science and two periods of mathematics.

In Mr. Silva's first year of teaching, Ms. Olvina, a paraprofessional, was assigned to work with him in one of his science and one of his math classes to support the learning of several students with special needs. In his second year, Ms. Spaulding, a special educator who was hired at the same time as Mr. Silva, co-taught with him for one science class, and Ms. Olvina continued to provide support to students in one of Mr. Silva's other science classes and in one math class. This was Ms. Spaulding's first co-teaching experience. Although she would have preferred to teach language arts and social studies, her content-area strengths, she enjoyed getting to know more about the science curriculum and Mr. Silva's hands-on activities, cooperative-learning lessons, and strategies for making the content more comprehensible for English language learners. Mr. Silva thought that their first co-teaching experience worked relatively well. His big concern was that Ms. Spaulding was often pulled away from their classroom to attend emergency special education–related meetings with the principal, parents, students, and other teachers. Ms. Spaulding feels that Mr. Silva's lessons might be even more interesting and effective for the students if there were a greater use of technology.

This year, the school has been restructured into transdisciplinary teams, each of which will be jointly responsible for the education of a common group of students. The restructuring is the next step in the district's ongoing journey to detrack students in all of the content areas and to integrate the curriculum and faculty in heterogeneous, family-like clusters through 90-minute block-scheduling arrangements. Mr. Silva, Ms. Spaulding, Ms. Olvina, and a language arts and social studies teacher, Ms. Kurtz, have been clustered together as a teaching team. They must organize themselves and their instruction to ensure that the educational needs of all the students under their charge are met. As in all of the clusters, the students are heterogeneously grouped. The class size averages 26, with the natural proportion of students with varying characteristics and needs (e.g., students eligible for GATE services, Title 1, and English language learning support). A slightly disproportionate number of students are eligible for special education in this cluster (i.e., 17% compared with the district average of 13%), which has allowed for a full-time special educator and paraprofessional to be assigned to this team.

To support faculty and staff with the transformation to transdisciplinary teams, the central office has purchased several sets of DVDs and books regarding differentiated instruction, collaborative learning, co-teaching, and collaborating with students in instruction and decision making; these are available in a professional-development library that has been set up at each school in the district. These resources are frequently used during professional learning community (PLC) activities at the school sites. In addition, the district's inservice training events are focused expressly on developing teachers' co-teaching skills. Release time and substitutes have been provided so that every team can visit and talk with teachers at other middle schools and high schools that already have some experience with co-teaching and integrated-curriculum teaching arrangements.

A High School Co-Teaching Team

Mr. Woo is a high school social studies teacher who has been teaching for 12 years. He is very concerned with covering the curriculum and addressing social studies curriculum standards. His U.S. history class is a required course for high school graduation, and, although some might consider the content dry or boring, he works hard to develop instruction that will activate student interest. For example, he uses various active learning techniques (e.g., partner and cooperative group learning, role-plays, and debate); he places technology into the hands of the students; he arranges to take the class on field trips to government meetings, including meetings of the state board of education and county and state legislative committees. He strongly endorses service learning, a district graduation requirement, so he incorporates into the course syllabus and grading criteria multiple ways in which students can show what they know through community involvement.

Mr. Woo is known throughout the school for his high expectations of every student in his class. Although students consider his course one of the toughest, they routinely report liking it more than most of those they take.

Mr. Viana is a special educator who has been working with students in the 11th and 12th grades for 15 years. For the first time, he has been assigned to co-teach, and it happens to be with Mr. Woo. Mr. Viana previously taught students with disabilities in a resource room. Students came to his resource room from their general education classrooms, and he focused on teaching study skills, providing homework support, modifying tests, and remediating deficits. As a high school student, he attended the school at which he currently teaches, and he has lived in this community all of his life; he is a varsity track coach and is popular with the students and their parents, as well as with the faculty.

Mr. Woo is open to having another person, such as Mr. Viana, work as a co-teacher in his classroom. He is unsure of how to use this extra adult, however, because his students are so accustomed to supporting one another through the cooperative group learning and other active learning methods that he routinely employs. Mr. Woo is especially committed to student empowerment and worries that the special educator might attempt to hover, provide too much support, or prematurely intervene with unnecessary support in the students' group work or, conversely, that Mr. Viana might have nothing to do.

Mr. Viana is somewhat intimidated by Mr. Woo's reputation and his expertise in both content and instructional methodology. Like Mr. Woo, Mr. Viana is unsure of what his role will or should be in Mr. Woo's government classes.

ROLES AND RESPONSIBILITIES OF CO-TEACHING PARTNERS ■

There are many actions that co-teachers, including the co-teachers in the three teams just described, take before teaching, during teaching, and then after the lessons are taught. For example, before the lesson begins, co-teachers identify the resources and talents each member brings to the lesson, discuss the content areas that will be co-taught, analyze the students' needs in the class, and decide how student outcomes will be assessed. They often make up-front decisions, such as deciding which member of the co-teaching team will explain their arrangements to administrators and parents.

During teaching, effective co-teachers explain each teaching-team member's role to the students, dynamically communicate with each other to check perceptions, ask questions, reinforce each other, provide feedback, monitor student and teacher performance and compare with goals, and ask if progress is adequate or improvements are needed. Co-teaching teams can also arrange for a mentor or coach to observe their co-taught lessons and provide feedback to improve instructional outcomes.

After the lesson, effective co-teachers continue to communicate with and coach each other as they collaboratively reflect on the lessons just taught and plan future lessons and activities. They might decide to contact parents to support classroom activities, structure a skills-oriented lesson for students whom they have identified as needing extra instruction, or set up a new learning center to respond to students' interests. We believe that celebrating accomplishments, especially the small steps along the way, is an action to include after every lesson.

Some co-teacher actions must take place on a daily basis; others are necessary periodically or only once or twice a year. Examples of daily activities include giving feedback on homework and in-class assignments, recording student progress, and collecting necessary materials for each lesson. An activity that co-teachers should make sure to accomplish daily or weekly is to track their use of the various co-teaching approaches (i.e., supportive, parallel, complementary, and team), using the tracking form that appears in Table 3.2. This reflective exercise gives them feedback on which approaches they are currently utilizing and allows them to set goals to increase the use of the various approaches and minimize the use of supportive co-teaching. Additional weekly activities might include, for example, communicating with administrators and parents. Activities that occur only periodically include completing formal progress reports, conducting parent–teacher meetings, and structuring teaching assignments for the next year to include co-teaching.

■ ISSUES TO RESOLVE IN PLANNING CO-TEACHING LESSONS

As the previous discussion of actions that co-teachers take before, during, and after co-teaching suggests, members of a co-teaching team must clarify their roles related to various organizational, logistical, instructional, and communication issues. Table 3.3 highlights some of the questions that members of each team must answer for themselves. The sooner those co-teachers have the conversation about these questions, the better. Friend (2008) suggests that *pet peeves* are an important issue that should be discussed right up front. Returning to the marriage analogy, co-teachers might consider this set of conversations and agreements as their prenuptial conversation. It should be noted that answers to the questions change as team members have more experience with one another and with co-teaching. We therefore encourage co-teaching teams to periodically revisit and discuss the items in Table 3.3.

Co-teachers have found it helpful to decide on the actions for which they individually prefer to have input, primary responsibility, secondary responsibility, or equal responsibility. Table 3.4 offers an example of a

Table 3.2 Co-Teaching Tracking Form

Week of: _____

	Supportive	Parallel	Complementary	Team	Additional Notes
Monday					
Tuesday					
Wednesday					
Thursday					
Friday					
Notes and Plans for Next Week					

Use this tool to monitor, plan, and document your co-teaching experiences.

Supportive—One co-teacher takes the lead instructional role, and the others rotate among the students providing support. The co-teacher(s) taking the supportive role watches or listens as students work together, stepping in to provide assistance when necessary, while the other co-teacher continues to direct the lesson. The roles of lead and supportive co-teacher can be alternated.

Parallel—Two or more people work with or monitor different groups of students at the same time in different sections of the classroom. Co-teachers may rotate among the groups, and, sometimes there may be one group of students that works without a co-teacher for at least part of the time.

Complementary—All co-teachers have a role teaching the whole group. One may introduce the new academic content while the other makes it more accessible through complementary instruction (e.g., modeling how to take notes using different examples or analogies, paraphrasing, creating visuals).

Team—Co-teachers equitably share responsibility for what one teacher otherwise would have performed alone—namely, planning, teaching, and assessing the instruction of all assigned students. Co-teachers are comfortable using and do use each co-teaching approach based on the needs of students and the demands of the lesson.

Table 3.3 Co-Teaching Issues for Discussion and Planning

The strengths I bring to our team are . . .

Co-teacher A

- Content mastery
- Organized
- Hold high expectations for students

Co-teacher B

- Flexible
- Behavior management strategies
- Experience in differentiating for diverse learners
- Sense of humor

My fears about co-teaching are . . .

Co-teacher A

- Loss of control
- I am the only one held accountable as I am the instructor of record
- Watering down the curriculum
- Teaching with someone who doesn't know the curriculum

Co-teacher B

- Viewed as only a support person—not a real teacher
- Not being able to use my access skills
- Looking foolish teaching new content

Our 3 to 5 ground rules for operating as a team are . . .

1. What happens in Vegas stays in Vegas.

2. There will be no unspoken resentments. We will deal with any conflict in an open manner.

3. We will provide each other with only positive feedback for the first month.

Time for Planning

- How much time will we need?
- Where will we find the time that we need?
- How will we use our time together?
- What records can we keep to facilitate our planning?

Instruction

- What content will we include?
- Who will plan for what content?
- How will we share teaching responsibility?
- Who will adapt the curriculum and instructional and assessment procedures for select students?
- What are our strengths in the areas of curriculum, instruction, and assessment?
- What unique talents, interests, life experiences, and cultural heritage do each of us contribute to the instructional process?
- How will content be presented—will one person teach and the other(s) arrange and facilitate follow-up activities, or will all members share in the teaching of the lesson?

- How will we arrange to share our expertise? How can we arrange to observe one another and practice peer coaching?
- Will we rotate responsibilities?
- How will we assess the effectiveness of our instruction?

Student Behavior

- If we could each have only three class rules, what would those be?
- Who will decide on the disciplinary procedure?
- Who will carry out the disciplinary procedures and deliver consequences?
- How will we be consistent in dealing with behavior?
- How will we proactively address behavior?

Communication

- What types and frequency of communication do we each like to have with parents?
- How will we explain this collaborative teaching arrangement to the parents?
- Who will communicate with parents? Will there be shared responsibility for communication with parents of students with identified special education and other specialized needs, or will particular members of the co-teaching team have this responsibility?
- What frequency of communication do we each like to have with students?
- Who will communicate with students?
- How will we ensure regular communication with one another?
- Who will communicate with administrators?

Evaluation

- How will we monitor students' progress?
- How will we assess and grade students' performances?
- Who will evaluate which group of students—do team members collaborate in evaluating all students' performances, or is each team member primarily responsible for evaluating a subset of students?

Logistics

- How will we explain our co-teaching arrangement to the students and convey that we are equals in the classroom?
- How will we refer to each other in front of the students?
- How will teacher space be shared?
- How will the room be arranged?
- Who will complete the paperwork for students identified as eligible for special education?
- How will the decision be made to expand or contract team membership?
- How will a balance of decision-making power be maintained among co-teachers?

Pet Peeves

Co-Teacher A

- When my co-teacher shows up late
- When my partner misplaces his or her teaching materials and uses mine and I cannot locate my materials

Co-Teacher B

- When my co-teacher says "I" instead of "we" or "our"
- When a co-teacher doesn't follow through in preparing materials

Table 3.4   Sample Co-Teaching Roles and Responsibilities Matrix

Directions: Insert P, S, E, or I to designate level of responsibility. Plan to revise based on changes in co-teacher skills and/or student needs.

Responsibilities	Person Responsible			
	Name	Name	Name	Name
Develop units, projects, lessons				
Create advance organizers (e.g., concept map, lecture guide)				
Differentiate instruction				
Integrate technology into the lesson				
Monitor and assess student progress				
Assign grades				
Schedule/facilitate team meetings				
Assign responsibilities to paraprofessionals				
Train paraprofessionals				
Supervise paraprofessionals				
Recruit and train peer tutors				
Facilitate peer support and friendship				
Communicate with administrators				
Communicate with related service providers (e.g., speech)				
Communicate with parents				
Develop Individual Education Program (IEP) plans				
Other:				

CODE KEY:

        P = Primary responsibility

        S = Secondary responsibility

        E = Equal responsibility

        I = Input in the decision making

decision-making matrix that one co-teaching team created to help resolve their issues of how to distribute their roles and responsibilities. The matrix is not meant to be an exhaustive list of all of the responsibilities that a co-teaching team might take on, but rather a sampling of role-clarification decisions teachers frequently identify as important. Note that this team created a key that the co-teachers could use to indicate the degree to which each team member would take responsibility for a task (i.e., P = primary responsibility, S = secondary responsibility, E = equal responsibility, I = input in the decision making).

You will notice that Table 3.4 includes a subset of the issues that appear in Table 3.3, ones that this particular co-teaching team considered most important to attend to and track on a periodic basis. Table 3.4 could be viewed as the prenuptial agreement that resulted from the prenuptial conversation based on the items in Table 3.3. We encourage readers who are co-teachers or who become co-teachers to dip into the items in Table 3.3 to create their own version of Table 3.4.

HOW DO WE KNOW THAT ■ WE TRULY ARE CO-TEACHING?

The issues and responsibilities of co-teachers described in this chapter, as well as the research on collaborative teaming, reveal multiple dimensions of effective co-teaching. To highlight these dimensions, at the end of this book we offer (as Resource M) the Are We Really Co-Teachers? self-assessment, which co-teachers can use to track the progress of their co-teaching relationship. If you wish to preview this tool and use it as an advance organizer of information to come, please do so. You will find an example of its use in Table 11.3 in Chapter 11. If you do not use it as an advance organizer, know that it provides a nice synthesis of the information you will have read through Chapter 11. Finally, if you are interested in more details about the research and rationale for co-teaching on which this assessment is based, be sure to revisit Chapter 2.

PART II

The Four Approaches to Co-Teaching

In Part II, the elementary, middle-level, and high school co-teaching teams introduced in Chapter 3 are followed as they use each of the four co-teaching approaches. Chapter 4 describes and provides examples of *supportive* co-teaching and features vignettes of each of the three teams implementing the supportive approach across various curriculum areas. The chapter ends by analyzing how the cooperative process—face-to-face interaction, positive interdependence, interpersonal skills, monitoring, and accountability—was used by each of the three teams and by answering frequently asked questions about supportive co-teaching. Chapter 5 follows the same format as Chapter 4, but focuses on *parallel* co-teaching, highlighting seven variations of parallel co-teaching. Chapter 6 is devoted to *complementary* co-teaching, and Chapter 7 to the *team* co-teaching approach.

As you read about each of the four co-teaching approaches in the following chapters, you may find it helpful to use the advance organizer presented in Figure II.1 to compare and contrast what you are learning about the approaches. Can you detect the key features (i.e., differences) of each? What are some advantages and cautions for using each of the approaches? Also, as you read the chapters, you may discern that there are some common features or similarities across the four approaches that can be noted in the top section of Figure II.1. If using an advance organizer helps you organize information and solidify your learning, enjoy using this learning tool as you study the following chapters.

Figure II.1 Similarities and Differences of Supportive, Parallel, Complementary, and Team-Teaching Co-Teaching Approaches

Similarities Among the Four Co-Teaching Approaches		
Supportive Differences	Parallel Differences	Complementary Differences	Team Differences
Supportive Advantages	Parallel Advantages	Complementary Advantages	Team Advantages
Supportive Cautions	Parallel Cautions	Complementary Cautions	Team Cautions

The Supportive Co-Teaching Approach

4

Topics Included in This Chapter:

❖ Unique features, advantages of, and cautions associated with supportive co-teaching
❖ Vignettes: Supportive co-teaching
❖ Analyzing the cooperative process in the supportive co-teaching vignettes
❖ Frequently asked questions

With supportive co-teaching, often one teacher assumes primary responsibility for designing and delivering a lesson, and the other member(s) of the team provides support to some or all of the students in the class. Basically, one teacher leads, and the other supports. Said another way, one teacher functions as the sage on the stage, and the other functions as the guide on the side. Sometimes the lead teacher is primarily responsible for planning the content and the support person has less or little planning responsibility; sometimes co-teachers share equally in the planning and choose to use supportive co-teaching for a segment of their instruction because it is the most useful co-teaching arrangement. For example, at the beginning of a class, one co-teacher may take the lead, introducing the content and language objectives, while the other acts in a supportive role by collecting and scanning homework to see if students were successful in applying the content covered the day before.

It should be noted that who is in the lead and who is supporting does not need to remain the same throughout the lesson. For example, a general education classroom teacher may take primary responsibility for teaching the first part of a lesson, while a supporting co-teacher (e.g., special educator, speech and language therapist, paraprofessional, teacher of students who are learning English) circulates among the students monitoring academic and social progress, promoting peer interactions, or providing task assistance when needed. For the second part of the lesson, the co-teachers switch roles, with the classroom teacher circulating among students, providing immediate academic or behavioral support, while the other co-teacher takes the lead and introduces the next concept. Supportive co-teaching between a special and a general educator also might involve the supporting special educator reviewing a test-taking strategy with a student prior to a test, giving specific feedback to a student about his or her use of social skills in the general education classroom, or teaching a student how to use an augmentative communication system that is being used with classmates in the classroom. Still another example might involve co-teaching with someone who is expert in teaching students who are learning English. While the classroom teacher models a written language pattern orally and in writing (e.g., with a document camera, on a whiteboard, on easel paper), the co-teacher circulates around the classroom to check for the English language learners' understanding of the pattern and the associated writing assignment.

Often, when teachers begin to co-teach, they use the supportive co-teaching approach. It allows the co-teacher who is not the classroom teacher to observe the classroom routines, get to know the classroom teacher and students, and learn the preferred instructional strategies of the classroom teacher. Supportive co-teaching is also used when one of the members of the co-teaching team does not have curriculum content mastery and new content is being introduced. Teams with little to no planning time typically use the supportive co-teaching approach.

A caution when using the supportive co-teaching approach is that whoever is playing the support role (e.g., bilingual translator, special educator, paraprofessional) must not become "Velcroed" to individual students, functioning as a "hovercraft vehicle" blocking a student's interactions with other students. It is well documented that this is stigmatizing for both students and the support person, causing classmates to perceive that the student and support person are not genuine members of the classroom (Giangreco, Edelman, Luiselli, and MacFarland 1997). While there are advantages and disadvantages of each approach and a time and a place to use each approach, supportive co-teaching should, over time, become the least utilized of the four approaches because it does not allow the co-teacher in the supportive co-teaching role to adequately use her or his skill set to greatly influence instruction and make it more accessible for learners. Sometimes interventionists cast in the supportive role develop resentment because they feel that their professional skills are not being adequately used. Conversely, classroom teachers may resent their supportive co-teaching partner because they feel an unequal burden of responsibility for designing lessons, instructing, and assessing the progress of the learners.

■ VIGNETTES: SUPPORTIVE CO-TEACHING

If you peek into the classrooms of the co-teaching teams described in Chapter 3, you might see and hear the activities summarized in Table 4.1.

The following vignettes illustrate how supportive teaching might play out in elementary, middle-level, and high school classrooms as co-teachers conduct standards-based lessons.

An Elementary Co-Teaching Team

During math, Ms. Gilpatrick (the teacher) and Ms. Hernandez (the paraprofessional) are in the classroom. Ms. Gilpatrick begins by leading a large-group activity in which she checks students' understanding of number recognition for the numbers 0 through 9 with whole-class choral response and by calling on individual students. Following this activity, Ms. Gilpatrick checks for understanding of the concept of *more* because this is a vocabulary term used when describing the addition process (e.g., *What does 2 oranges plus 1 more orange equal?*). She then models several examples of single-digit addition, using real objects to match written numbers to show the concept as well as the operation of addition.

Students' desks are arranged so that every student has a table partner. The co-teachers distribute to each pair a small container of colored, interconnecting blocks, which the students can use to solve several addition problems that have been written on the board. Each student also has a number line taped to the top of his or her desk. Students have had previous instruction and practice on how to use the number line and blocks to arrive at a total. After a short period, partner pairs are called to the front of the room to show how they arrived at their solution. There are colored number lines and translucent two-dimensional blocks on the document projector that students can use to show the thinking and processes by which they arrived at their answers. The other students in the class also have attempted to solve the problem and have previously written the answers on their individual whiteboards, which they hold up after each pair's demonstration and explanation.

Following this guided practice, students are given a choice of three pages that contain problems they are to solve independent of the teacher's instruction: one with 4 problems, one with 6, and one with 10. All pairs are to complete a minimum of eight problems, but any pair can complete all three teacher-designed worksheets for additional practice. Students are instructed to be prepared to explain how they arrived at each answer to the teacher, the paraprofessional, another classmate, or the entire class.

Ms. Hernandez and Ms. Gilpatrick have had no time to plan. Ms. Hernandez arrives just as Ms. Gilpatrick finishes modeling the examples for single-digit addition in large-group instruction. Ms. Hernandez walks around to check with the students as they use the manipulatives and write their answers on the whiteboards. She continues to circulate around the room, asking and answering questions and providing support as needed during the time that partners complete the worksheets. She ensures that students with special needs, those who receive Title I tutorials, and those who are learning English can follow the instructions and perform the addition procedures. She pays particular attention to Elisa, the student with autism, but observes her from a distance rather than sitting by her, thus fostering Elisa's independence. In addition to asking questions of other partner pairs, Ms. Hernandez periodically asks Elisa or her partner to show how they arrived at the answers to their problems.

A Middle-Level Co-Teaching Team

Mr. Silva (the science and math teacher with an endorsement to teach students who are English language learners) wants students to compare and contrast animals that reside in various environments (e.g., ocean, desert, mountain) and learn about environmental damage or threats to each of these ecosystems. Mr. Silva posts the content and language objectives prior to class. While Ms. Spaulding references the objectives and solicits rationale from the students as to why it is important to learn the content of the lesson, Mr. Silva collects the students' homework. Working in groups (i.e., five groups of four and two groups of three), students are asked to create two visual representations: One will depict the similarities and differences between the environments, and the other will represent some of the environmental concerns for each of the three ecosystems.

At this time, Ms. Spaulding (a special educator) is in the science class with Mr. Silva, and Ms. Olvina (a paraprofessional) is with Ms. Kurtz in her language arts class. Mr. Silva and Ms. Spaulding previously collaborated and assigned students to heterogeneous groups, avoiding best friends and worst enemies in the groups and assuring diversity across gender, race, language, and ability. Some students use Venn diagrams; others create tables; others draw, cut out, or download pictures from the Internet or use other materials to represent the ecosystems graphically. Mr. Silva teaches, checks understanding, monitors group interactions, and answers students' questions. Ms. Spaulding quietly observes various students to help Mr. Silva plan for future modifications, roles within groups, and future grouping suggestions. Ms. Spaulding also collects data on students' level of participation in their groups and demonstration of social skills (e.g., turn taking).

After the lesson, Mr. Silva and Ms. Spaulding meet briefly to discuss what occurred in this lesson. They take turns describing what went well, what they would change the next time they teach this unit, and to what extent they fulfilled their agreed-on tasks. They also take time to outline their plan for the next unit of study (specifically, group composition, content modifications, social skills to teach and monitor). Ms. Spaulding shares with Mr. Silva some online resources she discovered when she did an Internet search. He promises to review them and to subsequently discuss with Ms. Spaulding and the other members of the middle-level teaching team, Ms. Olvina and Ms. Kurtz, how these resources might be integrated into the upcoming unit.

A High School Co-Teaching Team

During a common planning period the week before they are scheduled to co-teach five classes, Mr. Woo (the social studies teacher) and Mr. Viana (the special educator) met to address several issues. They used the matrix shown in Table 3.3 (in Chapter 3) to help determine the appropriate goals and activities for each of the classes, clarified Mr. Viana's responsibilities, and decided how to group students for the various learning activities. Based on his knowledge of students' strengths and needs, Mr. Viana suggested which students should work together, indicating specific roles within the cooperative learning groups that some learners might take (e.g., a student who is not reading at grade level could function as a timekeeper). Mr. Woo explained that if students have questions, he wanted Mr. Viana to encourage them to ask one another to solve the problem before asking an adult for help. Mr. Woo identified four of the eight groups he wanted Mr. Viana to monitor for academic work, role performance, and use of social skills.

On the following Monday, Mr. Woo and Mr. Viana check in with each other briefly before the start of the class. Mr. Viana passes out clicker handsets to the students while Mr. Woo reviews the objectives. Mr. Woo and Mr. Viana decided to use the clicker handsets to informally assess students' knowledge of the three branches of government. Based on the informal assessment results, the co-teachers make an on-the-spot adjustment for one group by assigning a fourth member with some knowledge of the branch of government that will be assigned to that group. In addition, Mr. Viana believes one student in that particular group will benefit from this additional peer support and modeling.

Mr. Woo introduces the activities, explaining the academic and social (i.e., reaching consensus, listening, equal participation) objectives, and telling the students that they will have a common goal. He describes the individual roles (e.g., timekeeper, recorder) within the groups, notes that each student will be held accountable, and outlines the criteria for success. The class is divided into thirds. Each third is further divided into groups of three. Mr. Woo asks the students questions to check their understanding of the directions and criteria for success he has just explained.

Each third of the class is to learn and be prepared to teach about one of the three branches of government (i.e., legislative, judicial, and executive). Students within each "expert group" will become experts on their branch of government through a variety of means, such as online resources available from museums, government entities, universities, and popular news publications and networks; textbooks, news magazines, and other printed materials; DVDs, videos; and interviews. In 2 days' time, after students have become experts in their areas, Mr. Woo will reconfigure the groups to include an expert with knowledge of each of the three branches of government. This will allow students to jigsaw their information, teach one another, and then apply their collective knowledge to determine the role of each branch of government when given a set of scenarios (e.g., declaring war, how a bill becomes a law, raising taxes, determining guilt, sentencing, the possibility of pardoning those who violate the law).

Mr. Viana passes out the task instructions, a list of resources, and some materials to each of the expert groups. As students get organized to begin studying their respective branch of government, Mr. Woo and Mr. Viana move among the groups to monitor student understanding of the assignment, role performance, and use of small-group social skills. Mr. Woo monitors the time and gives the class a 5-minute warning that the period is almost over so that groups can wrap up.

ANALYZING THE COOPERATIVE PROCESS IN THE SUPPORTIVE CO-TEACHING VIGNETTES

The cooperative process differed when supportive co-teaching was applied at three levels—elementary, middle school, and high school. The five elements of the cooperative process are face-to-face interaction, positive interdependence, interpersonal skills, monitoring, and accountability.

All three supportive co-teaching vignettes show that the co-teachers interacted face-to-face during the teaching of the lesson, while both the middle school and high school supportive co-teaching teams also met face-to-face after the lesson. The high school supportive co-teaching team met before, during, and after the lesson. Positive interdependence is evident in all three vignettes; each supportive co-teaching team had a division of labor (although the elementary team had an unspecified agreement). Interpersonal communication skills were evident in the high school supportive co-teaching vignette, especially when Mr. Woo communicated

Table 4.1 The Many Faces of Co-Teaching: Co-Teaching Teams' Use of Supportive Co-Teaching

Meet the Co-Teachers	Co-Teacher Roles	Curriculum Area(s)	Teaching Learning Strategies	Planning Method
Elementary				
Ms. Gilpatrick, classroom teacher	Leads the lesson	Mathematics	Manipulative and number line; partner learning	On-the-spot planning
Ms. Hernandez, paraprofessional	Circulates to check understanding and task completion			
Middle Level				
Mr. Silva, science and math teacher	Leads the lesson	Science	Cooperative group learning; multiage grouping	Reflective guided planning
Ms. Spaulding, special educator	Observes to plan for future groupings			
High School				
Mr. Woo, social studies teacher	Leads the lesson	Social studies	Cooperative group learning (jigsaw with expert groups), authentic assessment, computer technology	Preplanning
Mr. Viana, special educator	Suggests student group membership, encourages students to use problem-solving methods, passes out papers, and, along with the teacher, monitors the group interactions			

how he wanted Mr. Viana to interact with the students. Monitoring effectiveness of the lessons occurred on the spot for all three supportive co-teaching teams. In addition, the middle school and high school co-teachers included a debriefing time to discuss what went well, what needed to be done differently, and what would be done next time. Accountability was implied in the vignettes, with the high school co-teachers being more articulate about how they held each other accountable for the tasks they agreed to achieve.

We advocate that supportive co-teachers incorporate as many elements of the cooperative process as possible. This happens when co-teachers experience face-to-face interactions, realize that they are positively interdependent, use their social interpersonal skills, monitor how well they work together, and hold each other accountable for the tasks they set for each other. The research is clear that when all five elements are present, the quality of the co-teaching relationship improves. And when the quality of the co-teaching relationship improves, the outcomes in terms of student achievement are positively affected.

FREQUENTLY ASKED QUESTIONS

We have interviewed many co-teachers, students, parents, administrators, and advocates for the use of co-teaching arrangements in the classroom. The following questions are those asked most frequently when people first learn about the supportive co-teaching approach.

1. What is the most difficult problem to overcome when working with a paraprofessional and a classroom teacher using the supportive co-teaching approach?

No matter whether it is a classroom teacher, a special educator, or a paraprofessional who is playing the supportive role, the supportive co-teacher must not become "Velcroed" to individual students. He or she should not function as a hovercraft vehicle blocking a student's interactions with other students. Hovering can stigmatize the student. It also runs the risk of stigmatizing a co-teaching team member who works predominantly with one student. Students from preschool through high school explain that if a teacher is glued to a particular student, the teacher becomes a barrier to other children's desire to interact socially with that child. Not only that, students often raise this question: "If the special teacher helps me, will people think that I'm a special education student?" (Villa and Thousand 2002, 304). An important component of successful supportive co-teaching is ensuring that students perceive each member of the co-teaching team (special educator, regular educator, or paraprofessional) as their teacher.

We hope you agree that the vignettes featured in this chapter show how the supportive co-teaching teams organized their interaction so that students perceived each of the co-teachers as their teacher. Administratively, to avoid stigmatization further, the job definition for paraprofessionals hired to work with individual children with special needs can include responsibilities for all the children in the classroom.

2. Does supportive co-teaching always occur inside the classroom?

We suggest that the place co-teachers should work most often is the classroom in which all the children meet. Occasionally, however, co-teachers may work for a short period with an individual child

(Continued)

(Continued)

or a group of children outside the classroom, in the library, or in the computer lab. If you choose to use this approach, we advise that, to avoid stigmatization of students or instructional personnel, the same students or member of the co-teaching team should not always be the ones leaving the general education classroom.

3. I'm a professional special educator who has just been assigned to work as a co-teacher with a general educator. How do I avoid acting in a subsidiary role by just walking around and helping the students?

Are you worried that you'll go into a classroom and just drift around, working with one or two students, waiting and watching the flow of the classroom teacher's lesson? This indicates your concern that all of the skills you've acquired will not necessarily be used. One way to address this concern is for co-teachers to learn to use the other approaches to co-teaching described in subsequent chapters of this book. Then you and your co-teacher can agree to a goal that will help your relationship capitalize on all four approaches instead of relying on only one. The benefits of the increased awareness that all educators bring to their co-teaching partnerships far outweigh the temporary discomfort that occurs when a team is just beginning to use the supportive co-teaching approach. It is not uncommon for special educators and support personnel to discover, when they enter a general education classroom, that it is a very different world from the one-on-one or small-group instruction typically found in resource rooms or self-contained classrooms. With a supportive co-teaching arrangement, both co-teachers have the chance to become familiar with each other's curriculum and teaching techniques. The goal is to nurture and enrich the relationship so that both co-teachers can experience an evolution of their skills. Remember that this involves taking time to talk, establish trust, and communicate. Expanding your co-teaching repertoire beyond just the supportive approach avoids the special educators' resenting the classroom teachers for not valuing them and allowing them to use their skills and avoids the classroom teachers' resenting the special educators because they feel they are left with the majority of the responsibility for planning, teaching, and assessing the learners in the classroom.

The Parallel Co-Teaching Approach

5

Topics Included in This Chapter:

❖ Unique features, advantages of, and cautions associated with parallel co-teaching
❖ Vignettes: Parallel co-teaching
❖ Analyzing the cooperative process in the parallel co-teaching vignettes
❖ Frequently asked questions

Parallel co-teaching occurs when co-teachers instruct, monitor, or facilitate the work of different groups of students at the same time in the classroom. A benefit of parallel co-teaching is that it decreases the student-to-teacher ratio, allowing for increased individualization, differentiation, and data collection to meet students' needs. It also makes it easier for co-teaching personnel to establish closer positive relationships with the students in their small group(s). Parallel co-teachers may teach the same or different content. They may split the class evenly among themselves, or one person may work with the majority of the students while another works with a small subgroup of the class. One variation on parallel co-teaching, often referred to as *station teaching*, involves one group of students working with one co-teacher, another group working with a classroom support person (e.g., special educator, paraprofessional), perhaps a third group working with yet another support person, and a fourth group working independently. Over the course of one or several class periods, students rotate among all of the stations and their respective co-teachers. Parallel co-teaching provides an opportunity for less teacher talk and greater student-to-student interaction with partners, in stations, or in groups, as co-teachers monitor or facilitate the work of different groups. In summary, parallel co-teaching has many faces. Table 5.1 briefly describes several variations of parallel co-teaching.

There are several cautions that co-teachers must beware of when using the parallel co-teaching approach. One caution is to beware of elevated noise levels that can become uncomfortably high when numerous activities are occurring in the same classroom. A second caution is to beware of failing to adequately prepare other co-teachers so that they are able to deliver instruction to their group or at their station as intended. Since in parallel co-teaching all instructional personnel are busy teaching, members of the co-teaching team cannot monitor one other while they are simultaneously co-teaching in order to ensure "instruction integrity."

43

A final and very important caution co-teachers must guard against is creating a special class within a class or an island in the mainstream by repeatedly homogeneously grouping lower-performing students together. Such configurations can result in lower student achievement (Marzano, Pickering, and Pollack, 2001) and stigmatization of students and the co-teacher working with such groups. Instead, groupings should be fluid, flexible, and, for the most part, heterogeneous in composition. Groupings may be made for a multitude of different purposes (e.g., student interest, learning strengths and modalities, planned diversity in background knowledge). When teachers homogeneously group students for targeted instruction such as during a response to intervention Tier 2 intervention block, the groupings should based upon data rather than labels. There also should be shared responsibility among co-teachers for teaching all students, over time, regardless of the groups in which students might be placed.

■ VIGNETTES: PARALLEL CO-TEACHING

Let's once again peek into the classrooms of our elementary, middle-level, and high school teams as they teach standards-based lessons. Table 5.2 summarizes the variations of parallel co-teaching and the diverse instructional methods used by these teams.

Table 5.1   Examples of Parallel Co-Teaching Structures With Co-Teachers Teaching the Same or Different Content

Split Class. Each co-teacher is responsible for a particular group of students, monitoring understanding of a lesson, providing guided instruction, or reteaching the group, if necessary.

Station Teaching or Learning Centers. Each co-teacher is responsible for assembling, guiding, and monitoring one or more learning centers or stations.

Co-Teachers Rotate. The co-teachers rotate among the two or more groups of students, with each co-teacher teaching a different component of the lesson. This is similar to station teaching or learning centers, except that in this case the teachers rotate from group to group rather than having groups of students rotate from station to station.

Cooperative Group Monitoring. Each co-teacher takes responsibility for monitoring and providing feedback and assistance to a given number of cooperative groups of students.

Experiment or Lab Monitoring. Each co-teacher monitors and assists a given number of laboratory groups, providing guided instruction to groups requiring additional support.

Learning Style Focus. One co-teacher works with a group of students using primarily visual strategies, another co-teacher works with a group using primarily auditory strategies, and yet another may work with a group using kinesthetic strategies.

Supplementary Instruction. One co-teacher works with the rest of the class on a concept or assignment, skill, or learning strategy. The other co-teacher (a) provides extra guidance on the concept or assignment to students who are self-identified or teacher-identified as needing extra assistance, (b) instructs students to apply or generalize the skill to a relevant community environment, (c) provides a targeted group of students with guided practice in how to apply the learning strategy to the content being addressed, or (d) provides enrichment activities.

Table 5.2 The Many Faces of Co-Teaching: Co-Teaching Teams' Use of Parallel Co-Teaching

Meet the Co-Teachers	Co-Teacher Roles	Curriculum Area(s)	Teaching Learning Strategies	Planning Method
Elementary				
Ms. Gilpatrick, classroom teacher	Station teaching—the three co-teachers each guide one station	Literacy	Station teaching	Preplanning and postinstruction debriefing
Ms. Nugent, speech and language therapist			Visual and kinesthetic demonstration	
Ms. Hernandez, paraprofessional	One independent station		Modeling and guided practice	On-the-spot briefing of paraprofessional
			Motivation through friendly *beat the teacher* competition and choice in practice options	
Middle Level				
Mr. Silva, science and math teacher	Split class	Interdisciplinary, thematic unit integrating language arts, math, science, and social studies	Interdisciplinary, thematic instruction	Preplanning
Ms. Spaulding, special educator	Same content		Differentiation of materials	
Ms. Kurt, language arts and social studies teacher	Alternating instructors		Frequent monitoring and adjusting	
Ms. Olvina, paraprofessional				
High School				
Mr. Woo, social studies teacher	Large- and small-group split class	Social studies test preparation	Individualized and differentiated direct instruction	On-the-spot division of labor
Mr. Viana, special educator	Different content	Assistance in planning for a major homework assignment	Guided assistance	Individual planning
			Self-correction	Check-in prior to lesson delivery

An Elementary Co-Teaching Team

Ms. Gilpatrick (the classroom teacher) and Ms. Nugent (the speech and language therapist) now meet weekly to plan. They are trying out parallel co-teaching, in which each works with different groups of children at the same time. In preparing to introduce the class to compound words, they created materials the week before.

Ms. Hernandez (the paraprofessional assigned part time to their classroom) arrives. Ms. Nugent briefs her while Ms. Gilpatrick takes attendance, collects permission slips for an upcoming field trip, and makes the daily announcements. Ms. Nugent quickly explains the instructional objectives of the week and how Ms. Hernandez will support students at the station to which she has been assigned, as well as how each of the other three stations will work.

To introduce compound words, Ms. Gilpatrick and Ms. Nugent have planned a team co-teaching introduction. They stand at the front of the room, each holding a large piece of construction paper with a word written on it (Ms. Gilpatrick has the word *cup;* Ms. Nugent has the word *cake*). Ms. Gilpatrick has students identify the word she is holding with a choral response. Ms. Nugent does the same for her word. Next, the two teachers move together to form a single compound word (*cupcake*). Ms. Gilpatrick and Ms. Nugent ask the students, through choral response, to identify each of the words they are holding up on construction paper and then to identify the compound word formed when they are joined. The two teachers repeat this modeling for an additional six compound words. Next, Ms. Gilpatrick assigns students to one of four stations through which all students will rotate over the course of the morning.

Ms. Hernandez is at the first station. She has several identical piles of simple words (written on flash cards) that can be combined to make compound words. Ms. Hernandez pairs the students, gives each pair one pile of words, and instructs students to sit together on the neighboring rug area to create from their flash cards as many compound words as they can in 5 minutes. She first models a couple of examples using her pile of words. Then she sets a timer and challenges pairs to beat her in creating compound words that make sense by recording their words on a teacher-made word chart with 10 entry spaces per side. As the students work, Ms. Hernandez closely observes and reinforces their creation of compound words; intervenes with a question, if a word is not a "real" word; and provides guided support to any pairs who need it. Elisa, the student with autism, is strategically paired with a classmate who is especially skilled at imitating the teachers' models and guiding classmates to complete a task. Ms. Hernandez pays extra attention to this partnership to ensure that they are able to create words, but she does not intervene unless it is clear that they need support.

When the timer goes off, pairs share their words. Ms. Hernandez writes them on chart paper, putting check marks next to compound words that more than one group created. Students initial the chart while she congratulates them on beating her in the number and creativity of their words. If there is time left, the students are given some new flash cards with additional words to work with to add even more compound words to their list.

With each new group, Ms. Hernandez provides the same instructions so that the groups will be motivated to compete with the teacher. The station proves highly motivating to the students. In the afternoon, Ms. Gilpatrick shares the composite list of words with the whole class (Ms. Hernandez is now working with another teacher) so that students can celebrate their competence in creating compound words.

Ms. Nugent is at the second station. She and the students are seated around a kidney-shaped table, with Ms. Nugent on one side and the students sitting in a semi-circle on the other side, allowing Ms. Nugent to observe and interact easily with all students in the group. Each student is given a piece of paper that contains a word bank from which to combine words to make a compound word that makes sense in one of several sentences also written on the page. Ms. Nugent has the students rotate reading each of the sentences prior to looking at the word bank so that they understand the context of the activity. She then models a couple of examples with a different word bank and different sentences on the large whiteboard behind her that is in full view of all students in her group. Moving to papers she handed out, she ensures that students complete the exercise by providing guided practice until she observes that each student can work independently. She has a second and third practice page ready for students who move more quickly so that they can practice independently.

Ms. Nugent keeps data on each of the groups that rotate through her station, noting the level of support each student needs. She shares these data with Ms. Gilpatrick at their next planning meeting.

Ms. Gilpatrick is seated at the third station on a carpeted area with a large whiteboard, a dozen erasable markers, paper, and several big books, each of which includes compound words. On the left and right sides of the whiteboard, she has listed several words that can be combined to make compound words. She models how to connect words on the left and right to create words that make sense and has individual students come forward to model connecting a few more. She then forms pairs and has each pair select and scan one big book, underlining with erasable markers all of the compound words they can find. She debriefs by having pairs show and tell their compound words to other group members. Next, she gives each student a piece of paper with the two ends of the paper folded inward to create a kind of door; when opened, the door reveals the inside of the paper. She has created samples with a single word on each flap, and together the two words form a compound word; when the flaps are opened, the two separate words appear inside, melded into the single compound word. Ms. Gilpatrick guides students through the process of creating this visual representation for the first word that each pair found in their big books. She then challenges the students to go through and create opening doors for the remaining words in their big books until the time is up. Students leave with their compound-word creations to take home and share with their parents.

At the fourth station, set up as an independent practice station, students work in pairs at one of five classroom laptop computers to create sentences that include compound words the students formulated at previous stations. The first students at this station have not yet been to another station, so they are given a list of words they can combine and use in a sentence. Each pair is to create at least three sentences, each with a different compound word. Pairs earn bonus points that can be traded for free time on Friday if they create more than three correct sentences with compound words. At this station, students also practice their technology skills by pulling up the program they are to use to compose the sentences, putting their names at the top of the document, spell-checking the document, saving the document to the desktop, printing the document, and placing it in the teacher inbox. This procedure for producing work at the computer has been rehearsed as a classroom routine. This fourth station allows students to demonstrate independence while doing a meaningful and relevant language arts task.

Students at the fourth station know they are free to go to any of the adults in the room for assistance after they have consulted their peers who are working at other computers. The co-teachers in this class want students to rely on their peers to help them problem solve their own issues, and this task provides a natural opportunity for them to do so.

All students rotate through all four stations. The task at each station takes approximately 15 minutes. At this point in the year, students are quite capable of actively engaging for this period of time, with teacher support and intervention as needed.

A Middle-Level Co-Teaching Team

The middle school has embarked on a journey to develop transdisciplinary teaming and curriculum integration. This team—Mr. Silva (the math and science teacher with an endorsement for teaching English language learners), Ms. Spaulding (the special educator), Ms. Kurtz (the language arts and social studies teacher), and Ms. Olvina (the paraprofessional assigned to the team)—has arranged with the principal to have a common preparation period that backs up to their lunchtime. This allows them to meet to discuss curriculum, teaming, and specific student issues. The team's first endeavor is to create an integrated unit of study about the historical tension between progress and preservation, with a focus on global environmental issues. The team members are excited; they all see ways in which math, science, and literature can tie into this social studies–based theme.

During the unit, students will read literature that deals with environmental issues. For instance, Rachel Carson's classic, *Silent Spring* (2001), will bridge language arts and science. In language arts, students will examine the persuasive literary elements in the text. In science, students will read for information, identifying the negative impact of pesticides on the food chain and the lives of birds and other wildlife.

Language arts and social studies are integrated through a series of lessons that develop students' skills in debating and delivering persuasive speeches regarding the positive and negative impact of progress on the health, quality of life, economic situation, and other aspects of various societies. In this way, Ms. Kurtz addresses key middle-level language arts standards related to speaking and reasoning and key social studies objectives regarding reasoning and environmental issues in international settings as well as the United States. Ms. Kurtz is comfortable giving Ms. Olvina more than a behind-the-scenes role, so while Ms. Kurtz works with half of the groups, who are developing persuasive speeches and debates, Ms. Olvina works with the other half. They rotate between groups from one day to the next so that the classroom teacher can monitor all students and all students see that both Ms. Olvina and Ms. Kurtz have expertise and can be of assistance.

Mr. Silva and Ms. Spaulding are enjoying the chance to connect science and math with literature and social studies creatively through the theme of progress versus preservation. For math, they have planned for students to do calculations; produce charts, graphs, and tables; and make projections based on current data regarding the destruction of various rainforests, smog levels in major cities worldwide, the effects of smog and other contaminants on life expectancies, and the human and financial costs of these and other forms of progress. Mr. Silva will introduce a unit on probability and have students apply what they are learning to science by having them forecast possible destruction-versus-preservation scenarios locally, nationally, and internationally. The co-teaching team has asked the librarian teacher to bookmark a diverse array of Internet sites on the classroom and library computers so that students can begin to collect data.

For science, the team decided to connect the scientific and social roles of organizations and agencies such as the United Nations, the Environmental Protection Agency, and the U.S. Department of Agriculture, as well as other government entities and the courts. Although this is traditionally thought of as social studies content, Ms. Kurtz agreed to plan with Mr. Silva and Ms. Spaulding to ensure that the content was included as part of the science lessons. Mr. Silva and Ms. Spaulding also are taking the lead on introducing *Silent Spring,* using it as scientific evidence of environmental damage. Together they generated a series of questions on the progress-versus-preservation theme for students to consider as they read the book.

To differentiate instruction, they set up their lessons so that students can read the book in a variety of ways. In addition to the original printed format, text-to-speech software and audiotapes of the book read by students from a previous year's class are available to those who learn more easily through auditory versus visual means, find the text beyond their reading decoding or comprehension skill levels, or enjoy and learn best from having two forms of content input (e.g., auditory and visual). The book is also available on classroom and library computers in a rewritten, simplified format and in larger print (accessed from the Braille Institute's library for a student with visual impairments who was in this class 2 years earlier). It is available in a Spanish translation so that students who are primarily Spanish speakers may read both books simultaneously, thus ensuring access to the content of the book and development of English comprehension for those learning English. For other students who are studying Spanish as a second or third language, the simultaneous reading of English and Spanish text promotes their Spanish literacy development. All of these materials and accommodations are made available to every student in the class.

In terms of co-teaching, Mr. Silva and Ms. Spaulding have decided that they can best provide students in this lesson with individualized support by dividing the class in half, with each teacher taking 13 of the 26 students. They have learned that this is a form of parallel co-teaching. They think that parallel co-teaching really suits how they will use *Silent Spring*.

In setting up parallel co-teaching, Mr. Silva and Ms. Spaulding first spend 5 minutes showing three short video clips. The video clips were the first-, second-, and third-place winners of the European Environmental Agencies competition (2012), which asked young people in Europe to submit a short video depicting their ideas for a sustainable future. Following the video clips, Mr. Silva introduces *Silent Spring* to the entire class and tells the students the questions they are to answer. He then explains that each teacher will work with half of the class so that everyone gets attention from one of the teachers. He further explains that both groups will be working on the same goals and will have a variety of resources for accessing the content of the book (as described previously). He then divides the class. Both his group and Ms. Spaulding's are heterogeneous in terms of students' gender, reading level, and eligibility for special services (e.g., special education, gifted and talented education). The only deliberate clustering of students is done to ensure that the two students who are learning English and who speak Spanish as their primary language are with Mr. Silva because he is a proficient Spanish speaker and is certified as a teacher of English as a second language. He wants to make sure that he can check the students' understanding of content; differentiate materials and scaffold the instruction if needed and provide the option for the students to produce their work in Spanish rather than or in addition to English if they desire. These two students are new to the class and district and are still being assessed for their level of proficiency in English.

In both Mr. Silva's and Ms. Spaulding's groups, students are seated in desks in a semicircle arrangement facing their teacher's desk. The two instructors alternate between giving short task instructions and rotating among the 13 students to check for student engagement, answer questions, pose questions, and provide positive feedback for work engagement. They also pair students to do reciprocal reading at various intervals and assemble students into triads and quads to discuss questions jointly and speculate on responses before they formulate their individual answers. This parallel co-teaching arrangement allows each teacher to monitor easily and readily a smaller number of students; flexibly group and regroup students to maintain their interest and create synergy and higher-level thinking through conversation; gather diagnostic information about students' interests, motivational factors, and literacy skills; and individualize accommodations for students as needed (e.g., use of audiotapes with a tape recorder and headset for students who are falling behind in the reading).

A High School Co-Teaching Team

Leading up to the time that this lesson was developed, Mr. Woo (the social studies teacher) and Mr. Viana (the special educator) had taken advantage of the fact that there are two educators in the classroom in order to designate Fridays as a day to experiment with dividing the class between the two instructors. From week to week, they reconstitute the membership of their respective groups so that there is no stigma of any sort attached to working with one or the other of the educators. They both agreed that it was important to keep group membership flexible, based on the content and the purpose of a lesson and students' background knowledge and strengths. They have done some dividing of the class prior to this lesson, usually when certain groups of students needed some reteaching or an enrichment exercise. They have also divided the class based on the learning styles of students, with one teacher working primarily with visual learners and the other primarily with auditory learners.

Preparation for this particular social studies lesson on the role of the United Nations was done on the spot the day before. Mr. Woo and Mr. Viana agreed to the lesson's objectives and structure and then went off on their own to plan their materials and the details of how they would structure their specific activities. Right before class, they checked in with one another to be sure that they both still agreed to the class structure and their roles and to ensure that if either one had any questions or concerns, they were addressed before the students arrived.

This class period is divided into two parts. During the first part of the class, Mr. Woo takes the majority of the class and focuses on preparing them for a homework assignment on the history, role, and impact of the League of Nations and the United Nations. Mr. Viana works with the remaining smaller group of students, with whom he reviews the questions answered incorrectly on the previous day's test. Students will have a chance to retake the test and improve their scores later in the week.

During the second half of the class, Mr. Woo assigns independent work in which students analyze international treaties and charters such as the Geneva Accord. Mr. Viana is available to answer questions from any of the students and monitors them as they work. Mr. Woo sits at a table at the side of the room and works with a small group of students who have voluntarily signed up in advance for more guided assistance in getting started on the assignment. Included are two students whom Mr. Woo and Mr. Viana asked to join the group, knowing they would need extra clarification and support to initiate this assignment.

■ ANALYZING THE COOPERATIVE PROCESS IN THE PARALLEL CO-TEACHING VIGNETTES

The cooperative process as applied to parallel co-teaching can be quite varied, as shown in these elementary, middle school, and high school vignettes. Parallel co-teaching differs from supportive co-teaching, yet both can occur within the same lesson. Co-teacher roles and responsibilities shift based on the nature of the instructional activity, learners' needs, and other variables. In the case of the middle school co-teaching team, the desire to implement interdisciplinary thematic units helped the co-teachers decide how to divide the teaching responsibilities to capitalize on their strengths and interests. In parallel co-teaching, students do not necessarily have the opportunity to see their teachers collaborate in communication and instruction. It is clear, however, that students do experience the more intensive attention and monitoring that each co-teacher provides.

The five elements of the cooperative teaching process (face-to-face interaction, positive interdependence, interpersonal skills, monitoring, accountability) are illustrated in some way by all three of the co-teaching teams in the parallel co-teaching vignettes. All three teams experienced face-to-face interaction by including a preplanning component to their relationship. All teams met regularly in some configuration. Of the three teams, the middle school team was most deliberate in its planning, having arranged for a common preparation period to plan and process lesson implementation. The elementary educators met weekly, with on-the-spot briefing of the paraprofessional when she was unable to attend planning meetings. Even though the high school team used on-the-spot division of labor for its respective student subgroups and planned for the groups separately, the co-teachers briefly met before instruction to check in with one another regarding their agreed-on teaching roles and the overall lesson plan.

All three co-teaching teams experienced positive interdependence, which is necessary for success in parallel co-teaching. In the elementary station-teaching example, all three teachers needed one another to facilitate each of the stations. The teachers' lively, physical demonstration of how to bring together two words to create a compound word is an excellent example of positive interdependence. Because parallel co-teachers teach separately from one another, they experience resource interdependence through their division of labor. The middle school team illustrated this when Ms. Kurtz gave Mr. Silva her resources so that he could take on her usual role of introducing the literature to be read in the unit and managing some social studies activities.

All three teams exercised interpersonal skills such as negotiation, consensual agreement, and creativity through their planning. Perhaps trust is the most important quality required of and demonstrated by members of the three co-teaching teams. The three elementary co-teachers trusted that the other two would facilitate their respective stations as planned. In the middle school team, the language arts and social studies co-teacher trusted that the math and science and special education co-teachers would introduce and use the literature as planned and deliver the lesson on the scientific roles of social agencies as planned. The high school co-teachers trusted that each person would independently complete the agreed-on individual planning and be prepared for the next day's parallel co-teaching lesson.

Monitoring effectiveness and individual accountability is probably the most difficult to accomplish in parallel versus other forms of co-teaching. Parallel co-teachers are not readily available to monitor and hold one another accountable for their instruction; they are engaged in teaching their own group and may not even be in the same physical space to observe and interact with each other. Monitoring effectiveness is implied in all three vignettes; the co-teachers all had planning times during which they could debrief about self-monitored successes or challenges of the lessons. Accountability also is implied because the co-teachers trusted one another to deliver instruction without direct monitoring. Trust is built on past accountability. It may not be clearly stated, but can you see how the co-teachers were accountable for their roles and responsibilities?

FREQUENTLY ASKED QUESTIONS

The following are among the questions people ask when they are considering the use of parallel co-teaching.

1. If we group by disability labels, learning styles, perceived ability in a subject, or other traits such as gender, won't that produce stigmatization?

We warn against the possibility of creating a special class within a class by routinely grouping the same students in the same groups. We want to decrease the stigmatization that labels can create. In addition, homogeneously grouping students of low ability may result in lower achievement scores (Marzano, Pickering, and Pollock 2001, 84). Placement of students in groups should not be a life sentence. Furthermore, assigning students into groups should be a fluid and flexible process based on data. Placement of students in a group should never be based on their sharing a particular label such as being eligible for special education, because all students with the same label are not the same, and their abilities, challenges, and learning styles will not be the same. We recommend that co-teachers deliberately assign students to groups to make them heterogeneous whenever possible. Heterogeneous grouping allows students to learn with others who have different ways of approaching learning and thinking. Heterogeneous grouping stretches students to learn new ways of approaching problems, new questions to ask, and new styles of learning and yields positive achievement and social skills gains. Co-teachers are encouraged to group and regroup students frequently, as there are many different purposes for assigning students to work in a group. Frequent rotation of group members reduces any stigmatization that would result if students with similar kinds of learning needs were permanently grouped for long periods of time.

2. Should students stay primarily with the same co-teacher?

In parallel co-teaching, as in other forms of co-teaching, it is beneficial for students to rotate among the different team members. This avoids stigmatization of students or teachers that might arise if someone other than the classroom teacher, such as the special educator or paraprofessional, always teaches one set of students. By interacting with multiple instructors, students stretch their thinking and learning approaches as they experience the differing content expertise and instructional approaches of each co-teacher. Rotating students among co-teachers ensures that the professional educators as well as paraprofessionals, each of whom may have different strengths, instruct all students. In addition, struggling learners can benefit from the informed problem solving in which co-teachers can engage, given their firsthand knowledge of the students' learning characteristics.

3. How can we ensure quality control of the instruction provided by the other co-teacher(s) when we are busy with another group of students and may not even be in the same room?

This is a valid teacher concern, particularly when a co-teacher is a paraprofessional, a community volunteer, a student teacher, or an older cross-aged tutor, any of whom may have little experience taking full responsibility for a learning situation without direct teacher monitoring. Parallel co-teaching works best when co-teachers plan and debrief on a regular basis. Doing so provides the opportunity to include time to evaluate the successes and challenges that occurred while parallel co-teaching. Another way to enhance the likelihood that others will conduct their co-teaching responsibilities with integrity (i.e., as designed and intended) is for co-teachers to model briefly, before a lesson, each of the lesson's activities. Furthermore, during the co-teaching lesson, students may be assigned an independent task that does not require a co-teacher's guidance, thus releasing that co-teacher to observe, be available for questions, and provide guidance or feedback to other co-teachers. The idea here is to create structures before and during the operation of parallel co-teaching that allow for the co-teachers to be well prepared, confident in one another and in themselves, and available to each other.

The Complementary Co-Teaching Approach

6

Topics Included in This Chapter:

❖ Unique features, advantages of, and cautions associated with complementary co-teaching

❖ Vignettes: Complementary co-teaching teams in action

❖ Analyzing the cooperative process in the complementary co-teaching vignettes

❖ Frequently asked questions

Complementary co-teaching occurs when a co-teacher does something to enhance or augment the instruction provided by the other co-teacher(s) to assist students in accessing the content being taught. Within this model, one co-teacher often takes primary responsibility for presenting new academic content while the other supplements the instruction with analogies, different examples, or slowing down the pace of instruction. Both co-teachers share in the delivery of the information, sometimes with a varied delivery method. One co-teacher may lecture or read aloud while the other writes notes that are projected on a Smart Board, showing students how to follow along in their study guide. One co-teacher might paraphrase the other co-teacher's statements. Sometimes, one of the complementary co-teaching partners may preteach vocabulary, idioms, or figurative language. The complementary co-teacher might also preteach the content of roles for successful cooperative group learning and then monitor as students practice the roles during the other co-teacher's lesson. The general educator might teach a lesson while the special educator demonstrates (on the document projector or the white board) how to take notes on key points. Or the special educator might lecture while the general educator uses a graphic organizer on the document projector to assist students in organizing facts as differentiated from opinions. A complementary co-teacher can ask questions to check understanding of content, principles, or facts or task directions. Through these types of actions, the complementary co-teacher is positively influencing instruction even if she or he does not have the same level of content mastery as the core content teacher.

Co-teachers who employ the complementary approach are cautioned not to forget to monitor the learners. Sometimes co-teachers get so excited "performing on the stage" with their colleague that they forget to monitor the learners as closely as they did when they employed the supportive or parallel co-teaching approaches. They also must guard against too much teacher talk, repeating one another's statements or forgetting to solicit student input. Finally, complementary co-teachers can get in a rut, with one co-teacher always taking the role of content expert and the other, the complementary role. This can lead students to typecast the content teacher as the "real" teacher. To ward off this pitfall, be sure to plan for *role release*, the exchange of content and complementary roles, so that all co-teachers are perceived as "real" teachers. An added benefit of role release is that it gives the person who starts off as the complementary co-teacher the chance to really learn the content. As any teacher will testify, you really get to understand a concept, skill, or procedure when you have to teach it to another person.

■ VIGNETTES: COMPLEMENTARY CO-TEACHING TEAMS IN ACTION

Let's peek into the classrooms of the co-teaching teams to see how they teach standards-based lessons through complementary co-teaching. As shown in Table 6.1, they are demonstrating a variety of teaching and learning strategies, as well as different planning methods.

An Elementary Co-Teaching Team

In this lesson, Ms. Gilpatrick (the classroom teacher), Ms. Nugent (the speech and language therapist), and Ms. Hernandez (the paraprofessional) have complementary roles in a science lesson in which students compare and contrast the seeds of various fruits. In planning the lesson, all three met with the gifted and talented program coordinator for about 20 minutes to tap her expertise regarding multisensory activities. On the day of the lesson, the gifted and talented coordinator cannot be in the classroom, but her expertise is represented in the lesson's design.

Ms. Hernandez, who is musically talented, begins the class by playing a simple song about fruits that the students have been practicing. Students and co-teachers sing along. Ms. Gilpatrick then asks the students what they think they will be studying today, and they all chorally respond, "Fruit!" She says, "Yes" and begins holding up various fruits (e.g., grapes, banana, apple, peach, orange) as the students identify them in choral response. While she does this, Ms. Nugent, a talented artist, draws and colors in the fruits on the board with colored markers, also labeling each fruit as it is presented.

Ms. Gilpatrick explains to the students that they are to work in pairs with their tablemates to create a chart about the seeds of each of five fruits. In the chart, they are to describe the color, shape, size, and amount of seeds in each fruit. As Ms. Gilpatrick explains the task, Ms. Hernandez passes out to each student a grape that has been cut in half so that the seeds inside can be seen. It should be noted here that Elisa, the student with autism, is seated with a classmate to whom she is especially responsive when she needs to stay on task.

As Ms. Gilpatrick asks students questions about each of the dimensions of the grape seed, Ms. Nugent records the students' responses on a large chart on the board. The dimensions—size, color, shape, and amount—also are written on the board so that students may refer to them when they are working with the other fruits.

Size	Tiny, small, big
Color	Brown, white, black, red
Shape	Oval, round
Amount	One, a few, lots

After showing this chart, Ms. Nugent distributes copies of it to each pair of students. At the same time, Ms. Gilpatrick checks for understanding by asking students to raise their hand if they know how to explain what to do; she calls on one of the seven students who raise their hands to explain and praises the student for sharing. All three co-teachers then distribute one fruit at a time for each pair to examine; each fruit has been cut in half so that students can see the seed(s) inside. The pairs study the fruit and complete the chart.

As students work in pairs, the three adults circulate around the room to monitor students' engagement and to probe them about their findings. Ms. Hernandez is assigned to keep a particular eye on Elisa and her partner to be sure that they are engaged and to provide redirection or support, if needed.

When students have completed their task, they are encouraged to draw and color the seeds for each of their fruits and to taste the fruits they have been examining. This "sponges up" what might otherwise be "dead time" for groups that finish early and provides students motivation for task completion.

Ms. Gilpatrick asks students to stand up around the room holding their charts. She calls on pairs randomly to share their findings, while Ms. Nugent records their results on a large chart on the board.

The lesson concludes with Ms. Hernandez leading the fruit song that the students already know. She introduces a new verse that celebrates the seeds of the fruits the students examined. She had composed the verse spontaneously as the groups were working and, with Ms. Gilpatrick's permission, wrote the words in large print on chart paper so that students could follow along. The students sing the new verse twice. Ms. Gilpatrick tells them that Ms. Hernandez created it especially for them and that they will have a chance to practice it all week. Finally, Ms. Nugent previews the follow-up activity of creating a fruit-and-seed collage. Ms. Gilpatrick reminds them that they will continue to observe the plants that they have planted and will record the observations in their learning logs.

A Middle-Level Co-Teaching Team

Ms. Kurtz (the language arts and social studies teacher) and Ms. Olvina (the paraprofessional) have been discussing the confusion that students often have in trying to differentiate among synonyms, antonyms, and homonyms. This conversation leads to an on-the-spot plan to use the game of Charades as an introduction to cooperative group-learning activities (round-robin, Go Fish–type of practice for determining synonyms, antonyms, and homonyms). Ms. Olvina volunteers to think of a few examples to use in Charades. As the class begins, Ms. Kurtz asks, "Who here knows how to play Charades or Go Fish?" She calls on a couple of students to explain the games briefly and then informs the class that today's lesson on synonyms, antonyms, and homonyms will involve both games.

Ms. Kurtz first provides a definition and gives several examples of antonyms, synonyms, and homonyms. She then says, "OK, let's play Charades for antonyms!" Ms. Olvina gets in front of the class and models a charade for a pair of antonyms. The students guess until the correct answer is given. Ms. Olvina challenges them to an even tougher one, and students guess again. Ms. Kurtz then asks if any students have an antonym in mind to stump the class. Before they model them, she has the students who volunteer whisper the antonyms in her ear to be sure that they are, in fact, antonyms.

Ms. Olvina says that she is sure to be able to stump the class on her synonym charade. She performs it, and students guess. Again, two or three student volunteers model additional synonyms. Ms. Olvina repeats her challenge, this time for a homonym pair. New students act out homonym charades.

Ms. Kurtz sets up a transition to the next activity by telling students that, in pairs, they will have 8 minutes to come up with at least two synonyms, two antonyms, and two homonyms that are really hard to figure out. She tells them that they have access to the computer, dictionaries, and thesauruses and that when they are finished, they are to come to her or Ms. Olvina to check their answers. Ms. Olvina projects a listing of the student pairs that Ms. Kurtz had previously determined.

Ms. Kurtz and Ms. Olvina move around the room to monitor students' progress on the task, suggesting resources, such as the online thesaurus accessible through the iPad provided to all students, to pairs that appear to be struggling. Ms. Kurtz has identified a few students whom she believes will need "starter" words. She has prepared a stack of cards, half of which she passes to Ms. Olvina. The two co-teachers share the responsibility for observing the pairs in which these students are working and are prepared to pass them a starter word, if needed.

After 10 minutes, Ms. Kurtz congratulates the pairs on their work and has them sign and pass to Ms. Olvina their worksheets. She then has two sets of partners sit at round tables to create six groups of four. A remaining pair is split across two quads to create two groups of five students. Each table has a can of Popsicle sticks with words written on them. Ms. Kurtz explains that the students will have 8 minutes to play a variation of Go Fish by taking turns drawing sticks from the can in a clockwise, round-robin manner and stating out loud a homonym, synonym, or antonym for the word they have drawn.

Teammates have two rounds to guess what the word on the stick might be, guessing homonyms, synonyms, or antonyms. When someone guesses correctly, the stick holder must show the stick. If no one guesses after two rounds, the students holding the Popsicle sticks tell their tablemates what word is written on their sticks.

Ms. Kurtz sets a timer for 8 minutes and tells the groups that the person in each group who is seated closest to her is the first person to pull a stick. Then, both Ms. Kurtz and Ms. Olvina roam among the groups listening for examples of homonyms, antonyms, and synonyms to share with the class during the closure to the lesson.

Ms. Kurtz and Ms. Olvina start to wrap up the lesson by applauding the students for a great fishing expedition, and Ms. Kurtz asks for a couple of fish stories about a really difficult or funny synonym, antonym, or homonym pair. Ms. Kurtz and Ms. Olvina each share a couple of examples they heard as they monitored groups. Ms. Kurtz then announces a flash round. She offers a word, asking first for a homonym, next for an antonym, then for a synonym, and finally for the same word in another language. She asks Ms. Olvina to lead a second round, passing her a couple of words. They end the lesson by giving each other a high five with big smiles and laughs.

A High School Co-Teaching Team

The students in Mr. Woo's and Mr. Viana's government class are about to prepare for two major assignments. The first is a field experience visiting a government meeting. The second is an interview of a public government official. Both of these field experiences are ones that the students have anticipated with excitement and ones for which the instructors have emphasized the importance of being prepared and behaving professionally. Today's lesson focuses on preparing students for their visitation to government meetings.

Mr. Woo begins the class by asking students, "What do you think we should be looking for? What do you think we should have as requirements for our report of the experience? How should the report be formatted? How long should the report be? In what varied ways might you share the report with your classmates and other interested parties?" Within 15 minutes, the class comes to agreement on a structure for observing and then reporting about the meeting. By the time they are finished, Mr. Viana (the special educator) has typed this format into the computer, printed a form for every student, and quickly projected the form. As Mr. Woo briefly introduces a DVD clip of a meeting from the previous year, Mr. Viana distributes the form to all of the students. Mr. Woo directs them to use the form to take notes while they are watching the DVD clip. While the clip is playing, Mr. Viana creates and projects a model of what the students' reports should look like. Following the DVD, Mr. Woo leads the students through an examination of Mr. Viana's notes, so that they can compare their attempts with the standard the teachers expect of their actual meeting report.

In the second half of the class, Mr. Woo leads a similar discussion with the students about the content and format of their upcoming interview with a government official. Again, they come up with an agreed-on format, which Mr. Viana types, prints, and distributes. As he does this, Mr. Woo offers the students a list of the possible local and regional officials whom they might interview and asks the students if they know of any others.

Mr. Woo then has students brainstorm possible questions that they might ask a government official. Mr. Viana records these on the board. All questions are accepted as potentially good questions. Mr. Woo describes the job of the president of the district's school board and asks students, in pairs, to generate three questions appropriate to ask this person. Mr. Woo samples at least one question from each pair while Mr. Viana records the questions on the board. Mr. Woo then teaches the students a process for prioritizing questions in which they each get four colored dots to vote for their preferred questions. They may distribute their four dots among one, two, three, or four questions. Students line up at the board to vote. Mr. Viana tallies the votes as Mr. Woo announces that the president of the school board will come to class the next day so that Mr. Woo can model the interviewing process using the students' most-voted-for questions.

The following day, Mr. Woo interviews the school board president, while Mr. Viana records the president's responses and projects it with the document projector, using the questions and formats that the class developed. The purpose of this exercise is to offer the students a concrete model of professional behavior in interviewing and the detail with which the instructors expect students to take notes in an interview. The school board president opens the class to a question-and-answer period for the students. After she leaves, Mr. Woo reviews the notes Mr. Viana prepared and again engages the students in a discussion to determine the format, length, and due date of the interview report. Mr. Viana records these requirements and the format on the computer, prints copies, and distributes them to students while Mr. Woo goes over the list of officials whom students can interview. Mr. Woo closes the lesson by previewing the next day's class, in which students will sign up for particular officials, develop interviews, and rehearse questions with classmates.

After class, Mr. Viana suggests to Mr. Woo that some students may need some accommodations in how they perform and record the interviews. For example, he suggests that some students might feel more comfortable interviewing in pairs. He also suggests that for students who may have difficulty listening and simultaneously recording answers, they could be allowed to record, videotape, or create a podcast of their interview and transcribe it later. Finally, Mr. Viana suggests that it might be a good idea to pair all students thoughtfully so that students with differing strengths (e.g., interpersonal vs. verbal-linguistic, listening vs. writing) could support one another to create a better report. Mr. Woo agrees that all of these are great options for differentiating the assignment and suggests that in the next class, before they engage students in creating their interviews, Mr. Viana should discuss with the students the various options for conducting and recording the interview. Mr. Viana agrees, and they leave to teach their respective next-period classes.

Table 6.1 The Many Faces of Co-Teaching: Co-Teaching Teams' Use of Complementary Co-Teaching

Meet the Co-Teachers	Co-Teacher Roles	Curriculum Area(s)	Teaching Learning Strategies	Planning Method
Elementary				
Ms. Gilpatrick, classroom teacher	Leads the lesson and explains the task, distributes materials, and monitors student progress	Science	Constructivist learning	Preplanning
Ms. Hernandez, paraprofessional	Incorporates art and music, distributes materials, and monitors student progress			
Ms. Nugent, speech and language therapist	Incorporates notes on blackboard, previews next activities, distributes materials, and monitors student progress			
Middle Level				
Ms. Kurtz, language arts and social studies teacher	Leads the lesson, explains the task, and monitors and gives feedback to students	Language arts	Multicultural education strategies	Preplanning and on-the-spot planning
Ms. Olvina, paraprofessional	Models how to play the game and monitors and gives feedback to students		Game format for application practice	
High School				
Mr. Woo, social studies teacher	Leads the lesson	Social studies	Cooperative group learning (jigsaw with structured social and task roles)	Preplanning and on-the-spot planning
Mr. Viana, special educator	Records notes to model note taking and suggests future accommodations			

ANALYZING THE COOPERATIVE ■ PROCESS IN THE COMPLEMENTARY CO-TEACHING VIGNETTES

The five elements of the cooperative process differ when complementary co-teaching is applied at the various levels—elementary, middle level, and high school. The cooperative process gains in depth as the co-teaching team members shift from supplementary to parallel to complementary co-teaching. Co-teaching roles and responsibilities also shift based on the nature of the instructional activity, the preferences and experience of the members of the team, and the needs of their learners. Most important, students in classrooms in which complementary co-teaching is practiced have the opportunity to see how their teachers communicate, establish equity and parity, and share authority.

As we have noted previously, the five elements of the cooperative process are face-to-face interaction, positive interdependence, interpersonal skills, monitoring, and accountability. In the complementary co-teaching vignettes, all three teams added a preplanning component to enrich their face-to-face interactions. Their division of labor allowed them to experience positive interdependence, perhaps most vividly portrayed by the elementary team, who allowed the students to experience their individual talents (music and artistic expression). The three teams exercised their interpersonal skills by communicating with each other both before and during the lessons. All three teams monitored their effectiveness during their debriefing sessions in preparation for the next day's lesson. It may not be clearly stated, but can you see how the team members held each other accountable for the roles and responsibilities that had developed?

We advocate that complementary co-teachers include as many elements of the cooperative process as possible. This happens when co-teachers experience frequent face-to-face interactions, realize exactly how they are positively interdependent, make opportunities to practice their social interpersonal skills, monitor how well they work together, and hold each other accountable for the tasks they have agreed to perform.

FREQUENTLY ASKED QUESTIONS

People ask several questions when they consider the option of complementary co-teaching. You might have similar questions.

1. How can you expect a special educator or a teacher of students who are learning English to be an effective complementary co-teacher in a high school science class where content mastery is so important?

It is to be expected that there will be a learning curve for anyone who is entering the science classroom—or the mathematics, foreign language, or social studies classroom. Adding to their knowledge base, updating their skills in teaching new content, and learning new dimensions of the teaching/learning

(Continued)

(Continued)

process are part of the professional responsibility of all educators and one reason that professional-development activities are so important. For example, a special educator assigned to work with a science co-teacher can enroll in online courses such as those sponsored by the National Science Teachers Association (http://learningcenter.nsta.org/products/online_courses). Similarly, general educators who are assigned to work with special educators can engage in the reciprocal responsibility of acquiring learning strategies and/or knowledge about the educational adaptations suitable for students in their classrooms (see, for example, the tutorial for learning a reading strategy for teenagers and other resources at the IRIS center, http://www.iriscenter.com/palshs/chalcycle.htm).

Co-teaching team members may need to structure observation and processing time for those who need to become acclimated to the content and procedures of particular classes. We have great admiration for the co-teachers who have stepped up to the cognitive demands of learning enough of the subject matter—sometimes, seemingly, just barely enough—to stay one page or one chapter ahead of the students. As adults who have successfully completed their elementary, secondary, and postsecondary education opportunities, the special educator and the teacher of students who are learning English have the skills to acquire new knowledge, assimilate it, and support young people as they learn it. Science textbooks provide ample resources such as chapter outlines, previews, summaries, glossaries, and test banks. Students also can share what they know in the language of the beginner and thus better communicate with the co-teacher who is also a beginning learner in the subject. We, too, have experienced reluctance to jump into a new area of knowledge, yet each time we have done so, we have come through our trepidations with newfound knowledge, increased content mastery, enhanced skills and strategies, and improved self-confidence.

Finally, remember that not all members of the co-teaching team need to have the same level of curriculum content mastery and that, over time, all members of a co-teaching team can acquire the content knowledge and the skills modeled by their co-teaching partners. A benefit of co-teaching is that as co-teachers pool their respective expertise, they also exchange and enhance one another's diverse knowledge, skills, and strengths.

2. As a complementary co-teacher, for what specifically am I responsible? I'm still unclear about this.

This is a good example of a question about role clarification. We suggest that people on the co-teaching team literally step apart from one another and write the following: "What are the questions that confuse you?" Questions about role clarification tend to fall into categories such as planning, instructing, grading, communicating with parents, and managing the discipline in the classroom. Here are a few examples:

- How do team members arrange to share their expertise?
- Who plans for what content?
- Who will adapt curriculum and instruction?

Do these questions sound familiar? They were first introduced within the context of roles and responsibilities. These questions continually arise as co-teachers move from supportive to parallel to complementary to team-teaching co-teaching approaches. The answers to these questions will change depending on the experience of the co-teachers and the needs of the students for whom they are responsible.

Please forgive the ambiguity of the answer to this question. The answers are within each co-teaching team member and must be collaboratively developed. Some co-teaching team members will need to envision the big picture to contextualize their role. Others will need a step-by-step (sometimes even a minute-by-minute) agenda. We encourage each co-teaching team member to be respectful of the others' learning and working styles.

The Team-Teaching Co-Teaching Approach

7

Topics Included in This Chapter:

❖ Unique features, advantages of, and cautions associated with team co-teaching
❖ Vignettes: Team teaching co-teaching
❖ Analyzing the cooperative process in the team-teaching co-teaching vignettes
❖ Frequently asked questions

Team co-teaching occurs when two or more people do what the traditional teacher used to do. Specifically, they share responsibility for planning, teaching, and assessing progress of students in the class(es) that they teach together. Team co-teaching is a sophisticated process that has a beautiful flow to it. In keeping with the marriage or committed partnership analogy introduced earlier, when co-teachers use the team co-teaching approach, they are like a couple who know their partner so well that they dance beautifully together. Their dance is similar to a tango. It is complex, sophisticated, and intimate; and the partners must have practiced, be flexible, trust one another, and anticipate each other's moves.

Both co-teachers plan and design the lesson or unit and then simultaneously deliver or take turns delivering various components of the lesson. It may look as if they've orchestrated the lesson in such a way that one person assumes greater responsibility for the introduction of the activities or the lesson and another takes greater responsibility for the closure and facilitation of students' individual practice. Or it might look like tag-team or turn teaching in which they consistently and fluidly go back and forth in sharing responsibilities throughout the lesson, appearing to finish one another's sentences. Some team-teaching teams rotate responsibility for the different aspects of a lesson or unit among the members each time they co-teach so that each person gets a chance to teach each element of the lesson or unit.

It may take time for co-teachers to shift from supportive, parallel, and complementary co-teaching arrangements to achieve team co-teaching. Team co-teaching usually requires more face-to-face planning time than do the other co-teaching approaches. Decisions about who teaches what are mutually determined and based on variables such as each person's curriculum content mastery, preferences, and professional training or background. The goal is for co-teachers to move in and out of each of the four co-teaching approaches, often within a single lesson, based on the needs of the diverse learners whom they are teaching. As for cautions, as with complementary co-teaching, co-teachers employing the team co-teaching approach must remember to not get so engaged in the act of teaching that they forget to closely monitor the students in the class. They also must guard against too much teacher talk, repeating one another's statements, "stepping on one another's toes" by interrupting at inopportune times, or forgetting to solicit student input or prompt student conversation.

In team co-teaching arrangements, the equity and parity of the team members is obvious from their roles in the classroom. For example, you may find two teacher desks in the classroom and all teachers' names on the classroom door and on papers that are sent home. Both instructors' names may appear as instructors of record. Moreover, all co-teachers participate equally at conferences as well as other meetings with students' families (e.g., Individual Education Program meetings, for students with disabilities).

■ VIGNETTES: TEAM TEACHING CO-TEACHING

Let's look into the classrooms for a final time as the co-teaching teams team co-teach standards-based lessons. As summarized in Table 7.1, they are demonstrating a wide variety of best practices for instructional methods and a range of planning models as they team co-teach.

Table 7.1 The Many Faces of Co-Teaching: Co-Teaching Teams' Use of Team Teaching

Meet the Co-Teachers	Co-Teacher Roles	Curriculum Area(s)	Teaching Learning Strategies	Planning Method
Elementary				
Ms. Gilpatrick, classroom teacher	Distribute responsibility with joint delivery	Problem solving	Creative problem solving	Preplanning
Ms. Nugent, speech and language therapist				
Middle Level				
Mr. Silva, science and math teacher	Split class	Science	Multiple intelligences theory	Pre- and postplanning
Ms. Spaulding, special educator	Same content			
Ms. Kurt, language arts and social studies teachers	Alternating instructors		Think-pair-share quick cooperative learning structure	
Ms. Olvina, paraprofessional				
High School				
Mr. Woo, social studies teacher	Distribute responsibility with joint delivery	Social studies	Cooperative group learning—base team and expert groups	Preplanning
Mr. Viana, special educator			Application of small group social skill	

An Elementary Co-Teaching Team

Ms. Gilpatrick (the classroom teacher) holds weekly class meetings with students and convenes additional meetings at other times as needed. She has been working with the students on problem solving since the beginning of the school year. At this weekly class meeting, she plans to problem solve repeated problems seen on the playground. Ms. Nugent (the speech and language therapist) arrives with a box that contains written note cards that describe some of the playground problems. The problem-solving process the two have agreed to use is SODAS (Hazel et al. 1995), one that Ms. Nugent has used successfully with students for years. SODAS is an acronym for situation-options-disadvantages-advantages-solution. A template for the SODAS process is shown in Table 7.2.

Ms. Gilpatrick convenes and explains the purpose of this week's class meeting. The first problem randomly drawn from the box states, "A student calls another student's mother a name, and the students get into a fistfight on the playground." Ms. Gilpatrick puts a transparency of the SODAS template on the overhead projector as Ms. Nugent asks the students to identify the problem situation. Ms. Gilpatrick calls on a student who correctly identifies the problem situation. Ms. Nugent writes the identified situation on the overhead form. Ms. Nugent asks students to identify some options for solving this problem. Ms. Gilpatrick and Ms. Nugent alternate taking turns calling on students to share their ideas. Five options are generated, and Ms. Gilpatrick adds a sixth. Ms. Nugent records the information on the transparency.

The next step involves identifying disadvantages for each of the options. Ms. Nugent and Ms. Gilpatrick model talking about disadvantages of the first option, while Ms. Gilpatrick records disadvantages on the transparency. Then Ms. Nugent asks the students to turn to a neighbor and discuss possible disadvantages of the second option. After 1 minute, Ms. Gilpatrick calls on various students, and Ms. Nugent records the disadvantages that they share. The co-teachers repeat this process for the remaining options, alternating the roles of calling on the students and recording their answers.

Ms. Gilpatrick and Ms. Nugent model and record a discussion about the possible advantages of the first option and then ask the students to work in pairs to identify advantages for the remaining five options. Elisa, the student with autism, is partnered with a classmate who is especially good at giving Elisa the time she usually needs to generate ideas. When students are ready, Ms. Gilpatrick calls on them, and Ms. Nugent records their answers on the transparency. When this is done, Ms. Nugent rereads all of the disadvantages and asks the students to identify the worst disadvantages by raising their hands for no more than three choices when the item is reread. Ms. Gilpatrick tallies their responses and puts a box around the three disadvantages that had the most votes.

Ms. Gilpatrick and Ms. Nugent repeat the process for the advantages. This time, Ms. Gilpatrick reads and Ms. Nugent tallies responses and puts a circle around the advantages with the most votes. Ms. Gilpatrick directs the students to turn to a different partner to identify the possible solution(s) that would achieve the best advantages and avoid the worst disadvantages. After a couple minutes, Ms. Nugent asks the students to report their answers, and Ms. Gilpatrick tallies the results. Ms. Gilpatrick explains that if the scenario were real, the two students who had fought would be expected to use SODAS to come up with an alternate response to fighting if a problem like this were to occur again.

Ms. Nugent asks students how the SODAS problem-solving process might help them solve problems on the playground, in class, and at home. Ms. Gilpatrick and

Table 7.2   The SODAS Problem-Solving Process

SODAS

Situation (Define the problem)

_____

_____

_____

_____

Options

1. _____ 2. _____ 3. _____

Disadvantages

a. _____ a. _____ a. _____

b. _____ b. _____ b. _____

c. _____ c. _____ c. _____

d. _____ d. _____ d. _____

Advantages

a. _____ a. _____ a. _____

b. _____ b. _____ b. _____

c. _____ c._____ c. _____

d. _____ d. _____ d. _____

Solution

_____

_____

_____

If you agree to a solution, make a plan.
(Who will do what, when? How you know if the plan is working?)

_____

_____

_____

_____

_____

Ms. Nugent close the lesson by each sharing an example of how they have used SODAS in their personal lives and telling the students that they will practice using SODAS to solve problems throughout the year.

A Middle-Level Co-Teaching Team

Mr. Silva (the science and math teacher with an endorsement to teach students who are English language learners) recently attended a workshop at which he heard Thomas Armstrong talk about the use of multiple intelligences (MI) theory (Armstrong 2009). In the workshop, Armstrong gave an example of how MI theory could be used to teach Boyle's law. Boyle's law explains the inverse relationship between the volume and pressure of a gas if temperature remains constant. Coincidentally, Boyle's law is related to one of the seventh- and eighth-grade standards in physics that Mr. Silva must address.

Mr. Silva explains MI theory and Boyle's law to both Ms. Spaulding (the special educator) and Ms. Olvina (the paraprofessional) during a planning session. Ms. Spaulding agrees that using MI theory would be a great way to teach Boyle's law. She is already familiar with the theory and is really looking forward to team teaching this lesson and having the chance to apply MI theory in a content area.

During planning, Mr. Silva and Ms. Spaulding prepare a visual presentation. Ms. Olvina spontaneously creates a rap that reinforces the main concepts of the law. She records it so that it can be played in the class, even though she is not going to be there because she will be co-teaching with Ms. Kurtz (the language arts teacher) at that time.

Ms. Spaulding starts the lesson with an overview of MI theory and the eight intelligences—verbal-linguistic (word smart), logical-mathematical (logic smart), visual-spatial (picture smart), bodily-kinesthetic (body smart), musical (music smart), naturalist (nature smart), interpersonal (people smart), and intrapersonal (self smart). As Ms. Spaulding describes each intelligence, Mr. Silva points to its representation on the MI Pizza visual projected on the screen, which is reproduced in Figure 7.1.

Mr. Silva then asks students to identify their own top two intelligences and one that is currently least developed for them. He explains that everyone has all intelligences in different proportions and that intelligence may change over time with opportunities to learn. Like a muscle, intelligence grows with exercise.

As Mr. Silva names each intelligence, students raise their hands if it is one of their top two. Ms. Spaulding tallies responses on the MI Pizza visual projected with the document camera and creates a class profile of strength intelligences. Ms. Spaulding uses this as an opportunity to talk about how no one intelligence is better than another. Ms. Spaulding reveals her strength intelligences (i.e., body smart, people smart, picture smart), and Mr. Silva reveals his (i.e., logic smart, word smart, nature smart). Ms. Olvina and Ms. Kurtz have given permission to reveal their strengths; they both are people smart. In addition, Ms. Olvina is music smart, and Ms. Kurtz is word smart.

Mr. Silva states, "Today we are planning to teach you about a gas law named after a man, Robert Boyle. Now be honest, how many of you are excited to learn about this law?" Of the 26 students, 5 raise their hands. Mr. Silva asks, "How many of you might be interested in learning about this law if it was taught through the use of MI?" Now 22 of the 26 students raise their hands.

Mr. Silva says that some students who are word smart might understand by reading the definition of Boyle's law, which Ms. Spaulding projects on a screen.

Figure 7.1   The Multiple Intelligence Pizza

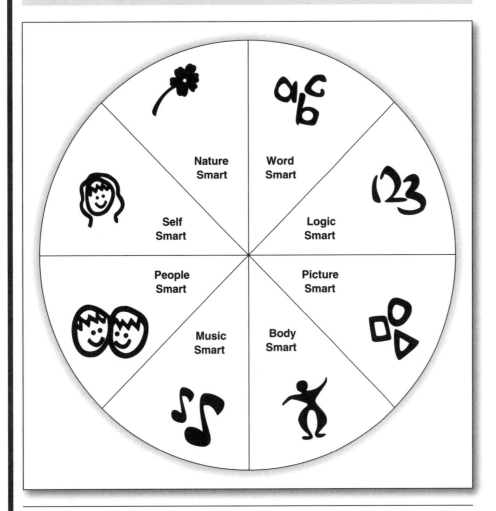

Source: From Figure 4.1 (p. 46) *Multiple Intelligences in the Classroom, 3rd edition,* by Thomas Armstrong, Alexandria, VA: ASCD ©2009 by Thomas Armstrong; Reprinted with permission of ASCD.

Ms. Spaulding reads the law and asks, "How many of you understand Boyle's law by reading the definition or hearing me read it to you?" Only a few students raise their hands. Mr. Silva says, "Some of you are logic smart, so you might understand if I give you the formula." Ms. Spaulding projects the formula and briefly explains it. She asks, "How many of you now think you understand Boyle's law?" A few more students raise their hands.

To use bodily-kinesthetic (body smart) intelligence to facilitate understanding, Mr. Silva asks the students to suck oxygen into their mouths and inflate both cheeks. Ms. Spaulding models this. Mr. Silva then has everyone push all of the air into one cheek, and asks, "What happened to the pressure in the one cheek when the volume was decreased?" The students answer that they felt that one side had more pressure when the volume was cut in half.

To use visual-spatial (picture smart) intelligence, Mr. Silva passes out balloons while Ms. Spaulding directs students to blow up and tie their balloons. Mr. Silva then has students squeeze the balloon to decrease the balloon's volume. As the students comply, several balloons pop. Ms. Spaulding asks the students to describe what just happened. As they do, Mr. Silva draws a V (volume) and a P (pressure) on the board, with an arrow pointing down next to the V and an arrow pointing up next to the P, graphically illustrating that as the volume of a gas goes down, the pressure goes up. Mr. Silva next holds up a balloon pinched midway by his hand. When he has the students' attention, he releases his hand, and the pressure releases.

Ms. Spaulding asks students to speculate about the relationship between volume and pressure that he has just illustrated. As they correctly respond, Ms. Spaulding draws an arrow pointing up next to the V and an arrow pointing down next to the P, indicating that as the volume increases, the pressure decreases.

To use the naturalist (nature smart) intelligence to help students learn about Boyle's law, Mr. Silva, a scuba diver, explains how when people dive, they have to control their rate of assent to the surface to avoid getting the bends. He explains this in terms of Boyle's law—the inverse relationship between the pressure and volume of a gas.

To use musical intelligences to activate learning, Mr. Silva plays the recording of Ms. Olvina's rap about Boyle's law while Ms. Spaulding projects the words of the song on a screen. Students listen once and then, as a class, all sing "The Boyle's Law Rap."

Mr. Silva and Ms. Spaulding use students' interpersonal (people smart) intelligence in a think-pair-share cooperative activity in which students explain Boyle's law in their own words to a partner and then identify the intelligence activities that most helped them understand the law and why.

To use the intrapersonal (self smart) intelligence to help students learn about Boyle's law, Mr. Silva asks them to think of a time when they felt under lots of pressure and to identify how much psychological or thinking space (or volume) they felt they had. Then Ms. Silva asks the students to think of a time when the pressure was low and to identify how much psychological space (volume) was available to them. The students are asked to record their observations in their learning logs and to be prepared to share their answers at the beginning of the next day's class.

To close, Mr. Silva asks, "Who now completely understands Boyle's law?" All but two students raise their hands. Ms. Spaulding asks, "Who found MI helpful in learning about Boyle's law?" Everybody raises his or her hands. They do the same when she asks if they want to use MI to learn other things in science. In the remaining minutes of the class, the MI rap is played again, and the students sing along.

In a debriefing session after the lesson, Mr. Silva and Ms. Spaulding excitedly talk about how enlightening the lesson had been. Mr. Silva said, "I think we can use multiple intelligences in other ways, too. We can use it to assess learning in different ways, like Ms. Olvina showing understanding of Boyle's law by using her musical intelligence to develop a rap." Ms. Spaulding agrees, and the two brainstorm ways to use MI theory to promote and assess students' learning in the next week's lessons.

A High School Co-Teaching Team

Mr. Woo (the social studies teacher) and Mr. Viana (the special educator) spent two planning sessions getting ready for a 2-week unit in which students will learn about primaries, campaign finance, conventions, and election processes, including the Electoral College. In the first session, Mr. Viana admitted that he has always been a little confused about why, in a democracy, it is not simple majority rule. Mr. Woo said, "I am sure you are not alone, so let's arrange for our students to discuss whether the Electoral College process should be maintained or abolished."

To examine the Electoral College, they decided to use a classic jigsaw cooperative group methodology, with base teams and expert groups. The 4-day lesson would start with students preparing in expert groups on the first day. On the second day, experts teach one another in base teams and come to decisions about whether the Electoral College should be abolished or maintained. On the third day, students share results of surveys of community members' understanding of and desire to keep or abolish the Electoral College and develop a class-wide summary chart of survey results. On the fourth day, base teams synthesize their work by composing a 200- to 300-word letter to the editor of the local newspaper explaining their position on the Electoral College's value and how they came to that position (e.g., community opinion survey, outcomes of past presidents elected through this process). What follows are details of the first 2 days of the lesson.

Mr. Woo begins by asking students, "What do you know about the process for becoming the president of the United States?" Someone states that the majority of people voting elect the president. Several students disagree and speak about the Electoral College. One student says that you can be elected even if you do not have the majority of votes. Mr. Woo asks the students how the Electoral College works. The students admit that they don't really understand the process. Mr. Viana admits to the students that he is not clear on how it works either. Mr. Woo states that by the end of the day's class, everyone should understand the process.

Mr. Woo assigns students to small cooperative groups and explains the cooperative group jigsaw in which each person is responsible for learning and teaching critical content to the base team. He says that the ultimate goals of each team are to determine the pros and cons of maintaining or abolishing the Electoral College system and to reach consensus about whether to maintain or abolish the Electoral College and provide rationale to support the group's decision.

Within each base team, the members are given a vignette in which a president came into power not by majority vote but by election within the Electoral College or a decision made within the House of Representatives. Included in the vignette is the actual election process along with the historical context of the time that this president was in office and the significant accomplishments or perceived failures (or both) within his or her presidential term. Members are given an overview of the Electoral College—how it came about, the rationale for it, and how it works.

Mr. Viana explains that students will first work individually to become experts on their material, as they are responsible for teaching it to the other members of the team. After all members have read and studied their materials, they are paired with a person from another team who has the exact same materials in order to check jointly for understanding and prepare the key points for instructing the other team members about their content. While the students are working, both teachers monitor students' work by walking around the room.

After 10 minutes, Mr. Viana directs the pairs of students to get into a larger expert group with people from the remaining groups that have been studying the same content. In the expert group, they are to review the content and prepare materials—visuals, flowcharts, bullet points, and so on—that will help them teach their classmates. Twenty minutes later, Mr. Woo disbands the expert groups and sends students back to their base teams. Mr. Viana and Mr. Woo provide the students with feedback on their use of cooperative, academic, and social skills; thank them for their great work; and briefly describe what students will do the next day in base teams. They tell the students that they want to check their understanding of the next day's activities. They give them think time, ask them to share with a partner, and randomly call on several students to summarize the next day's planned activities.

On the second day, Mr. Woo asks students, "What is it that we did yesterday to prepare for today? What is the task we are going to complete by the end of the day?" He and Mr. Viana randomly call on students to answer the questions. Mr. Woo then tells the students that they will have 30 minutes for base team members to teach their information to one another.

Mr. Woo describes the rotating roles of speaker, clarifier, and timekeeper. The speaker has 7 minutes to teach information and 3 minutes to answer questions. The clarifier is responsible for leading listeners to ask clarifying questions in the last 3 minutes. The timekeeper gives the speaker 5-, 7-, and 9-minute warnings as time elapses. Mr. Viana checks students' understanding of the three roles.

Mr. Viana clarifies the social skills that the students will be expected to use (i.e., active listening, turn taking, and encouraging others to speak) by reviewing charts of what each social skill looks and sounds like, which the students prepared earlier in the year. Mr. Woo tells the students that both teachers will observe them to be sure they are using the social skills while working.

Mr. Woo and Mr. Viana rotate among the base teams, complimenting members on their teaching and use of social skills. At the end of the instructional period, Mr. Viana asks students to give examples of active listening demonstrated by their team. Both he and Mr. Woo provide additional examples from their observations. Mr. Woo asks the students to identify the pros and cons of maintaining the Electoral College, and Mr. Viana records and projects the information. Mr. Viana asks for the results of the various groups' decisions either to maintain or to abolish the Electoral College. Mr. Woo records these data. Mr. Woo and Mr. Viana assign homework, which is for each person to interview at least four people, no more than two of whom are family members. They are to ask the following:

- How does the Electoral College work?
- Should it be maintained or abolished?
- Why should it be maintained or abolished?

Mr. Woo distributes forms for students to use to record information gathered during the interviews while Mr. Viana previews the unit activities and timelines.

■ ANALYZING THE COOPERATIVE PROCESS IN THE TEAM-TEACHING CO-TEACHING VIGNETTES

In these vignettes, you might have noticed that team co-teaching requires more trust, confidence, communication, and face-to-face planning time than the other co-teaching approaches. As stated previously, the five elements of the cooperative process are face-to-face interaction, positive interdependence, interpersonal skills, monitoring, and accountability. In the team co-teaching vignettes, all three teams relied on preplanning face-to-face interaction. The elementary team spent the least amount of time engaged in formal preplanning, indicating that they had a high level of trust and had taught in a similar fashion previously. In its preplanning, the middle-level team included other persons who had different areas of strength as resources when designing the lesson. By dividing the tasks according to co-teachers' strengths, each of the teams experienced a form of positive interdependence. All three teams rotated some of the responsibilities among the team members, and, in addition, the high school team divided some tasks among the members based on content mastery. For example, the classroom teacher had a greater role in explaining the academic content, and the special educator assumed greater responsibility for explaining social skills and facilitating students' use of the social skills when they worked in cooperative learning groups. The three teams exercised their interpersonal skills by communicating with each other both before and during the lessons. Accountability can be detected in the various ways that effectiveness was monitored. Accountability is strongest among the members of the middle-level team, as they debriefed about lessons in preparation for future lessons. We advocate that co-teachers who team co-teach incorporate as many elements of the cooperative process as possible into their interactions before, during, and after co-teaching.

FREQUENTLY ASKED QUESTIONS

The following are among the questions people ask when they are considering the use of the team co-teaching approach.

1. Should personnel who are team co-teaching remain together, or should one of them follow the students whom they have been supporting to the next grade level, working with new teachers at that level?

We know that it takes time for the team co-teaching relationship to develop. We've heard from many classroom teachers that attempting to team teach can be really frustrating for them when personnel changes from year to year. They work together for an entire year and get to a certain point, and then they have to start over again the following year with a brand new person. Classroom teachers often report that changing co-teaching partners often thwarts their development as co-teachers. Support personnel such as special educators, Title I personnel, instructors for students learning English, and those who provide gifted and talented education also express concern about changing co-teaching partners. Their concern, particularly at the middle and high school levels, has to do with mastering new content. For example, they might have been assigned to co-teach in a specific content area (e.g., biology), acquiring more familiarity with the content, and then they are transferred to another academic area (e.g., algebra) in which they will learn a whole new set of academic principles, concepts, facts, and skills.

On the other hand, there are benefits to the students and to the new teachers of students who are at risk for school failure if teaching personnel who know the students accompany them to the next grade and work with other teacher(s) at that level. If the students go to a new class with someone who has supported them before, such as a special educator, students are less likely to fall through the cracks. The new teacher immediately has access to a knowledgeable, built-in resource person.

(Continued)

(Continued)

In co-teaching, as in life, there are no perfect solutions. There are advantages and disadvantages associated with staying with the teacher or accompanying the students. It is up to the team members to explore the advantages and disadvantages of each option and to choose the solution that is best for the students they teach. Our observation of co-teaching teams reveals that in elementary schools, about half of the teams decide to stay together and half decide to follow the students. In the upper grades, we tend to see more of the co-teaching teams staying together, with team members citing mastering the complex curriculum as one of the main reasons for doing so.

2. How long will it take for co-teaching teams to evolve to the team co-teaching stage?

First, we want to emphasize that each co-teaching approach is a valid option. Second, we encourage you to avoid referring to "evolving" or "stages" because these terms imply a hierarchy. Although it is true that many co-teachers begin with the supportive and parallel co-teaching approaches, others often start with team teaching. Third, there is no one answer to this question—only multiple options.

Some teachers decide to use the team co-teaching approach within a few weeks of working together. Other teachers may require a year or more to see that the team co-teaching approach might be useful given the needs of their students and the curricula they are teaching. The amount of time required varies because of many factors, including the teaching competencies and subject matter expertise of the co-teachers, the time co-teachers devote to the cooperative process itself, the time available for collaborative planning and teaching, the willingness to develop a working relationship among the members of the co-teaching team, and the needs of the students.

In fact, one of the best ways to learn to co-teach is to co-teach, to learn by doing. We have each learned a new skill this way, in particular when we practice with someone who is just a little bit more skilled than we are. We propose a framework to help guide the decisions about who should co-teach; this framework is based on two of the many factors involved: willingness to co-teach and skills or ability to co-teach. The Willingness to Co-Teach scale can vary from *low willingness* to *high willingness.* The Capability to Co-Teach scale also varies from *low capability* to *high capability.* As shown in Figure 7.2, this results in a four-quadrant taxonomy.

In Quadrant A, when co-teachers are both capable and willing, their use of all four approaches to co-teaching can be developed quickly. For co-teachers in Quadrant B, who are capable but not so willing, it may take a little more time. For co-teachers in Quadrant C, who are willing but not so capable, more time may be needed for them to develop the teaching competencies that are needed for successful co-teaching to occur.

For those in Quadrant D, who are neither willing nor capable, it may be necessary to provide systematic professional development opportunities such as those described in Chapter 12 and logistical administrative supports such as those described in Chapter 10. The zone of proximal development (Vygotsky 1987) offers a theoretical framework to describe how teachers learn from each other while they actually conduct co-teaching activities. A *zone of proximal development* (ZPD) is defined as a particular range of ability with and without assistance from a teacher or a more capable peer (Vygotsky 1987). Vygotsky emphasizes that what children can do with the assistance of others is even more indicative of their mental development than what they can do alone. We believe that this is also true for teachers: What teachers can do with the assistance of others is even more indicative of their capabilities than what they can do alone.

To scaffold teachers effectively within their ZPDs, there should be an awareness of the reciprocal roles that can be assumed throughout the co-teaching process: A teacher-peer models the co-teaching behavior, that co-teaching behavior is then imitated, the model fades out instruction, and the teacher practices reciprocal teaching (scaffolding others) until the co-teaching skill is mastered. Supports and demands for co-teaching may be adjusted depending on the co-teacher's placement in the taxonomy.

Figure 7.2   The Zone of Proximal Development for Co-Teachers

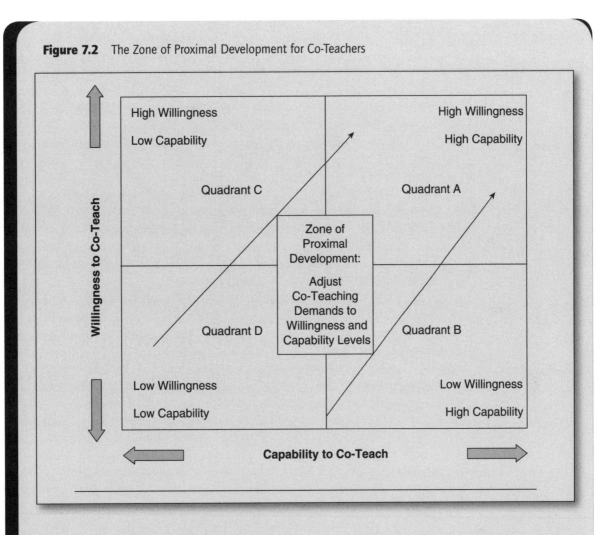

To illustrate, when co-teachers are neither willing nor capable (Quadrant D), a lower demand for co-teaching would be expected, along with more support required to learn the skills and develop the willingness. Teachers in Quadrant D might start with one period a day as a supportive co-teacher and then move to a parallel teaching arrangement as they experience the natural reinforcement of seeing children succeed.

When co-teachers are willing and capable (Quadrant A), they can continue to accept a high level of responsibility for co-teaching assignments and, at the same time, expand their skills in mentoring and coaching others. Co-teachers who are capable but not so willing (Quadrant B) might take the opportunity to interview other co-teaching teams in action to discover how perceived barriers were addressed. In this way, the unwilling co-teachers might become more willing to co-teach. When co-teachers are willing but not so capable (Quadrant C), specific supports for developing teaching skills such as cooperative learning would help the co-teachers learn the communication and leadership skills necessary for children to be successful in group work and, at the same time, co-teachers would be learning the skills to practice within their own co-teaching team work.

In summary, it is important to honor where people are in their co-teaching journeys and treat them with respect, regardless of the quadrant in which you or they may currently fall. The quadrant can help you and your co-teachers plan for and lobby for professional development and administrative support as described in Chapter 10 so that you and your students can experience the benefits of co-teaching.

Part II Summary

As you read about each of the co-teaching approaches in the previous chapters, you may have used the advance organizer presented in Figure II.1 in the introduction to Part II to compare and contrast what you learned about the four approaches. Did you detect key features (i.e., differences) of each approach? What were some cautions for using each of the four approaches? What did you conclude were some common features or similarities across the four co-teaching approaches? Whether or not you used the advance organizer to summarize your discoveries regarding the four co-teaching approaches, you may find the comparisons among the approaches presented in Figure II.2 useful as a summary of Chapters 4 through 7. Note that the content of this table is not intended to present all that there is to know about the four approaches but as a selection of some of the common and differing dimensions as well as cautions associated with the supportive, parallel, complementary, and team co-teaching approaches.

Figure II.2 Similarities and Differences of Supportive, Parallel, Complementary, and Team Co-Teaching Approaches

Similarities and Differences Among the Four Co-Teaching Approaches

- Two or more co-teachers are in the classroom.
- They capitalize on specific strengths and expertise of both co-teachers.
- They provide greater teacher-to-student ratios and additional one-on-one support for students in the classroom.
- All approaches have benefits and cautions associated with their use.
- Students are primarily heterogeneously grouped by mixed abilities and interests.
- There are shared responsibilities.
- Each approach requires trust, communication, planning time, and coordination of effort. (Note: The need for all of these elements increases as you move from supportive to parallel, parallel to complementary, and complementary to team-teaching co-teaching.)

Supportive Differences	Parallel Differences	Complementary Differences	Team-Teaching Differences
One co-teacher is in the lead role; the other provides support. Who is in the lead and who provides support may change during a lesson.	Co-teachers work, monitor, or facilitate different groups of students in the same room. (There are at least seven different options for arranging the groups.)	One co-teacher teaches content; the other facilitates access (e.g. clarifies, paraphrases, simplifies, provides visual scaffolding, records content.) One co-teacher may preteach specific study or social skills and monitors students' use of them; the other teaches the academic content.	Both co-teachers are equally responsible for planning, instruction of content, assessment, and grade assignment. This approach requires the greatest amount of planning time, trust, communication, and coordination of effort.

Supportive Advantages	Parallel Advantages	Complementary Advantages	Team-Teaching Advantages
Allows immediate support (academic or behavioral) to students. Can be used when there is little or no planning time. A way for a new member of a co-teaching team to get to know other co-teachers, the students, the curriculum, and the classroom routines. New content is introduced by the teacher with the greatest content mastery. Allows the supportive co-teacher to monitor and collect data.	Reduces the student-to-teacher ratio (divide and conquer). Increases teacher feedback to students. Each co-teacher instructs and uses instructional expertise. Co-teachers can be viewed as equal partners. Allows for greater individualization, data collection, monitoring, and relationship building with students. Students have greater opportunities to work alone or engage in conversation and peer-mediated instruction with partners, at stations, or in cooperative groups.	Complementary "experts of access," regardless of their level of content mastery, influence instruction by making content more accessible. Co-teachers are viewed as teachers of all students in the classroom.	All co-teachers are viewed as equal and as teachers of all students. Content experts acquire and practice access skills. Access experts acquire and practice content skills. It is difficult to identify who is the "content" vs. the "access" expert.

Supportive Cautions	Parallel Cautions	Complementary Cautions	Team-Teaching Cautions
Beware of the "Velcro effect," where the supportive co-teacher hovers over one or selected students, stigmatizing both the student(s) and the co-teacher. Beware of making the supportive co-teacher the "discipline police," materials copier, or in-class paper grader rather than an instructor. Beware of ineffective use of the supportive co-teacher's (e.g., special educator, ELL specialist) expertise. Beware of resentment if the skills of the supportive co-teacher (e.g. special educator) are not being used or the lead co-teacher (e.g. content teacher) feels an unequal burden of responsibility. Beware of staying "stuck" in the supportive role due to lack of planning time.	Beware of creating a special class within the class and lowering student achievement by homogeneously grouping lower-performing students together. Beware that the noise level can become uncomfortably high when numerous activities are occurring in the same room. Beware of failing to adequately prepare other co-teachers to ensure that they deliver instruction as intended, since co-teachers cannot monitor one another while all are simultaneously co-teaching different groups.	Beware of failing to closely monitor students as co-teachers co-instruct in the front of the class. Beware of too much teacher talk, repetition, and reduced student–student interaction. Beware of "stepping on one another's toes." Beware of "typecasting" the co-teacher delivering content as the "real" or "expert" teacher. Beware of failing to plan for "role release" or "role exchange," so that all co-teachers get a chance to lead instruction of the content.	Beware of failing to closely monitor students as co-teachers co-instruct in the front of the class. Beware of too much teacher talk, repetition, and reduced student–student interaction. Beware of "stepping on one another's toes."

PART III

Changing Roles and Responsibilities

The two chapters in Part III examine how the roles of paraprofessionals and students change when they are engaged as co-teachers in the classroom. Chapter 8 traces the history of paraprofessionals in schools; introduces a paraprofessional and her team; and follows her team as she engages in supportive, parallel, and complementary co-teaching roles in a single lesson. This vignette is followed by an examination of the benefits of having paraprofessionals co-teach, the variety of roles and responsibilities of paraprofessionals in co-teaching classrooms, the unique challenges faced by paraprofessional co-teachers, and cautions for paraprofessional co-teachers to avoid when engaged in each of the four co-teaching approaches. Chapter 9 looks at the role of students as co-teachers and introduces five vignettes in which elementary through high school students engage as instructors in very different ways. The remainder of the chapter examines the emerging research base on students as co-teachers and offers suggestions on how to prepare students for and assess them in the co-teaching role.

The Role of Paraprofessionals in Co-Teaching

8

Have you ever wondered about the role of paraprofessionals in co-teaching? In our work with co-teachers, we have faced numerous questions about the various roles of paraprofessionals in inclusive classrooms. In this chapter, we examine these roles. Through a vignette, we offer examples of how a paraprofessional can contribute effectively as a co-teacher in the classroom. We summarize potential benefits of having a paraprofessional in the classroom as a co-teacher. We also examine the critical issues of paraprofessional training and supervision as well as cautions about employing paraprofessionals as co-teachers. Readers interested in further information about paraprofessionals performing as co-teachers are referred to the Nevin, Villa, and Thousand's 2008 text, *A Guide to Co-Teaching With Paraeducators: Practical Tips for K–12 Educators.*

HISTORY OF PARAPROFESSIONALS IN EDUCATION

The history of paraprofessionals began in the 1950s, when paraprofessionals were introduced into schools to provide teachers with more time for planning for instruction. For the most part, early paraprofessionals performed clerical services such as duplication of materials or management of students in noninstructional settings (e.g., lunchroom, playground). Then in the 1970s, federal legislation was passed that guaranteed students with disabilities access to free public education. With steady movement toward general education being the preferred primary placement for students with disabilities, the paraprofessional's role has transformed to being primarily instructional in nature, especially when supporting students in the general education setting (Giangreco, Smith, and Pinckney 2006; Giangreco, Suter, and Doyle 2010; Nevin, Thousand, and Villa 2008; Pickett and Gerlach 2003; and Pickett, Likins, Morgan, Gerlach, and Wallace 2007).

The numbers evidence the increased reliance on paraprofessionals to assist in differentiating instruction in the classroom. For example, a comprehensive study of K–12 staffing patterns in all 50 U.S. states revealed that from 1993 to 2000, the number of paraprofessionals in classrooms increased 65%, from approximately 319,000 to more than 525,000 (National Center for Education Statistics 2000). Of these, 55% were employed in inclusive and other educational settings supporting students with disabilities, 25% were assigned to support students in compensatory programs (e.g., as Title I aides or multilingual aides), and the remaining 20% worked in learning environments such as libraries, media centers, and computer laboratories. Notably, by 2004 (just 4 years later), the number of instructional paraprofessionals had increased to 633,671; the majority were assigned to special education teachers and other instructional assistance. Other roles that paraprofessionals were assigned included teaching children in Title 1 programs, ESL/bilingual classrooms, and library/media centers (National Center for Educational Statistics 2007). These data reveal the predominant instructional nature of today's paraprofessionals, as do the various titles given to individuals in this position—teaching assistant, paraprofessional, instructional aide, and educational technician, to name a few.

National surveys of paraprofessionals reveal that many are co-teaching with their general education or special education teachers (e.g., Liston, Nevin, and Malian 2009; Olshefski 2006). In the work of Liston and colleagues, respondents reported that they provided one-to-one instruction, small-group instruction, working with peer tutors, and supervising learning centers (one of the four approaches to co-teaching). They had learned a variety of techniques such as direct instruction in reading and math, cooperative group learning, hands-on teaching, computer-assisted instruction, educational games from Internet websites, and community-based instruction. Themes related to their advice for other paraprofessionals included "Be willing to ask" and "Be flexible." Many echoed the sentiment of one paraprofessional who wrote on her survey, "It is a joy to be in this work" (p. 11). A recent statewide survey of 1,800 paraprofessionals by Fisher and Pleasants (2011) emphasized the importance of paraprofessionals as instructional team members.

Given that hundreds of thousands of paraprofessionals are assigned to instruct in elementary, middle-level, and high school classrooms, the following three questions naturally arise:

1. Can paraprofessionals be co-teachers?

2. What are the appropriate co-teaching roles for paraprofessionals?

3. What supports do paraprofessionals need to become and perform as effective co-teachers?

Let's examine the first question by revisiting the teaching teams introduced in Chapter 3. Recall that in the elementary team, Ms. Hernandez, the part-time paraprofessional who attends the university in hopes of becoming a teacher, joins the first-grade classroom teacher, Ms. Gilpatrick, for 3 hours a day during literacy instruction. Also, Ms. Nugent, the school's new speech and language therapist, joins the team as a collaborating teacher. Recall also the transdisciplinary middle-level teaching team. This team comprises two content area teachers—Mr. Silva, the bilingual math and science teacher, and Ms. Kurtz, the language arts and social studies teacher—Ms. Spaulding, the team's special educator, and Ms. Olvina, the paraprofessional who is assigned to one of Mr. Silva's science classes and one of his math classes. With the addition of a paraprofessional as integral to each team, students were more likely to receive individualized instruction to meet their needs.

To approach the second question—whether a paraprofessional can play any of the supportive, parallel, complementary, and team-teaching roles—take a moment to revisit Chapters 4 through 7, which describe the co-teaching approaches. As we track the elementary team members through their experiences with the four co-teaching approaches, we learn how Ms. Hernandez successfully works with her collaborating teachers using the supportive, parallel, and complementary co-teaching approaches. As we trace the middle-level team's journey from supportive to team-teaching instructional arrangements, we learn how Ms. Olvina naturally uses all four of the co-teaching approaches. For all four approaches, then, it is possible for paraprofessionals to provide meaningful instruction, although our experience has been that to use the complementary and team-teaching approaches, the paraprofessional's roles and responsibilities require, at the very least, time for planning, careful training, and supervision. Issues of paraprofessional training and supervision for co-teaching are critical ones that are frequently discussed in the literature (Ashbaker and Morgan 2005; French 2002; Gerlach 2006; Picket and Gerlach 2003; Pickett et al. 2007). Therefore, at the end of this chapter, we examine these issues and offer some advice to co-teachers.

Meet a Paraprofessional and Her Elementary Co-Teachers

The role of the paraprofessional as a co-teacher is best illustrated by examples. To supplement the examples of the elementary and middle-level co-teaching teams described in Chapters 4 through 7, we introduce you to the following elementary team, on which Ms. Katz is the assigned paraprofessional.

Who Are Our Co-Teachers?

Table 8.1 introduces you to the team members by name, job role, and the curriculum area(s) for which each person is responsible.

Table 8.1 Meet the Co-Teaching Team Members

Co-Teaching Team Members	Co-Teaching Role	Curriculum Area(s)
Mr. Jeffries	Fourth-grade classroom teacher	All core areas
Ms. Katz	Paraprofessional	Language arts, science/health
Mr. Riehl	Speech and language therapist	Social studies
Ms. Hoosokowa	Special educator	Math

Mr. Jeffries, a fourth-grade teacher, has been teaching for 3 years. Currently, he teaches 26 students—three are eligible for special education as well as speech and language services, one is eligible for gifted and talented services, five are eligible for Title I support, and three are students who are learning English. Two students are eligible for special education. Andreas, a boy with autism, and Wendy, a girl with Down syndrome, require additional peer, adult, or technological support at times throughout the day.

As a first-year co-teacher, Mr. Jeffries is eager to appear competent to all who enter his classroom but fears that his teacher-preparation program and previous experiences have not adequately prepared him to co-teach or design lessons for such a diverse array of students. He acknowledges that the composition of his class is more diverse than previous years. He has been assigned to co-teach and collaboratively plan with a variety of people. He is to co-teach with Ms. Katz, a paraprofessional, daily during language arts and three times a week in science/health; with Mr. Riehl, a speech and language therapist, three times a week during social studies; and with Ms. Hoosokowa, a special educator, four times a week during math. In addition to meeting and planning with these folks, Mr. Jeffries is expected to collaboratively plan monthly with the teacher who works with students eligible for free and reduced lunch, the consultant who works with students who are gifted and talented, and the teacher for students learning English. Although Mr. Jeffries welcomes all of the support, he feels a bit overwhelmed with the number of people with whom he must interact and with the number of meetings that he must attend.

Ms. Katz has worked as a paraprofessional in the same school district for 4 years. This is her first year at this particular elementary school. In previous years, she provided instruction and support to students who were seated at the back of classrooms, or she supported certain students by sitting next to them during other class activities. Also, she has performed many clerical duties (e.g., copying worksheets, recording grades, making modified materials). Her supervisor, Ms. Hoosokowa, tells Ms. Katz that she will now function primarily as a supportive or parallel co-teacher with Mr. Jeffries during language arts and science/health classes. She learns about the various learning profiles of the students in Mr. Jeffries's class and is told that her responsibility is to promote independence and interaction with peers rather than codependence with the paraprofessional. Ms. Katz comments that this is a departure from her traditional responsibilities and is uncertain about how to function in the classroom. She wonders how acceptable these new responsibilities and roles will be to Mr. Jeffries. Ms. Hoosokowa promises to meet with Ms. Katz and Mr. Jeffries weekly and to occasionally observe, coach, or co-teach to model practices and approaches for Mr. Jeffries and Ms. Katz to use during their team-taught language arts and science/health classes.

Getting Ready to Co-Teach

Ms. Katz is required to attend 2 days of training prior to the beginning of the school year. The training, designed and delivered by Ms. Hoosokowa and Mr. Riehl, emphasizes skills development for paraprofessionals. However, when Mr. Jeffries reviewed the list of strategies Ms. Katz would learn (i.e., developing positive supports for responding to challenging behavior, differentiating instruction based on learning profiles, using educational technology to support diverse learners, facilitating peer support, co-teaching, and learning the roles and responsibilities in inclusive classrooms), he asked if he could attend. Ms. Hoosokowa and Ms. Katz were thrilled that he wanted to attend. Ms. Hoosokowa talked with Mr. Riehl, and they decided to open the training session to any professional staff member who might want to participate. Ms. Katz learns that she will participate in twice-monthly, hour-and-a-half training meetings for all district paraprofessionals. Mr. Jeffries is surprised and impressed that Ms. Katz will have ongoing professional development while co-teaching in his class.

Ongoing Planning for Co-Teaching

During the first week of school, Ms. Katz, Ms. Hoosokowa, and Mr. Jeffries identify the need for and initiate a weekly 45-minute collaborative meeting time. Once a month when they review the progress of target students and discuss further accommodations or modifications for any learner who appears to be struggling, they are joined by Mr. Riehl as well as the teacher who works with students eligible for free and reduced lunch, the consultant who works with students who are gifted and talented, and the teacher for students learning English. On a daily basis, Ms. Katz meets with Mr. Jeffries for 10 minutes before the language arts class in order to review and finalize the procedures that each will follow during the lesson. Ms. Katz is comfortable meeting with Ms. Hoosokowa on an as-needed basis.

A PARAPROFESSIONAL IN THE ROLE OF SUPPORTIVE, PARALLEL, AND COMPLEMENTARY CO-TEACHER

The Big Picture

It is 1 month into the school year, and Ms. Katz is feeling comfortable in her role as a member of the teaching team. Ms. Hoosokowa has observed and given feedback three times. In meetings with Mr. Jeffries, Ms. Katz feels her ideas are respected and welcomed. Mr. Jeffries has said on more than one occasion that her contributions in the classroom are valued. Ms. Katz is especially pleased that Ms. Hoosokowa has noticed academic, social, and communication progress shown by both Andreas, a boy with autism, and Wendy, a girl with Down syndrome.

Mr. Jeffries is amazed at how efficient and productive the weekly planning meetings have become. He, too, has noticed and is excited about the progress all of his students are making. He is pleased with the lessons that the team has implemented. He has shared the lessons with other fourth-grade teachers, noting how grateful he's become for his teammates' knowledge and perspectives. He would like to continue to learn effective teaching strategies and has decided to earn a master's degree in special education or instructional leadership.

A Sample Lesson: Supportive, Parallel, and Complementary Co-Teaching in Action

Mr. Jeffries and Ms. Katz outline a 3-day language arts lesson on character development and plot for the next week (see Resource G for the lesson plan). As usual, they agree to create a positive tone by greeting students as they enter the classroom. Mr. Jeffries opens the lesson with an anticipatory set, a brief reading, and a minilecture on and review of character development and plot. Meanwhile, Ms. Katz is in the supportive co-teaching role and positions herself near Andreas because he sometimes gets confused about expectations for the lesson. Most of the time, Andreas wants to join the activity, and sometimes he needs a short break prior to settling into the activity. At these times, Ms. Katz suggests that he move to a table at the side of the room for a few moments or go for a walk prior to beginning the activity. Being in the supportive co-teaching role, Ms. Katz is free to provide the adult support or supervision that Andreas needs.

Strategically seated close to the front of the room near Mr. Jeffries, Wendy works with a group of her peers who can be strong academic, social, and communication models for her. At the beginning of a language arts activity, Wendy sometimes needs to be reminded to put away her other materials and get organized for the current activity. Again, because Ms. Katz is in the supportive co-teaching role at the opening of the lesson, she is free to assist Wendy, if needed. Also, Ms. Katz works in the supportive role at the beginning of the lesson by circulating among all of the students to check their completion of the language arts homework.

After the anticipatory set, minilecture, and a brief reading, Mr. Jeffries asks students questions about the characters in the story and the plot. Ms. Katz shifts to the complementary co-teaching role. She complements Mr. Jeffries's teaching by writing clarifying comments or examples of his questions on the board. Next, Ms. Katz switches roles with Mr. Jeffries; she takes the lead, assigning students to one of three learning stations. In this parallel co-teaching arrangement, one group, of which Andreas is a member, works at Station 1 with Mr. Jeffries to examine character development in a trade book they all read together. A second group works with Ms. Katz at Station 2, where students compose and illustrate their own stories. Ms. Katz is ready to explain how students might develop their characters fully and how they can make the plot more interesting. She coaches the students at her station to provide peer-editing suggestions to improve each other's characters and plots.

Wendy is a member of the third group of students, who are working independently at Station 3. These students choose their own stories, read, and then focus on the character and plot development. Here, students have the choice of accessing content either by reading alone, reading the same book with a peer, or reading with text-to-speech software, an accommodation for Wendy's Individual Education Program. Wendy and all of her classmates know that if she needs help with her computer, headset, or the text-to-speech software, she is expected to ask a peer for assistance before asking for help from Mr. Katz or Mr. Jeffries. Two other classmates who like to use the text-to-speech software because it helps them learn correct pronunciation of English vocabulary often join Wendy.

Students rotate through each of the three stations over the course of 3 days. On the third day, Mr. Jeffries and Ms. Katz exchange stations. Mr. Jeffries facilitates student writing at Station 2, and Ms. Katz is at Station 1, where students all read the same book together. They agreed to do this strategic swap in parallel co-teaching roles so that Mr. Jeffries can observe Wendy, whose turn it is at Station 2, and thus authentically assess her present level of performance in writing and illustrating an original story (one of the fourth-grade standards on the high-stakes statewide assessment test). As accommodations for Wendy, the co-teaching team has set up this station so that (a) she can first dictate parts of her story to a peer or to Mr. Jeffries, who writes her ideas, and (b) the dictated notes are then transferred to text with the *Alpha*, a keyboarding and writing tool. Peers are available to assist with illustrating, if Wendy so desires. Andreas is working at the independent reading station, with Ms. Katz as the group facilitator. A different book, at a more difficult reading level, will be assigned for the group to read at this station on the third day.

Both Andreas and Wendy have individualized behavior contracts and checklists that Ms. Hoosokowa developed and provided to Mr. Jeffries. At the end of each language arts period, Ms. Katz, in the parallel co-teacher role, meets with Wendy and then Andreas to discuss and record measures of their academic, social, communication, and independent behaviors; concurrently, Mr. Jeffries assigns homework and directs the other students to clean up the classroom. Wendy and Andreas then take their checklists to Mr. Jeffries, who reviews them and awards their earned points. He exchanges exuberant high fives with many of the students who are happy with the products they have created.

At their subsequent planning meeting, Mr. Jeffries and Ms. Katz reflect on the 3-day lesson (see Resource G for the lesson plan). They agree that they liked the flow in and out of supportive, complementary, and parallel co-teaching approaches so much that they want to continue designing lessons this way. They brainstorm how to include others (e.g., parent volunteers, fifth or sixth graders, the librarian) who could facilitate a fourth learning station, so as to increase the amount of individualized attention and coaching that each student could then enjoy. They decide to ask Ms. Hoosokowa to facilitate a learning station. This would allow her to directly observe how the students with disabilities are not only surviving but thriving in the co-taught classroom.

Analyzing the Cooperative Process for a Paraprofessional as a Co-Teacher

Because you were introduced to the five basic elements that comprise the cooperative process for working within co-teaching teams in Chapters 4 through 7, we invite you to analyze this co-teaching team. In what ways have Ms. Katz, Mr. Jeffries, and Ms. Hoosokowa structured their work together? Do you see how they have set up frequent face-to-face interaction (daily as well as monthly), setting mutual goals so that they reciprocate and exchange roles (positive interdependence)? What specific interpersonal skills do you think were important in ensuring the success of this co-teaching team? In what ways were supervision and training provided to all team members? How did Mr. Jeffries and Ms. Katz share the monitoring of student progress and accountability? Do you agree that this team has mastered the cooperative process for creating a viable co-teaching team? What other considerations for determining effectiveness did they consider?

■ BENEFITS OF PARAPROFESSIONALS AS CO-TEACHERS

Researchers and practitioners alike agree that multiple benefits occur when paraprofessionals join co-teacher teams (Nevin, Thousand, and Villa 2008). The benefits are organized by their role in inclusion and differentiation of instruction, their role as cultural ambassadors, and their role in recruiting paraprofessionals into the teaching force.

Inclusion and Differentiation of Instruction

Researchers and practitioners mention the importance of and need for instructional assistants in order to instruct students with identified disabilities alongside their general education peers (Downing, Ryndak, and Clark 2000; Liston et al. 2009; Marks, Schrader, and Levine 1999; Mueller and Murphy 2001; Piletic, Davis, and Aschemeier 2005; Riggs and Mueller 2001). Co-teachers in inclusive settings have not been silent about their reliance on and appreciation of paraprofessionals (e.g., Salazar and Nevin 2005). For instance, Nevin and colleagues (2007) describe co-teachers' perceptions of the added value that paraprofessionals bring. In particular, the teacher-to-student ratio is increased, thus allowing for increased personalization of instructional programs.

Cultural Ambassadors

In their comprehensive study of paraprofessionals in two large school districts in Southern California, Rueda and Monzo (2002) state that the knowledge of the multicultural and multilingual communities from which paraprofessionals hail is essential in helping teachers tap into their students' prior knowledge and interests. This is especially true if a teacher is monolingual and his or her students are culturally and linguistically diverse. As a caution, Rueda and Monzo note that if school cultures don't support collaboration among teachers and paraprofessionals, teachers can remain unaware of the knowledge that paraprofessionals possess about students' cultures. Thus, teachers can fail to tap their paraprofessionals' expertise as cultural ambassadors.

Teacher Recruitment

As preservice teacher educators, we have met paraprofessionals who decide to become certified teachers; they are among the best first-year teachers who show high levels of confidence meeting the needs of diverse learners. Therefore, one benefit of having paraprofessionals serve as co-teachers, particularly in inclusive general education classrooms, is that they provide a solid foundation upon which to apply the theory and practices to which they are introduced in their teacher-preparation studies. There are currently teacher preparation programs in special education from which paraprofessionals are actively recruited for teaching certification (Littleton 1998; Rueda and Monzo 2002).

ROLES AND RESPONSIBILITIES OF ■ PARAPROFESSIONALS IN CO-TEACHING CLASSROOMS

Paraprofessionals take on many diverse roles. The literature on the day-to-day work of paraprofessionals is clear about the differentiated roles that paraprofessionals can and do perform. They are key players with classroom teachers who differentiate instruction through co-teaching and other techniques.

How do you decide a paraprofessional's role? Paraprofessionals and their teachers are encouraged to clearly articulate what the paraprofessional's role should be. The first recommendation to school districts and states is "to have a clear definition of the paraprofessional's role in the classroom and the related roles of the teacher and administrator" (Torrence-Mikulecky and Baber 2005, p. 1). Role clarification can be complex because a paraprofessional's role may change dramatically throughout the course of a school day depending on the changing needs of students and the decisions made by the professional educators who collectively decide the specifics of the job in each instructional situation. At least the following areas need to be clarified: (a) lesson planning, (b) delivery of instruction, (c) proactive and reactive responses to students' behaviors, (d) strategies for promoting ongoing communication, and (e) methods of student evaluation (Doyle 2002). Two other areas might include confidentiality and team participation (French 2003).

Remember that the job of the paraprofessional is to supplement the instruction of qualified teaching professionals under the direction of those professionals. In other words, it is the professional educator, not the paraprofessional, who is to take the lead in developing and directing the delivery of curriculum, instruction, and student assessments (French 2008). We all are encouraged to be clear about who will supervise paraprofessionals in inclusive settings, especially within a collaborative team approach (Pickett and Gerlach 2003). Such clarification of roles and responsibilities is important because the Elementary and Secondary Education Act (also known as No Child Left Behind Act) specifies that paraprofessionals who provide instruction in Title I-funded programs must provide services under the direct supervision of a highly qualified teacher (Title I, Section 1119(g)(2). There are two national resources that provide excellent support to assist paraprofessionals and their team members in clarifying the role of paraprofessionals and developing useful job descriptions. One is the PAR2A Center (www.paracenter.org) and the other is the National Resource Center for Paraprofessionals (www .nrcpara.org/).

Understanding the instructional cycle can guide decisions about the paraprofessional's role. First, teachers plan their units and lessons by (a) getting to know the students in the class, (b) deciding the content that is to be delivered and connecting it to common core curriculum standards that guide what students are expected to know or do, (c) deciding the teaching/learning activities that will best help students make sense of the content, and (d) deciding how outcomes will be assessed. Teacher plans include how they will adapt what typically has occurred in a classroom in order to allow a student who learns differently to access the general education curriculum. When teachers deliver or implement the planned lesson, they monitor and adjust their instruction during the lesson as they observe and collect anecdotal or more formal information on how students are responding to what they have planned. Finally, after the lesson, teachers reflect on the lesson and evaluate how successful it was in achieving the intended learning outcomes for the students.

Paraprofessionals in co-taught classrooms may be called upon to assist at any point of the instructional cycle. They may be asked to plan, teach, monitor student progress, collect data, and reflect on and evaluate instruction; and this may be done at the individual student level or for all of the students in a classroom.

■ CHALLENGES FOR PARAPROFESSIONALS AS CO-TEACHERS

Poorly Defined Roles

In the vignette above that describes Mr. Jeffries, Ms. Katz, and their support team, did you detect the variety of roles that Ms. Katz performed in the classroom? Research studies conducted over the last decade reveal a broad range of roles that paraprofessionals can and do play. For example, bilingual paraprofessionals have served as both instructors and translators for children who speak languages other than English (Ashbaker and Morgan 2005; Wenger et al. 2004). Paraprofessionals are instructors of small groups (Ashbaker and Morgan 2005), behavior managers (Perez and Murdock 1999; Young 1997), assistants in speech and language therapy (Radaszewski-Byrne 1997), and even job coaches (Rogan and Held 1999).

The range and flexibility of paraprofessionals' roles can be viewed as both a gift and a burden. On the one hand, role flexibility gives teachers and paraprofessionals the discretion to adjust a paraprofessional's job description based on the current needs of the students in a classroom. On the other hand, if job expectations are not clear, it can be confusing, not only to the paraprofessional but also to the teacher and students. Villa and Thousand (2005) emphasize the importance of at least some fundamental job clarity regarding collaborative partnerships:

Job titles and formal definitions determine the way that people behave. Thus, to further signal a change in culture (from a previously isolationist perspective of only one teacher in a classroom), we should formulate new policies and job descriptions that expect, inspect, and respect a collaborative ethic. (p. 69)

Doyle (2002), who has developed comprehensive paraprofessional training materials and guidelines, suggests that paraprofessionals and their co-teachers articulate roles for at least the following five key areas: lesson planning, delivery of instruction, responses to students' behaviors (both proactive and reactive), strategies to promote ongoing communication, and methods of student evaluation. Pickett and Gerlach (2003) offer two inventories. One assesses potential responsibilities of a paraprofessional in a classroom or school (i.e., delivery of instruction, activity preparation, supervision of groups of students, behavior management, ethics, team participation and membership, clerical work, home–school communication, and other special education duties). The other examines the skills and confidence of the paraprofessional in these same areas. A comparison of the lists of responsibilities can inform which tasks become immediate job responsibilities and which require further preparation. Especially important for co-teaching is a clear description of what are and are not a paraprofessional's job functions, which can include instruction, behavior management, materials preparation, collecting assessment information, and legal and ethical conduct.

Ambiguity in Supervision Responsibilities

Etscheidt (2005), in a comprehensive legal analysis of paraprofessional services for students with disabilities, reminds us that "paraprofessionals may not serve as the sole designer, delivery, or evaluator of a student's program" (p. 68). In other words, it is the teacher who has the responsibility for the education of all learners even when instructional and other tasks are delegated or mutually decided on by a teaching team. Paraprofessionals are school employees who teach under the supervision of other professional staff responsible for the design, modification, implementation, and assessment of instruction and learner progress. Thus, as national leaders in the training and supervision of paraprofessionals emphasize (Pickett and Gerlach 2003; Pickett et al. 2009), supervision of paraprofessionals must occur. Yet ambiguity about who is responsible for the supervision of paraprofessionals and how supervision should be accomplished remains a premier problem. Clearly, co-teaching among educators and paraprofessionals creates a unique opportunity for the regular, authentic, and ongoing observation, analysis, and coaching of paraprofessional effectiveness that is recommended by Morgan and Ashbaker (2001).

Inconsistent Initial and Ongoing Professional Development

Mueller (2002) refers to the *paraprofessional paradox* when she writes that "we have developed a service delivery system that depends heavily on relatively untrained, underpaid, and devalued staff members to provide complex instructional and behavioral programs to our most challenging students. Hello, what's wrong with this picture?" (p. 64). Clearly, administrators, teachers, and paraprofessionals themselves want to avoid this paradox, and there are no arguments against the notion that the best way to address such a paradox is to provide adequate preparation and supervision of paraprofessionals.

To help paraprofessionals and their supervisors assess their competence, Nancy French (2003), the founder and former executive director of the National Resource Center for Paraeducators (www.nrcpara.org), generated a useful self-assessment inventory for paraprofessionals to use for rating responsibilities in a classroom or school (i.e., delivery of instruction, activity preparation, supervision of groups of students, behavior management, ethics, team participation and membership, clerical work, home–school communication, and other special education duties). It is not necessary to use the exact items listed in this inventory or other inventories suggested in this book, such as the "We Really Co-Teachers?" self-assessment presented in Table 11.3 of Chapter 11. The idea is to list the day-to-day required duties and actions of a paraprofessional as well as the stated requirements of the job in the job description in order to determine what the paraprofessional needs to know and learn to do. A clear description and analysis of what are and are not a paraprofessional's job functions is especially important for paraprofessionals who work with co-teachers because co-teaching can require quite complex instructional, behavior-management, assessment, ethical, and interpersonal behaviors and responsibilities.

Inventories like this one can help paraprofessionals and supervisors decide the type and scope of professional development activities. The literature is rich in comprehensive paraprofessional development options (e.g., Bueno Center for Multicultural Education 1997; French 2003; Morgan, Forbush, and Avis 2001). A valuable resource to add to your support system is the annotated bibliography of paraprofessional training resources, which is updated regularly and published on the Web by the National Resource Center for Paraeducators (www.nrcpara.org/bibliography).

■ CAUTIONS TO PARAPROFESSIONALS AS CO-TEACHERS

At the end of the chapters on each of the four approaches to co-teaching, there are frequently asked questions that serve as cautions for co-teachers engaged in each of the approaches. The cautions apply equally to paraprofessionals. Several are worthy of repeating here, as they especially apply to paraprofessionals. For paraprofessionals in the supportive co-teaching role, be mindful not to become "Velcroed" to individual students or function as hovercraft vehicles blocking students' interactions with other students. This can result in isolation of both the student and the paraprofessional, leading other students to perceive that the support teacher and the student being supported are not genuine members of the classroom.

Table 8.2   An Inventory of Paraprofessional Preparedness

	Rating			
	Unprepared		Highly Skilled	
Job Responsibility	**1**	**2**	**3**	**4**
Delivery of Instruction				
1. observe and record student progress in academic areas				
2. assist to differentiate instruction				
3. help students in drill and practice (e.g., vocabulary, math facts)				
4. help students use computers and software				
5. engage in support, parallel, and complementary co-teaching as requested by supervising teachers				
Activity Preparation and Follow-Up				
6. distribute supplies, materials, books to students				
7. collect completed work from students				
8. operate equipment (e.g., tape recorders, DVD, LCD, and document projectors)				
Supervising Groups				
9. supervising students during lunch or recess				
10. escorting groups to library, gym, bathroom				
Behavior Management				
11. implement classroom discipline system				
12. observe and chart individual student behavior				
Ethics				
13. maintain confidentiality of information				
14. respect privacy of students and their families				
15. respect dignity and rights of every child (e.g., use person-first, disability-second language)				
16. maintain composure and emotional control when working with students				
Team Participation				
17. contribute ideas in team meetings				
18. engage in roles (e.g., timekeeper, encourager) as needed or requested during a meeting				
Clerical				
19. score objective tests and enter data in grade book				
20. organize, file, and copy teaching or assessment materials				

Source: Adapted from French, N. (2003). Management of paraeducators. In A. L. Pickett and K. Gerlach (Eds.), *Supervising paraeducators in school settings: A team approach* (2nd ed.). Austin, TX: Pro-Ed.

For paraprofessionals in the parallel co-teaching role, remember that it is possible to create a special class within a class by routinely working with the same group of students who are clustered homogeneously based on some dimension such as perceived ability, eligibility for special education, or status as an English learner. This can stigmatize the students and the paraprofessional as well as remove the opportunity for students to learn from other students who learn in different ways, which occurs when students are grouped heterogeneously.

For paraprofessionals in the complementary co-teaching role, remember that, as with a new co-teacher assigned to an unfamiliar content area, it is impossible for a paraprofessional to have complete knowledge of the content area from the very start. There are many ways to become more proficient in a content area (see the second frequently asked question in Chapter 6). Be sure to take the initiative and learn about what you don't know in whatever way is best for you to access and absorb new information. Also, remember that it is possible to step on the toes of a co-teaching partner when restating points. To ensure that this type of clarification for students is not perceived as a correction or evaluation, be sure to have the conversation about when and how it is OK to complement instruction. It may be that you have to work out a signaling system so that you know when one co-teacher wishes to jump in and add value to another's teaching.

For paraprofessionals who are fortunate enough to reach the point in their partnership with a co-teacher to team teach, remember that any paraprofessional may be reassigned at any point in time, no matter how great the co-teaching relationship is. It may be to students' benefit that you follow them to the next grade. It may be that there is a greater need for in-class support from a paraprofessional in another classroom, with another teacher, or in another subject area.

■ ASSESSING PARAPROFESSIONALS AS CO-TEACHERS

As is true of professional certificated or credentialed teachers who engage in co-teaching, paraprofessionals who work as co-teachers benefit and grow from receiving constructive feedback from colleagues or by evaluating their own performance against some standard. That standard might be the job description crafted for the paraprofessional position. Or it might be the results of assessing oneself using the Inventory of Paraprofessional Preparedness offered in Table 8.2.

FREQUENTLY ASKED QUESTIONS

1. What are potential legal challenges for paraprofessionals who work in inclusive classrooms?

Etscheidt (2005), in a comprehensive legal analysis of paraprofessional services for students with disabilities, reminds us that "paraprofessionals may not serve as the sole designer, deliverer, or evaluator of a student's program" (p. 68). Stated otherwise, it is the teacher who has the responsibility for the education of all learners, even when instructional and other tasks are delegated or mutually decided upon by a teaching team. Paraprofessionals are school employees who teach under the supervision of other professional staff responsible for the design, modification, implementation, and assessment of instruction and learner progress. Thus, Pickett and Gerlach (2003), national leaders in the training and supervision of paraprofessionals, emphasize the supervision of paraprofessionals. Yet ambiguity as to who is responsible for the supervision of paraprofessionals and how supervision should be accomplished remains a premier problem. Clearly, co-teaching among educators and paraprofessionals creates a unique opportunity for the regular, authentic, ongoing observation, analysis, and coaching of paraprofessional effectiveness recommended by Ashbaker and Morgan (2005).

2. I am concerned about co-teaching with a paraprofessional who is not well trained to work with students with special needs. Isn't it a problem that people with the least amount of preparation are assigned to support children who have the most intensive needs?

This is a legitimate concern and speaks to the need for systems to be in place to ensure that paraprofessionals *do* receive the training, supervision, and coaching they need to support the education of children with special needs in the inclusive classrooms to which they are assigned. There are many ways for paraprofessionals to receive initial and ongoing training. The key is to ensure that there are administrators and educational professionals who take the initiative and responsibility to make sure this training, in fact, does occur. Any paraprofessional can learn from on-the-job modeling and coaching with his or her co-teachers. It requires that a paraprofessional's co-teachers structure time (even if it is just a few minutes) for pre- and postinstructional conferences in which preparation for and feedback on instruction occurs. As an example of more formal instruction, a supervising special educator at a school site might work with the general education and paraprofessional co-teachers to show them both instructional and differentiation techniques they can use not only with students with special needs but with all students in the classroom. The paraprofessional could participate in training programs specially designed to provide them with methods for differentiating instruction, such as the training program developed by Doyle (2002) and referenced in this chapter. The paraprofessional could then share the new knowledge and skills with general education classroom co-teachers. In fact, a job responsibility for the special educator or other professional responsible for the supervision of a paraprofessional as well as the job description of the paraprofessional should include provisions for ongoing training and support in effective instruction, behavior management, and specific instructional methodologies for particular students.

The Role of Students as Co-Teachers

9

Topics Included in This Chapter:

❖ Vignettes: Students in co-teaching roles
❖ Analyzing the cooperative process in the student co-teaching vignettes
❖ Preparing students to be co-teachers
❖ The research base for students as co-teachers
❖ Assessing students as co-teachers
❖ Frequently asked questions

Recently, we observed a classroom of fourth and fifth graders who were actually co-teaching! In this chapter, we begin by defining *teaching* so that it is feasible to consider students as co-teachers. We briefly explain methods that allow students to become co-teachers, and through a variety of vignettes, we show the student co-teachers in action. We offer essential questions that must be answered when developing a peer-tutoring or adult–student co-teaching program. We summarize the emerging research base on students as co-teachers (including the barriers and disadvantages to students as co-teachers), provide a method for student co-teachers to be assessed, and pose and answer frequently asked questions to address the major barriers to implementing students as co-teachers. Readers interested in more information about collaborating with students as instructors and decision makers are referred to the Villa, Thousand, and Nevin 2010 text, *Collaborating With Students in Instruction and Decision Making: The Untapped Resource.*

What is teaching? We believe that to tap the vast resources the student body offers, we should use the broadest possible answers to this question. If you consult any dictionary, you will find a plethora of meanings that the English language attributes to the word *teaching*. For example, to teach is to impart knowledge or skills. To teach is to give instruction. To teach is to cause to learn by experience or example. To teach is to advocate or preach. On the other hand, to instruct or to tutor or to train to educate implies methodological knowledge in addition to content knowledge. Students can and should become co-teachers. They effectively collaborate in school activities such as serving on school committees, being advocates for classmates and themselves, planning and evaluating instruction from their teachers, providing assistance in making friends, developing accommodations, leading their own person-centered meetings, and serving as tutors and co-teachers (Villa, Thousand, and Nevin 2010). In fact, children and youth who learn and practice being student co-teachers are more likely to grow into adults who are more effective advocates for themselves. They are likely to become more effective members of work teams, their families, and their communities. In other words, when students are co-teachers, they can embody all the verbs that are associated with the word *teaching*. They can tutor, instruct, impart knowledge, assess progress, demonstrate examples, act out the procedures as a model, and so on. In Chapter 2, we emphasized the reasons co-teaching is important in 21st-century schools. We want to emphasize here our most important reason for co-teaching: It allows students to experience and imitate the cooperative and collaborative skills that teachers show when they co-teach. All students benefit when their teachers share ideas, work cooperatively, and contribute to one another's learning. This often results in students becoming co-teachers themselves, as the following vignettes illustrate.

■ VIGNETTES: STUDENTS IN CO-TEACHING ROLES

Just as there are many faces of adult co-teachers, there are many ways for students to be co-teachers. Table 9.1 provides an overview of the roles and methods used by the student co-teacher teams described in this chapter.

Table 9.1 The Many Faces of Students as Co-Teachers

Meet the Student Partners	Adult Co-Teacher Partner(s)	Curriculum Areas	Co-Teaching Approach
Bill, high school senior, attending college-level classes in math during junior and senior years	Sharon, a high school math teacher	Sharon, high school mathematics teacher, supports Bill in acquiring deeper understanding of mathematics, assisting fellow students, and exploring teaching as a career	Supportive for the first 3 weeks, complementary for the next few weeks, team for the remaining time
Christine, a high school student with special needs Cat, a high school student who wanted to develop her teaching skills		Cat tutors Christine in the content of 11th-grade health class so that Christine learned to teach a unit on personal safety to a third-grade class	Supportive and complementary
Dave and Juan, reciprocal co-teachers	Elaine, a third-grade classroom teacher, and Laurie, a special educator	Elaine and Laurie teach reciprocal teaching to all students and structured a learning contract for Dave and Juan to be more successful in mathematics (acquisition of facts)	Complementary (each served as teacher and learner)
Denny, a fifth-grade student with gifts and talents who has difficulty with interpersonal skills	Cathy, a fifth-grade mathematics teacher, and Shamonique, a gifted and talented teacher	Cathy and Shamonique teach *friendly disagreeing* skills and math problem solving with an emphasis on explaining the reasoning processes	Parallel (for acquiring the friendly disagreeing skills) and supportive (for applying the friendly disagreeing skills)
Co-teaching students	Ms. Marquez, teacher of 25 ethnically and linguistically diverse first, second, and third graders	Ms. Marquez teaches students to teach each other the computer and other educational technology skills that they know	Complementary

Meet Bill and Sharon

During his senior year in high school, Bill experienced a unique partnership with his mathematics teacher that evolved from supportive to parallel to complementary co-teaching and culminated in team teaching.

"It is pretty neat when you can help out students who are having trouble learning, challenge someone like me at the same time, and it doesn't cost the school district a dime." Bill made this statement after he had exhausted his school's mathematics curriculum by his sophomore year and attended university mathematics courses in his junior and senior years. In his senior year, he arranged an independent study in mathematics that included team teaching with Sharon, who taught the high school's most advanced math class. Bill wanted to refine his instructional skills even though he also tutored many students in mathematics after school.

During the first week of the team-teaching arrangement, Bill observed Sharon. At the end of the second week, he began teaching the last 10 minutes of the class; he was responsible for introducing the math concept or operation that would be addressed in the next day's lesson. Sharon and Bill met daily to review and approve Bill's instructional plan for the minilessons. After a month, Bill taught his first full-length class and continued for the rest of the semester. When he was not instructing the group as a whole, he worked individually with students who had missed class or who had difficulty with a concept. He continued to observe Sharon's methods and conferred with her on a daily basis to receive feedback on his own teaching. Bill also asked for feedback from the students. He was available to help after school, and some students even called him at home for help. One student in the class commented, "Bill is easier to understand compared with the other teacher, and he uses better examples."

Bill's inclusion in the mathematics teaching team had other positive effects. He reported that he was advancing his math education and learning about people at the same time. He also noted that his self-confidence had improved. Having been a student in the same class only 2 years earlier, he empathized with the students' struggles with the material. He believed that the students recognized and appreciated this empathy. Sharon was impressed with the professional and serious manner with which Bill conducted himself, the students' positive responses to his presence as her co-teacher, and his progress in using effective instructional strategies.

Meet Christine and Cat

When Christine made a presentation before 200 parents, teachers, and administrators at her high school graduation, she stumbled slightly. The stumble came as she read something she had written 3 years earlier for a school newspaper article. She decided on the spot to make a modification. "I have…nothing…and I'm not handicapped," the 19-year-old proclaimed, and she immediately received a well-earned round of applause.

The applause came because the audience could see the newspaper article projected on the screen at the front of the room. In the article that she wrote as part of a journalism class she and her tutor had been taking, Christine explained, "I have Down syndrome, but I'm not handicapped." The modification represented Christine's anger at the labels placed on her and her refusal to accept the limitations that some labels imply.

Throughout her high school career, Christine enjoyed several types of peer support that made her full inclusion in a public high school possible. The peer support helped Christine enjoy meaningful relationships with those who became her tutors, tutees, friends, advocates, and recipients of her advocacy. During her freshman year, the peer support came in the form of the cheerleading squad, of which Christine was the student manager. During her sophomore year, Christine participated in a journalism class responsible for the production of a weekly school newspaper. Because it took her nearly five times longer to complete class assignments, her teachers sought a full-time partner for her. Cat, a fellow student journalist who had a study hall during the same period as Christine, volunteered. The two worked together twice a week during class and every day in the computer lab during study hall to produce "Christine's Corner," a column featuring the unique accomplishments of various students in the school.

During her junior year, Christine and Cat enrolled as second-year journalism students, resuming their partnership. Cat arranged to receive credit as a peer tutor for Christine. She planned, implemented, and evaluated daily lessons designed to assist Christine in completing health, journalism, and history assignments. She met weekly with her supervisor (a special educator who coordinated Christine's educational services), kept a journal, and learned Madeline Hunter's model of effective teaching (M. Hunter 1988, 1994; R. Hunter and Hunter 2006). With Christine as her tutee, Cat embarked on what developed into her future career as a teacher. Cat reported in her journal, "Not many kids my age get to sample the job that they hope to have five or six years down the road. Thanks to Christine, I get to do that. My transcript and portfolio will show that I've chosen this as an individualized course of study, and that should help me to get into the college I want."

Christine appreciated Cat's support. She explained, "It's boring having my teachers all day. I like having Cat as my tutor because we're friends and she is fun." Cat also participated with Christine in meetings with teachers, advocates, and administrators to plan for a smooth transition from high school to adult life. Christine noted, "I get scared. I don't know all those people, and sometimes I cry. That's why Cat helps me. She tells me it's okay, and she will stick up for me. After those meetings, we go to McDonald's and talk it over."

As much as Christine enjoyed the tutor–tutee relationship with Cat, she also wanted to reverse that arrangement so that she, too, was in the helping role. Christine did not have the content knowledge to assist Cat in all of her academic courses, so other opportunities were explored. What resulted was a weekly health lesson that Christine team taught with a third-grade teacher. Christine applied the knowledge she was acquiring in her 11th-grade health course to the personal safety unit offered to the third graders. Christine then evaluated her own performance by summarizing the lessons and the outcomes to Cat, who planned to be an elementary teacher. "I learned from Christine what worked and didn't work for little kids," Cat relayed. "By sharing her experiences with me, she helped me see that younger students have shorter attention spans. I'll remember that someday when I have a class of my own."

The coordinator for Christine's high school services wrote, "I feel extremely fortunate.... Christine, in my opinion, is a remarkable woman who has freely shared her thoughts and feelings with others. In return, she has been the recipient of support, respect, and unabashed admiration from some of the most unsuspecting and extraordinary adolescents I have known. She and her friends have taught me that camaraderie and common sense are far more useful than a master's degree and that some of the best educational resources come free of charge" (as reported by Harris 1994, 300).

Christine and Cat not only experienced the unique feeling that comes from helping; Christine developed a new co-teaching relationship with the third-grade teacher, which served as a key performance demonstration of her Individual Education Plan (IEP) speech and behavioral goals. Christine made an extra effort to improve her articulation and to model appropriate behavior for the third graders she taught each week. Her skills in the academic classes she was taking improved steadily as she learned to translate into her own words what she was learning. Cat, similarly, experienced the benefits of practicing her own career goals in meaningful and realistic ways.

Meet Dave and Juan

All the students in Elaine and Laurie's third-grade classroom learned how to be reciprocal co-teachers for acquisition of math facts. Each student co-teacher practiced sequential co-teaching steps using auditory, verbal, and written directions to match different learning styles. Elaine, the classroom teacher, and Laurie, a special educator, scheduled at least one opportunity per day for the student co-teachers to practice—approximately 10 minutes to allow for each partner to play the role of teacher and then switch to the role of learner. The students focused on six math facts per session (four known and two unknown or as yet not mastered), practicing with activities that matched various learning styles (e.g., auditory, visual, kinesthetic) until mastery occurred.

They noticed that Dave and Juan were two student co-teachers who frequently used derogatory put-down statements and failed to use praise, feedback, or other appropriate social skills they had learned during training. They also fought over the materials. Their progress in acquiring math facts as well as their written feedback, however, indicated that they perceived the sessions to be going well. When Elaine interviewed them about these concerns, Dave and Juan each accused the other. As reported by LaPlant and Zane (2002), Laurie provided additional social skills training, and both Laurie and Elaine demonstrated the social skills and supervised the tutoring sessions frequently. Dave and Juan developed more skills in making positive statements and sustaining positive interactions with one another. Elaine and Laurie then added two items to Dave and Juan's data-collection procedures: saying nice things and saying "thank you." Both Dave and Juan also kept a graph to give them a visual representation of their performance. Finally, Elaine and Laurie set up a contract whereby Dave and Juan collected jointly accrued points based on the number of times they both made positive statements. The points could be traded later for activities they both enjoyed (e.g., learning games, lunch with the supervisor). Not only were they learning more math facts, they treated each other with more respect, became friends, and eagerly volunteered to serve as co-teachers with other classmates.

Meet Denny, Cathy, and Shamonique

Denny (a pseudonym), a fifth-grade student who was gifted and talented and had challenging interpersonal behaviors, was in Cathy and Shamonique's classroom with 24 peers (Conn-Powers 2002). He often insisted that his ideas were the only correct ones and ridiculed his classmates. During a social studies lesson that required debate skills, Shamonique, the gifted and talented education co-teacher, taught the students a new skill—encouraging others by asking them, in a friendly way, to share their ideas for solutions—to use when they worked in groups. In this cooperative lesson, students were expected to use the skill at least twice during a 40-minute problem-solving session taught by Cathy, the fifth-grade mathematics co-teacher. In their groups, students were expected to solve an equation, explain their reasoning, apply computational skills, and use friendly disagreeing skills they had learned during social studies. Each group kept track of its friendly disagreeing skills by tallying members' use of the five ways to disagree. They referred to the posters that they had created in a previous lesson, which prominently displayed the five ways to disagree (see Table 9.2).

Table 9.2   Examples of Friendly Disagreeing Skills

Friendly Disagreeing Skills	What Words Might You Say?	What Might You See and Hear?
Ask for different opinions	Why do you think that is best? What is your answer?	Lean in, friendly face, mild tone of voice
Ask others to explain why	Will you show me how that works? Will you help me see how to solve the problem?	Lean in, friendly face, quizzical tone of voice
Add on or modify	Could we expand on your answer? How about if we added . . . ? Is it OK to change . . . ?	Lean in, friendly face, questioning tone of voice
Offer alternatives	Wouldn't this work too? What do you think about . . . ?	Lean in, friendly face, mild tone of voice
State disagreement	I have a different idea. Can I show you how my answer is different?	Lean in, friendly face, excited tone of voice

In addition, each group recorded its problem-solving strategies on the poster paper. The lesson overall was quite successful. All six groups met the criteria. Denny participated for the entire lesson, and his team members praised him for encouraging them to disagree with him. The impact of this positive peer pressure was powerful. While Denny played tetherball with another group from his class at recess, Shamonique overheard him use one of the friendly disagreeing skills, the alternative-idea method: "What do you think about this way to hit the ball?"

Meet Student Co-Teachers for Computer Use

Ms. Marquez, a classroom teacher in an ethnically and culturally diverse elementary magnet school for computing and technology, was considered an outstanding teacher. Her class consisted of 25 first, second, and third graders: 15 Anglo children, 8 Mexican Americans, 1 Chinese American, and 1 African American. The classroom seating and the placement of computers were flexible and adaptable to students' needs and the specific learning activity.

Ms. Marquez noticed that the children used the computers individually, in pairs, in larger groups, or with the teacher depending on the task and the students' computer skills or preferences. She assigned each student to be a study buddy with another student and reminded them that sharing and helping were expected. Study buddies were taught specific social skills for cooperation (e.g., sharing ideas, explaining answers) and were expected to produce an academic product from either a teacher-selected assignment or a student-selected assignment.

Learning styles and cultural differences were easily accommodated because Ms. Marquez selected software with animated graphics, sound output, sound input, or visual text to meet the auditory or visual learning styles of many children. In addition, the keyboard and mouse required kinesthetic learning (for more on effective instructional practices for students who are learning English, see Gersten and Baker 2000).

When it came to grouping students, Ms. Marquez reflected on Chisholm's (1995) research, which highlights the fact that gender is the only factor that appears when children are able to select their working groups: "Cross-gender groups at the computer were essentially non-existent" (p. 170). Consequently, Ms. Marquez ensured cross-gender groupings by assigning male and female students to work together on certain assignments. Later, one child explained that she worked with everybody (meaning both boys and girls), thus showcasing the egalitarian nature of the classroom.

■ ANALYZING THE COOPERATIVE PROCESS IN THE STUDENT CO-TEACHING VIGNETTES

These examples of student co-teachers illustrate the five elements of the cooperative process—face-to-face interaction, positive interdependence, interpersonal skills, monitoring, and accountability. We emphasize again that when these elements are present in a co-teaching partnership, in this case a student co-teaching partnership, the quality of the relationship often is more creative and yields better outcomes. The face-to-face interactions included student co-teachers in one-to-one tutorials (e.g., Dave and Juan, Christine and Cat during journalism class), small-group instruction (Ms. Marquez's students co-teaching each other computer skills, Denny and his classmates co-teaching their reasoning for math problem solving and keeping track of friendly disagreeing skills), and large-group instruction (Bill and Sharon co-teaching the math class). Positive interdependence varied according to the age and grade level of the student co-teachers (e.g., goal interdependence for Bill and Christine, reward interdependence for Dave and Juan). Social skills also varied according to the ages and needs of the student co-teachers (e.g., Christine improved her articulation so that the third graders could understand her; Denny learned to disagree in a friendly way that even helped him with a playground event). Methods to monitor and be accountable for progress included Dave and Juan's self-recorded graphs and the frequent feedback sessions between Bill and Sharon.

PREPARING STUDENTS TO BE ■
CO-TEACHERS

In this section, we describe the vital role that adults play in creating successful student co-teachers. We describe several instructional methods that support students to serve in co-teaching roles: cooperative learning, peer tutoring, dialogue teaching, and instructional conversation.

The vignettes show that adult co-teachers play a vital role in creating successful student co-teachers. For example, Bill needed the agreement of Sharon, the math teacher, to become her co-teacher. Christine and Cat exchanged teacher and learner roles during the debriefing session for Christine's teaching of the safety unit for third grade. In this way, Cat could hear how differently third graders learn compared with Christine's learning needs. Elaine and Laurie explicitly taught reciprocal peer tutoring skills to their third graders and provided additional supports for Dave and Juan. Denny's co-teachers, Cathy and Shamonique, arranged for all the fifth graders to learn how to disagree in a friendly way.

Students are more likely to become effective co-teachers when their co-teachers explicitly teach how to tutor or work as study buddies. Co-teachers with successful student co-teachers also make sure that student co-teachers enjoy the reciprocity involved in being both teacher and learner. Co-teachers create more opportunities for students to practice co-teaching skills when they set up *cooperative group learning* so that all members of the group can practice the communication skills involved in teaching others what they know. Denny's co-teachers used cooperative group learning with an emphasis on teaching the social skill of friendly disagreeing. Dave and Juan's co-teachers used structured peer tutoring to help students with emotional challenges become kinder and more effective partner learners. Ms. Marquez was a co-teacher with her students to ensure improved computer skills for all the children. Bill and Christine benefited from having their co-teachers (Sharon and Cat) work with them as coaches in developing teaching skills.

Co-teachers who rely on cooperative group learning make sure that students are responsible not only for their own learning but also for the learning of the other members of their group. They are responsible for showing certain social behaviors with their peers. The co-teacher's role shifts from that of a presenter of information to a facilitator of learning. There are five major tasks in a cooperative lesson: (1) clearly specifying the objectives, (2) making decisions about placing students in learning groups to ensure heterogeneity, (3) clearly explaining what learning activities are expected of the students and how they will demonstrate positive interdependence, (4) monitoring the cooperative interactions and intervening to provide task assistance (e.g., answer questions, teach task-related skills) or to increase students' interpersonal and group skills, and (5) evaluating student achievement and group effectiveness (Johnson, Johnson, and Holubec 1998).

There are several other instructional methods that encourage and prepare students to be co-teachers. *Dialogue teaching* may be the perfect method for those who have been silenced (e.g., students of color, those at risk, second-language learners, students with disabilities). Dialogue teaching means that students help to generate the curriculum, design their own instructional methods, and report their progress within a framework of consciousness-raising group dynamics (Kluth et al. 2002). Dialogue teaching also involves changing the pace of classroom speaking to allow more time to think before responding, valuing different types of contributions (e.g., laughter, gestures, typed words on a communication board), and making sure topics are important to the students (e.g., issues related to race, gender, class, ability). Co-teachers who practice dialogue teaching develop skills in listening to and differentially responding to their students' linguistic habits and verbal styles, especially for the students who are learning English as a second language or the students who are nonverbal. Student co-teachers who practice dialogue teaching can acquire powerful new awareness of their strengths and contributions.

Achievement increases when learners receive appropriate scaffolding of content instruction to help them learn English (Echevarria and Graves 1998; Graves, Gersten, and Haager 2004). Achievement also improves when teachers provide interactive and direct approaches to instruction for oral language, literacy, and academic content (Thomas and Collier 2001). Other effective techniques include guided practice, active learning, opportunities for frequent conversation in English, instructional presentations with multiple media, and curriculum modifications.

Instructional conversation (Garcia 2002, 2005), also referred to as the *discourse of sheltered instruction* (Echevarria and Graves 1998), is a particularly compelling teaching-learning process to use when the student co-teachers are also students who are learning English and are fluent in other languages. Student co-teachers who use instructional conversation learn how to encourage talking. They, as well as their partners in the co-teaching relationship, practice the give-and-take that is a hallmark of authentic conversation. This is different from the typical one-way teacher-to-student talk that often dominates classrooms, in which the teacher asks questions and the student answers. Instead, the co-teacher who uses instructional conversation accepts responses in either language (e.g., Spanish or English) and, in a response, models the English phraseology through restatements and furthering comments to discover more about what the speaker knows. The co-teacher who uses instructional conversation also ignores inappropriate responses or inaccurate usage, such as incomplete utterances to convey meaning, rather than providing immediate correction as is the usual method in traditional instruction. Instead, the co-teacher models appropriate constructive social interaction by continuing the conversation while modeling the correct usage. Co-teachers who practice instructional conversation often add a visual component by writing the words and sentence structures on a chalkboard or chart paper (an especially helpful technique for the specialized vocabulary that often appears in science and math subjects).

A common characteristic of these teaching and learning activities is that they encourage students in the co-teacher role. The outcome is that students receive the benefits of a more active role in communicating their understanding of the academic content. This, in turn, leads to increased retention and achievement.

The authors are familiar with numerous schools that have started formal peer tutoring and co-teaching programs (Villa et al., 2010). Peer tutors can tutor in a single classroom, across grades, or even across schools (e.g., middle-level learners tutoring in an elementary school). In our experience, the establishment of adult and student co-teaching teams primarily occurs at the high school level, but we have seen examples of high school-aged students co-teaching with adults in middle and elementary schools. High schools in California, Colorado, and Pennsylvania, with which the authors have assisted in the development of a co-teaching program, have had as few as 18 and as many as 50 high school juniors and seniors earning an elective credit by serving as members of adult and student co-teaching teams. Whether a school is interested in establishing a peer tutoring or a co-teaching program, there are at least six essential areas in which many questions are posed that must be answered when developing a formalized program (Villa et al. 2010). The essential questions are presented in Table 9.3.

Table 9.3   Essential Questions to Answer When Establishing Peer Tutor or Co-Teaching Programs

I. Identification	Who will participate?
II. Recruitment	What are the potential sources of tutors or co-teachers?
	How will potential participants and their families be informed?
	Who has received or who needs training in teaching skills?
III. Training	Who will conduct the training?
	Where will the training occur?
	What will be taught in each session?
	What materials are needed for teaching and how will the instructor use them?
	How will the peer tutor or co-teacher evaluate the quality and effectiveness of his or her own technical and interpersonal behavior?
IV. Delivery and Supervision	When, how often, and where will the instructional sessions occur?
	Who is responsible for supervision?
	How will you communicate with the classroom teacher, the special educator, and any others who are concerned with the tutor and/or co-teachers learners' performance?
V. Evaluation	How will you measure the students' progress?
	- tutor
	- tutee
	- co-teacher
VI. Reinforcement and Recognition	How will you provide recognition for partner learner/peer tutoring and co-teacher participation?

■ THE RESEARCH BASE FOR STUDENTS AS CO-TEACHERS

In this section, we summarize recent research in several areas: peer tutoring, partner learning, students in coaching roles in cooperative groups, and student-led conferences. Several theoretical frameworks undergird the research and practice base for students as co-teachers. For example, cognitive psychologists have verified that *reciprocal teaching* (see Palinscar and Brown 1984) is effective in significantly raising and maintaining the reading comprehension scores of poor readers. In a reciprocal teaching exchange, students alternate being the teacher who coaches the comprehension skills being practiced, similar to the way that Dave and Juan interacted to learn their math facts. Another theoretical framework that explains the success of students as co-teachers is *social learning theory* (Johnson and Johnson 1989, 2005). When students work as co-teachers, they form an interdependent relationship that allows them to learn from each other as they teach.

First, there is a strong body of research about the benefits of peer tutoring. Fuchs, Fuchs, Mathes, and Martinez (2002) and Fuchs, Fuchs, Thompson, and colleagues (2000), for example, show that peer tutoring helps teachers individualize learning materials to address a broader range of instructional needs. Students at risk for school failure in urban multicultural and disadvantaged neighborhoods also have increased their reading skills when the whole class engaged in peer tutoring (Kourea, Cartledge, and Musti-Rao 2007). When students co-teach in a peer-tutoring system, there are more opportunities to respond to and practice academic content than in more conventional teacher-directed lessons. There is also evidence that peer tutoring facilitates positive changes in students' social behaviors and school adjustment (Fuchs, Fuchs, Mathes et al. 2002). Moreover, Faltis (1993) and Walter (1998) cite peer tutoring and cooperative group learning as methods that are especially beneficial for students who are learning English.

Similarly, a rich research base documents the benefits of students as co-teachers within cooperative group-learning formats, especially for building relationships among diverse populations. Johnson and Johnson (1989, 2000, 2002, 2005) summarize the impact of cooperative learning on the processes of acceptance and rejection. When students experience cooperative group learning (i.e., positive interdependence, positive interpersonal social interactions, systematic feedback on their academic and social skills progress), they show more frequent and open communication, deeper understanding of other perspectives, more clearly differentiated views of each other, improved self-esteem, more successful achievement and productivity, and increased willingness to interact with others who are different from them. When students work in co-teaching roles, they experience elements similar to cooperative group learning. For example, positive interdependence occurs through shared goals and division of labor, student co-teachers must show good interpersonal and communication skills in the teacher role, and they both assess how their teaching is affecting their learners and receive feedback about their performance from the educator working with them in the co-teacher role.

In addition, there is a nascent body of literature that should encourage educators to continue exploring how best to achieve the student co-teacher role. For example, when students took on the role of reporting their own progress at family-teacher conferences, Countryman and Schroeder (1996) found that the positive evaluation data from students, parents, and teachers resulted in the decision to continue the practice for future conferences. Teachers at a middle school included their students as co-presenters when holding family–teacher conferences. The students led the meetings by introducing their family members to the teacher, showing their parents or family members selected examples of their work, explaining the progress they had made, and outlining the goals for the next marking period. Evaluation comments focused on the students' honesty in reporting their progress, increased student empowerment to be responsible for their own educational programs, and improved school–community relationships because of the more personal format.

ASSESSING STUDENTS AS CO-TEACHERS   ■

One way to assess students as they develop their co-teaching skills is to encourage them to self-evaluate by using the checklist shown in Table 9.4. Individually, each student co-teacher can use the checklist and then compare with his or her student co-teachers the Yes versus Not Yet assessments. This allows team members to have a starting point for discussing the strengths of the student co-teacher partnership thus far and target areas for improvement.

Student co-teachers can also complete the checklist jointly. Rather than coming to consensus on an item, we suggest that the team use a different approach to self-rating. We suggest that, for a team to give an item a *yes* rating, every member must definitively agree that a *yes* is appropriate. If any one team member is not sure about a *yes* rating, the response must remain *not yet*. This reduces the temptation to pressure the person with a differing perception to give in for the sake of consensus and, instead, encourages a real dialogue about the differing perspectives, perceptions, and experiences of members of a co-teaching team.

Others who are not on the team but who are requested to respond or who have a responsibility to observe the student co-teachers can use the checklist to provide constructive feedback (in much the same way that Laurie and Elaine did for Dave and Juan). We encourage student co-teachers to revisit the list frequently, talk about the items, and select some items to focus on for improvement. This is how independent, self-regulated learning develops!

Table 9.4 Checklist: Are You Really a Student Co-Teacher?

Directions: If you wonder whether your students are co-teachers, ask your students to check *Yes* or *Not Yet* to each of the following statements. Then add the number to discover their current Student Co-Teacher Score.

We know we are student co-teachers when we…	Yes	Not Yet
1. Explain instructional goals or objectives of a lesson.	_____	_____
2. Apply a scoring guide (rubric) to grade work produced.	_____	_____
3. Detect mistakes or misunderstandings.	_____	_____
4. Provide instructional feedback to correct mistakes without giving away the answers.	_____	_____
5. Celebrate the successes of our students.	_____	_____
6. Communicate with other co-teachers to plan, teach, and evaluate lessons.	_____	_____
7. Discuss concerns or disagreements freely with co-teaching partners.	_____	_____
8. Use a problem-solving method when faced with conflicts.	_____	_____
9. Ask for help when necessary.	_____	_____
10. Add item of interest to your own situation: _____.	_____	_____
Total		

FREQUENTLY ASKED QUESTIONS

1. Isn't it true that students are not developmentally mature enough to be capable of co-teaching? After all, it takes 4 years of college for teachers to learn the profession.

Yes, it is true that certification of teachers requires at least a 4-year college degree, methods classes, and understanding of learning and assessment techniques. However, we suggest that the goal is not to have students perform at the same level of proficiency as certified teachers. The most important strategy for overcoming the belief that students are not developmentally mature enough to serve as co-teachers is for the teacher to explicitly model and implement those strategies that facilitate students in partner-learning roles. School personnel must ensure that student co-teachers are trained, monitored, and provided with ongoing coaching and support. Moreover, school personnel can select instructional methods that set the context for students to practice co-teaching roles, such as cooperative group learning, peer tutoring, and dialogue teaching (as described earlier).

2. How can teachers justify taking time away from teaching the curriculum and helping students meet the standards for graduation to teach instructional methods to student co-teachers?

We agree that a major disadvantage of the use of student co-teachers is that it seems there isn't enough time in the school day to provide for all the required subjects. Conscientious teachers often worry that the time required to prepare students adequately to serve as co-teachers is time that could be better spent on teaching the curriculum. The structure of the typical school day requires that teachers guarantee that a specified number of minutes be used to teach mandated subjects. It could be argued that the time required to prepare students as co-teachers is time well spent; when students are trained as co-teachers, there is more one-on-one time available to meet the unique learning needs of more students.

In addition, we know some school districts require students to engage in service-learning activities as part of graduation requirements. Co-teaching roles can fulfill the spirit of service learning.

In fact, celebrating students as co-teachers can be perceived as the penultimate goal for teachers who practice co-teaching. Whether they use supportive, parallel, complementary, or team-teaching approaches, co-teachers model collaboration and communication for their students. Co-teaching teams can set the expectation among their students, other educators, and specialists that students will be members not only of student governance but also of peer support teams; learning teams; teams to plan Individual Education Programs; and teams to plan transitions from elementary to middle school, middle school to high school, or high school to life after school. Student co-teachers themselves become the most effective voices for showing and telling about the results. Creating a variety of methods for students to share their successes, trials, tribulations, and unexpected positive outcomes of being co-teachers is a powerful way to overcome barriers and disadvantages.

PART IV

Administrative Support and Professional Development

Part IV features five chapters that examine the logistical aspects of co-teaching and that illustrate the logistics in action with a co-teaching partnership. Chapter 10 is specifically written to provide administrators with ideas for facilitating change toward co-teaching by attending to five variables—vision, skills, incentives, resources, and action planning. Chapter 11 examines ways in which teacher-preparation programs can apply co-teaching training and coaching to enhance the quality of student-teaching clinical practice experiences and induct future teachers into co-teaching as an expected teaching practice. Chapter 12 describes how co-teachers can mesh planning with co-teaching by suggesting ways for creating and efficiently using planning time, providing an easy-to-use co-teaching lesson plan template, and offering an Are We Really Co-Teachers? self-assessment for promoting co-teachers' professional development. Chapter 13 builds upon the content of Chapter 12 and provides some advanced tips for avoiding potential pitfalls, tips that include communication, interpersonal relationship building, and conflict management. Chapter 14 pulls the content of the book together through the story of Nancy Keller's and Lia Cravedi's 2-year journey of developing a shared voice through co-teaching. Throughout the story, tips introduced in Chapter 13 are highlighted to illustrate how these two co-teachers worked to make their partnership flourish.

Training and Logistical Administrative Support for Co-Teaching

10

Topics Included in This Chapter:

❖ Building a vision
❖ Building the skills and capacity for co-teaching
❖ Incentives to engage people in co-teaching
❖ Resources for co-teaching
❖ Getting started: Planning and taking action
❖ Summary
❖ Frequently asked questions

Do you wonder how administrators spark an interest in co-teaching among their staff? Do you want to know the kinds of organizational support that administrators provide to facilitate the effective implementation of co-teaching approaches? Are you interested in learning how schools allocate resources to support co-teaching? These and other administrative, training, and logistical issues are discussed in this chapter as we examine five variables—vision, skills, incentives, resources, and action planning—that factor into a formula for facilitating change toward co-teaching (Villa and Thousand 2004). More specifically, this chapter describes ways to (1) build a vision of collaboration in planning and teaching within a school; (2) develop educators' skills and confidence as co-teachers; (3) create meaningful incentives for people to take the risk to embark on a co-teaching journey; (4) reorganize, schedule, and expand human and other resources for co-teaching; and (5) plan for and take actions designed to get school personnel excited about implementing co-teaching approaches.

■ BUILDING A VISION

School leaders involved in co-teaching stress the importance of clarifying for themselves, school personnel, and the community a vision based on assumptions that (1) all children are capable of learning, (2) all children have a right to an education with their peers in their community's schools, (3) everyone who provides instruction shares responsibility for the learning of every child in the school, and (4) co-teaching is an organizational and instructional strategy that benefits students and educators alike. Simply stating a vision, however, is not enough. School leaders need to foster widespread understanding and consensus regarding the vision.

Consensus Building Through an Examination of Rationales for Co-Teaching

One strategy for building a vision and consensus for co-teaching is to educate people about the rationales for and benefits of co-teaching, as discussed in Chapter 2 and illustrated in the vignettes and discussions throughout this book. Our experience tells us that in the process of building consensus, different people will find different rationales compelling. If we are to have any hope of shifting a person's belief in favor of co-teaching, we must first listen to and identify the person's concerns (questions, fears, nightmares, confusions) regarding co-teaching and supply him or her with the appropriate rationale that addresses those concerns.

Stated otherwise, as change agents, we first must solicit and listen to the concerns of everyone affected by a shift to co-teaching (which may be just about everyone—teachers, parents, students, community members). Next, we must use this information to determine which of the rationales speak to each individual's priority concerns. Fiscal and legal matters may speak to administrators and school board members; disappointing efficacy data about pullout programs versus inclusion and co-teaching may speak to parents and students; the fragmented and poorly coordinated nature of categorical support programs such as Title I, special education, gifted and talented education, bilingual education, and instruction of students learning English may speak to educators tired of isolation and endless hours of paperwork.

Information about the rationales that are important to various individuals may be communicated in any number of ways—through the structure of inservice training events, distribution of readings with follow-up discussions, videos of co-teachers, or visits to schools that have adopted co-teaching. Finally, once we are knowledgeable of concerns, we are in the position to address them seriously in any planning or implementation process by regularly and vigilantly asking, "How can we ensure that people's worst nightmares (concerns) about co-teaching do not come true?"

Consensus Building Through Respecting What We Expect

A vision and consensus for co-teaching can be fostered by actively respecting what we expect by encouraging, recognizing, and publicly acknowledging those educators who plunge in as early innovators and pioneers to model and actively promote the philosophy and practice of co-teaching. To determine what teachers find to be meaningful recognition, administrators need to ask them directly what they consider rewarding. For some teachers, public recognition for engaging in an innovation is rewarding. For others, public recognition would be embarrassing, but an opportunity to attend a conference on co-teaching would be a treat.

Building consensus for a vision is really about replacing an old culture with a new one and managing the personal loss that inevitably accompanies cultural change. New heroes and heroines, rituals and symbols, and histories must be constructed. New histories replace old ones when traditional solutions (e.g., adding yet another new pullout program or professional when children with new differences arrive at school) are publicly pointed out to be ineffective, inefficient, and counter to the desired vision and when collaboration among staff in planning and co-teaching is regularly and routinely celebrated.

Consensus Building by Clarifying How and When to Use Co-Teaching as a Strategy to Support Diverse Learners

Some school personnel appear to be confused about the purpose of co-teaching and when to engage in the practice. In some schools, co-teaching is incorrectly viewed as the only way to support students with disabilities in inclusive settings. Not every student eligible for special education needs to be placed in a co-taught classroom. Table 10.1 (and Resource I) describes various levels of support, including co-teaching, which can be made available for individual students. Members of the Individual Educational Program (IEP) team who are responsible for making placement decisions for students with disabilities are encouraged to review the table and identify the level of support that is needed.

Some students with and without disabilities may require additional support (e.g., study skills training, homework support, remediation) that school personnel may not be able to address adequately within the time available in a co-taught classroom. In response to this situation, many schools establish learning centers in which all students can receive extra or supplemental support and targeted instruction. Students may be assigned to a learning center during study hall or as an alternative to an elective for one period a day, or they may attend only as long as is necessary for them to master a specific skill. Staff members at one high school with which we are familiar use their library media center as the learning center. Every period of every day, one general education teacher and one special educator are assigned, as an official duty, to work with students in the learning center, which is housed in the library media center. In addition to the library media director and the general and special education personnel, trained peer tutors are available to provide tutorial and other assistance to their fellow students. Such an arrangement avoids stigmatization of students receiving support and allows all students, whether or not they are eligible for a particular support program, to receive assistance from teachers and peers on an as-needed basis. Additionally, in order to support students requiring supplemental or intensive interventions, some schools provide response to intervention (RTI) Tier II and III level services within general education classrooms through co-teaching arrangements (see Chapter 2 for a more detailed description of RTI). Other schools provide Tier II and Tier III services during intervention blocks either during the day or before or after normal school hours.

■ BUILDING THE SKILLS AND CAPACITY FOR CO-TEACHING

Unless educators believe they have the skills to co-teach, they will doubt their capacity to be good co-teachers. The more diverse the student body, the more skilled educators must be as a collective instructional force. We highlight the word *collective* to emphasize that educators of a co-teaching team need not have the same content and instructional skills; they do, however, need easy access to one another so that they can share their skills across students and classrooms. We further believe there is a core set of skills and strategies that all co-teachers need to acquire (over time) to meet diverse student needs and realize the research promise of co-teaching.

No matter how exciting or promising an innovation like co-teaching is, educators need training, guided practice, feedback, and opportunities to plan and problem solve with colleagues and to clarify the nuances of co-teaching. Furthermore, for the innovation to become the new culture, people must come to understand its significance for their personal and professional growth and for the growth of their students. Within the context of co-teaching, this places training front and center as a strategy for reducing anxiety and transforming the culture of the school. Because so many teachers report that neither their professional preparation nor their relatively isolated teaching experiences have adequately prepared them for co-teaching, it becomes a local school district's responsibility to develop and provide an ongoing comprehensive inservice training agenda. We emphasize the importance of giving people choice as to how they receive training (e.g., courses, mentoring, team teaching, summer institutes, workshop series, DVDs, book studies).

Who Receives Training?

As emphasized throughout this book, any member of the school and the greater community is a candidate for training because anyone can become a co-teacher. Although training may initially be organized for and delivered to innovators and early adopters in the school, eventually everyone involved—teachers, administrators, paraprofessionals, related service personnel, and students—needs to acquire a common core of knowledge about co-teaching. To excuse those who are reluctant, resistant, or apathetic from acquiring the disposition and skills to implement co-teaching divides people, promotes the development of factions, fosters resentment toward those who don't participate, reinforces a "this too will pass" mentality, and generally works against the development of a unified new culture.

Table 10.1   Levels of Student Support

Classroom Companion—One or more classmates support another student's participation in academic or elective classes. Support may include helping with mobility to and from class, carrying or remembering materials, taking notes, assisting in task completion, facilitating communication, and being role models for social/friendship interaction.
Consultation—Support staff meet regularly with the general education teacher to keep track of student progress, assess the need for supplemental materials, problem solve, and maintain positive and open communication. Students know that they can stop in or request assistance from support staff on a specific assignment or for general support.
Stop-In Support—Support staff observe students on a regular or periodic basis to determine possible needs, provide suggestions for curricular and instructional adaptations, and/or set up peer support systems. They maintain open communication with the classroom teacher and students.
Part-Time Daily Support—Support staff provide support to students at a predetermined time, on a rotating basis, or for specific assignments or activities. They maintain awareness of curriculum and assignments in order to encourage student productivity and provide additional tutorial or organizational support. Staff may also supply supplemental materials for classroom use.
In-Class Co-Teaching Support—A support staff member (e.g., special educator) is partnered for co-teaching to assist all students by moving around the room and providing support as needed, teaching small groups, or complementing instruction. This person collaborates with the general education teacher to develop and plan for specific support strategies and student needs.
Total Staff Support—A support staff member (e.g., paraprofessional) is assigned to support one or more target students, usually with significant academic or behavioral needs. Support staff may be in close proximity with the target student(s), facilitating interaction with classmates and the curriculum, and may assume responsibility for modifying, developing, or acquiring materials that support student engagement and success.

Common Core of Training

At a minimum, staff members need training in collaborative planning (Thousand and Villa 2000; Villa 2002a) and approaches to co-teaching such as those discussed throughout this text (Bauwens and Mueller 2000; Friend 1996; Villa 2002b). Other content includes differentiation and universal design approaches to instruction (Thousand, Villa, and Nevin 2007a, 2007b; Tomlinson 1999; Udvari-Solner, Villa, and Thousand 2002), cooperative group learning (Johnson and Johnson 2009; Villa, Thousand, and Nevin, 2010a, 2010b), and other areas (e.g., discipline) that they self-identify as priority areas for mutual skill development. Other resources for designing professional development activities include professional standards related to meeting the individual needs of learners and collaboration. For example, both special and general education members of a co-teaching team can improve their competencies by meeting the standards for special educators (Council for Exceptional Children 2009) and the InTASC standards for general educators (Council of Chief State School Officers 2011).

■ INCENTIVES TO ENGAGE PEOPLE IN CO-TEACHING

Without incentives that are meaningful to each person affected by the change toward co-teaching, the outcome may be passive or active resistance rather than excited engagement. Promoting co-teaching requires structuring incentives, notably a menu of incentives. In developing this, first be sure to focus on teams as well as individuals in order to highlight the importance of and pride in collaborative teaching efforts. Second, spend time "in the trenches" with teachers, support staff, and students who are involved in co-teaching. Discover what they are doing well that can be privately and publicly acknowledged. Third, ask staff members and students what they value as incentives. What is rewarding to one person may be of little significance to another. Some commonly identified teacher incentives include the following:

- Short notes of praise (e.g., "The students in your co-taught class seem excited about learning. Thanks for taking the risk and embarking on a co-teaching journey. I know you will have fun along the way.")
- Special training opportunities
- Mentoring of others new to co-teaching practices
- Travel to conferences or other schools engaged in co-teaching
- Regular forums for airing concerns and generating viable solutions
- Opportunities to make presentations at conferences, school board meetings, parent–teacher organizations, and community gatherings
- Modeling co-teaching for other teachers and administrators who visit your classroom
- Visits to co-taught classrooms to become familiar with other co-teachers and the practices they employ
- Off-campus retreats for collaborative planning efforts

Time: The Universal Incentive

Although many incentives are unique to individuals, one incentive is common to and highly valued by everyone engaged in co-teaching and other educational reforms: time—time for face-to-face interaction and time to plan, share, and reflect with colleagues. Many classroom teachers have told us that it is difficult to develop a co-teaching relationship when they cannot spend adequate time with their co-teaching partner(s). These teachers report that it is almost impossible to develop a trusting relationship with a co-teaching partner, decide on predictable co-teaching roles and responsibilities, or differentiate instruction when there is little planning time, when a partner fails to show up, when one partner is frequently pulled from the co-teaching classroom to handle emergencies, or when co-teachers are assigned to co-teach only 1 or 2 days a week.

The reality is that many special education and other support personnel have other mandated responsibilities and emergency situations that sometimes pull them out of co-taught classrooms. Administrators need to understand the necessity for continuity among co-teachers and work with classroom and support personnel to decrease the amount of time that support personnel are pulled from general education classrooms to handle behavioral emergencies, attend meetings, conduct assessments, and do paperwork.

Recognizing that forming a trusting co-teaching relationship is contingent on several variables (including frequency of contact, capability, willingness, and dependability), many school administrators promise general education teachers co-teaching support for a minimum of 4 out of 5 days a week. These administrators believe that four well-planned and purposeful co-taught lessons or class sessions are far better than five "fly by the seat of your pants" instructional sessions. The fifth day, the day that the support personnel are not necessarily in the class, is the same day each week, and the fact that the classroom teacher will be teaching alone that day is considered in the co-planning of instructional activities for that day. Support personnel use the fifth day for paperwork, assessment, planning meetings with co-teachers, and other meetings.

In addition, some schools schedule a meeting among support personnel for part of the fifth day so that they can collaboratively brainstorm strategies and supports that can be brought back to the co-taught classroom to support struggling learners. Consider the following example: A speech and language therapist is co-teaching several classes but is unable to provide direct service to all learners eligible for speech and language services in every classroom. Special educators, however, are co-teaching in all classrooms that include students eligible for speech and language services. During the weekly meeting occurring on the fifth day, the speech and language therapist can provide indirect service to the eligible learners by mentoring the special educators and enabling them to target oral and written language goals for eligible students in their co-taught classes. We encourage you to read the Frequently Asked Question at the end of Chapter 11 and examine Table 12.1 in Chapter 12 to learn about how some schools have provided the valuable incentive of time for collaborative meeting and planning.

Scheduling as an Incentive

Co-teaching is closely linked to scheduling. Scheduling practices can provide a powerful incentive or disincentive for co-teaching. For example, the scheduling practice of tracking students into ability groups and classes, such as concentrating special education–eligible and other at-risk students into the lower-track classes, is a huge barrier or disincentive for co-teaching. A research-supported, best educational practice is to group students heterogeneously by perceived ability or achievement. This means that classrooms should have a composition that closely reflects the natural proportion of students with and without identified special needs. On average in schools across the United States, 9% to 12% of students are eligible for special education. In any given classroom, therefore, the ideal would be to have not many more than that proportion of the students eligible for IEPs.

Some congregation of students with disabilities occurs when scheduling co-teaching personnel into the classes, but a recommended best practice is to keep the number of students with disabilities at no more than 5% above the mean for that school, thereby maintaining the natural proportion of students with disabilities to peers without disabilities. For example, if the natural proportion of students with disabilities were 12%, the recommended best practice would be to have no more than 17% of the student population eligible for special education in a co-taught classroom. A natural proportion allows for academic, social, and communication models; avoids stigmatization of students and personnel who support them; and follows the research-supported alternative of heterogeneous grouping (Johnson and Johnson 1999). It should be noted that some schools find it difficult at times to implement the recommended scheduling best practice of not exceeding more than 5% above the natural proportion. In those instances when it is necessary to place more students with identified needs into a classroom, administrators, teachers, and guidance personnel making placement decisions should endeavor to never exceed creating classrooms where more than one-third of the class are students eligible for special education or English language learning services and supports. To our knowledge, no leading co-teaching author or trainer has ever recommended exceeding this one-third cutoff point.

Professional Development as an Incentive

Many educators are motivated by professional development of their skills and knowledge (Cook 2004; Cramer et al. 2006; Hall and Hord 2001). Co-teaching experiences empower teachers to meet nationally recognized sets of standards specified for novice teachers and veteran teachers. The standards include competencies related to collaboration in order to differentiate instruction so as to increase student achievement. Once initial knowledge about a new instructional practice such as co-teaching has been acquired, follow-up application activities should reflect the best practices. We like to say, "Learning to co-teach is a journey, not a destination!" We have worked diligently with co-teachers and their administrators to prepare professional-development multimedia programs for developing not only their co-teaching skills but also their skills in differentiating instruction and engaging students as co-teachers (Thousand, Villa, and Nevin 2007a, 2007b; Villa, Thousand, and Nevin 2008; Villa, Thousand, and Nevin, 2010a, 2010b.). We cannot emphasize enough the power of including in such professional development activities anyone who might engage in or otherwise support co-teaching—speech-language professionals, paraprofessionals, school psychologists, teacher librarians, administrators, substitute teachers, student teachers, and so forth.

When co-teachers are provided with observational feedback and coaching, they are afforded the opportunity to (a) celebrate what they already are doing well, (b) be reminded of effective practices, and (c) set goals for continuing development as a co-teaching team. Figure 10.1 offers an example of the use of an Instructional Observation Form that we have found useful for collecting observational data on co-teachers' actions in the classroom and prompting co-teachers' reflections about their co-teaching experiences. The instructional observation form is divided into three sections. The first section examines content standards and objectives—*what is to be taught* in the lesson and the materials being used. The second section examines the product of instruction—*how students demonstrate and convey their learning.* The third and largest section of the observational form examines the processes of learning—*how instruction and differentiation help students make sense of the learning.* This third process section includes sections for the four co-teaching approaches (i.e., supportive, parallel, complementary, team) as well as the instructional formats, arrangements, and strategies that co-teachers might employ in their instruction. This Instructional Observation Form may be used by administrators, instructional coaches, fellow teachers who are observing and learning from one another, or the co-teachers themselves as they reflect on their instruction and plan for future lessons. For illustrative purposes, Figure 10.1 was completed during an observation of Ms. Spaulding and Mr. Silva, the middle-level science/math and special education co-teachers, delivering the parallel co-taught science lesson featured in Chapter 5. A blank instructional observation form appears as Resource O in the resource section of the book.

Figure 10.2 shows an example of the use of the Instructional Post-Observation Conference template for debriefing with and coaching co-teachers to engage in reflective conversations about their co-teaching experience. The conference begins with the co-teachers identifying what they perceive as having gone well in the lesson. This is followed by their analysis of what, if anything, they would do differently if they were to re-teach the lesson. Next, the co-teachers are asked to identify and describe which of the four co-teaching approaches they used and to discuss the frequency and duration of their co-teaching planning sessions. The coach then offers his or her analysis of the co-teaching approaches used, observations of what went well in the lesson, wonderings about what was observed or the thinking behind the design or delivery of the lesson, and suggestions for future planning and instruction. The conference closes with the co-teachers identifying their own learnings or *takeaways* from the co-teaching coaching session. Figure 10.2 was completed in a post-observation conference with Mr. Silva and Ms. Spaulding, immediately following the observation of the science lesson featured in Chapter 5. A blank Instructional Post-Observation Conference form can be found as Resource P in the resource section of this book.

Figure 10.1   Instructional Observation Form

Instructor(s): Mr. Silva Ms. Spaulding	Observer: Villa	Date: May 30		Room #: 212	Period/Time: 9:08am– 10:00am	Scheduled: ☑ Yes ☐ No
Grade: 8	Subject: Science	# of Students: present 24	absent 2	# of Sp Ed: 7	# TAG: 3	# ELL: 2

Content

Instructional Objective/Learning Outcome(s):
Unclear as it is not posted or referenced during the observation period.
Language Objective:
☑ Reading   ☐ Writing   ☑ Speaking   ☑ Listening

Purpose Posted for Students to See ☐ Yes ☑ No	Objective Referenced ☐ Yes ☑ No

Differentiated Materials ☑ Yes   ☐ No *text-to-speech software, adapted text, large print, Spanish translation*

Product

☐ Yes ☑ No   Learning outcomes demonstrated in multiple ways
☐ Yes ☐ No   Learning outcomes measured in a variety of ways – *unsure of what is planned*
☐ Yes ☑ No   Criteria for success explained

Process

Co-Teaching Approaches ☐ N/A ☐ Supportive ☑ Parallel ☐ Complementary ☐ Team	
Bell-to-Bell Instruction ☑ Yes ☐ No	Transition times are smooth ☐ Yes ☐ No ☑ Mostly
Think time provided ☑ Yes ☐ No ☐ N/A	Directions Clear ☐ Yes ☐ No ☑ Mostly
Checked for understanding of concepts/principles/facts ☑ Yes ☐ No	Checked for understanding of directions ☐ Yes ☑ No
Active Student Engagement ☐ Low ☑ Medium ☐ High	
Teacher asks higher level thinking questions ☑ Yes ☐ No ☐ N/A	
Students ask higher level thinking questions ☐ Yes ☑ No ☐ N/A	

Called on learners who didn't volunteer ☐ Yes ☑ No ☐ N/A

Utilized Think-Pair-Share & other quick cooperative structures ☑ Yes ☐ No

Frequency ☐ Low ☑ Medium ☐ High

☐ Formal ☑ Informal

Students required to speak in complete sentences ☐ Yes ☑ No

Level of teacher talk ☐ Low ☑ Medium ☐ High

Level of student talk ☐ Low ☑ Medium ☐ High

Students engaged in academic dialogue ☑ Yes ☐ No

Level ☐ Low ☑ Medium ☐ High

Teacher(s) was/were in control of the classroom ☑ Yes ☐ No

Positive Behavior Support Strategies employed ☑ Yes ☐ No

Degree used ☑ Low ☐ Medium ☐ High

Feeling Tone/Climate

☐ Positive ☑ Slightly Positive ☐ Neutral ☐ Slightly Negative ☐ Negative

---

Adapted Lectures ☐ Yes ☑ No _____

Activity Based ☐ Yes ☑ No _____

Simulation/Role Play ☐ Yes ☑ No _____

21st-century technology in the hands of teacher ☑ Yes ☐ No

21st-century technology in the hands of the students ☑ Yes ☐ No

---

Stations ☐ Yes ☑ No _____

Lecture/Pencil-Paper tasks ☑ Yes ☐ No _____

Whole Group ☑ Yes ☐ No	Research Based Strategies
Independent ☑ Yes ☐ No	☑ Yes ☐ No
Small Group ☑ Yes ☐ No	Application of Concepts from Multiple
Partner Work ☑ Yes ☐ No *reciprocal reading*	Intelligence Theory *visual/spatial,* *verbal/linguistic*
Cooperative Group Learning ☑ Yes ☐ No	☐ Yes ☐ No ☑ Somewhat
Teacher Directed Small Groups ☑ Yes ☐ No	All student monitored through the lesson
	☑ Yes ☐ No *when divided into 2 groups*

Instructional Sequence

- *Show video clips – re: sustainable future*
- *Introduce Silent Spring*
- *Explain task and identify resources*
- *Break class into 2 equal parts*
- *Combination of teacher directed, pairs, triads, quads, and individual*

Comments _____
_____
_____

Figure 10.2 Instructional Postconference Form

Name _____   **Date** _May 30_   **Time** _10:00 am - 10:30 am_

Length of time co-teaching: _2 months_

Teacher-Identified Approaches Used:

Supportive (**Parallel**) Complementary Team

Observer-Identified Approaches Used:

Supportive (**Parallel**) Complementary Team

Planning Time

Length: _35 minutes_

Frequency: _weekly_

Teacher(s)-identified "things" that went well:

Student engagement
- Variety of materials
- We are beginning to jell as a team.
- We covered everything we wanted to cover.

Teacher(s)-identified "things that they would do differently":

- Firm up transitions.
- Ask more higher-level thinking questions.
- Maybe find a DVD clip related to the book, Silent Spring and show that instead.

Observer-identified *things that went well:*

- Student interest (especially when showing video clips).
- Pacing - change of structure - large group, teacher-directed pairs, triads, quads.
- Variety of materials.
- Both teachers comfortable with content, students, and each other.

Observer wonderings:

- Why is the book being read in science class?
- What are the varied products students are expected to produce?
- What are the criteria for success?

Suggestions:

- Post and reference the content and language objectives.
- Clarify how learning outcomes will be demonstrated and the criteria for success.
- Check understanding of directions.
- During the whole-group instruction, call on learners who do not volunteer.
- Have the students generate higher-level questions.

Teacher(s)-identified next steps and *take aways:*

- Collect data on who responds to questions.
- Post and Reference objectives.
- Plan to use complementary and team-teaching approaches within 2 weeks.
- Explain criteria for success.

Members of co-teaching teams who have used or experienced the use of these two observation and coaching tools have remarked on the usefulness of both instruments in prompting objective and detailed self-examination of and conversation about both co-teaching and effective instruction.

Intrinsic Incentives

Although all of these extrinsic incentives are important, we have learned that genuine and sustainable changes in culture and dedication to co-teaching depend on people who are also reinforced by intrinsic motivators—their emotions, values, beliefs, and social bonds with colleagues. Intrinsic motivation includes recognizing one's increased effectiveness as evidenced by student success and happiness, feeling the pride in one's own professional risk taking and growth that accompanies recognition from respected colleagues and from students, and experiencing personal satisfaction with one's professional accomplishments.

RESOURCES FOR CO-TEACHING   ■

Resources for co-teaching may be technical and material (e.g., technology, curriculum materials) or organizational (e.g., how the school day, week, and year as well as the people within the organization are organized). Time is an example of an organizational resource (and incentive) that is in short supply in many schools. The previous discussion on incentives examined ways to gain more time for educators to plan, reflect, and collaborate with others. Clearly, educators' perception of the adequacy of the technological, material, and organizational resources available to them influences their work satisfaction. Nevertheless, the human resource—teachers' relationships with other adults and with the students, as well as the unique gifts, talents, and traits that each person offers—is most important to school health and improvement and to the success of co-teaching.

Redefining Roles

We propose that for educators to access most readily the resources of other educational personnel, everyone in the school system must stop thinking and acting in standard, isolated ways. Everyone must relinquish traditional roles, drop distinct professional labels, and redistribute job functions across any number of other people. Flexibility and fluidity are the main aims of role redefinition. Exactly who does what from one year to the next should evolve, determined by the needs of students and the complementary skills (and needs) of the educators distributing job functions among themselves.

Job titles and formal definitions sometimes determine how people behave. Thus, to further signal and symbolize a change in culture, new policies and job descriptions should be formulated to expect, inspect, and respect the collaborative ethic and practice of co-teaching. We are familiar with a number of school districts that have done this by creating a single job description for all professional educators (e.g., classroom teachers, special educators, school nurse, guidance personnel) that identifies collaboration in planning and teaching as expected job functions.

Allocating Resources for Co-Teaching

Allocating human resources to classrooms for the purpose of co-teaching should ideally be a collaborative responsibility involving general education classroom teachers, support personnel, and administrators of both general and special education programs (Thousand, Villa, and Nevin 2006). The overall responsibility for allocating or scheduling human resources resides with the administrator who can design a master schedule to allow the special educators and other support personnel—such as Title I, gifted and talented, and English-language instructors, as well as speech and language personnel—to be free to co-teach with their general education co-teaching partners. There is no one way to schedule co-teaching, but scheduling should always be based on an in-depth understanding of both student needs and existing human resources. What follows are elementary, middle-level, and high school examples of resource allocation through scheduling.

Resource Allocation at the Elementary Level

In some elementary schools committed to co-teaching, classroom teachers are told that they will receive co-teaching support in at least two academic content areas. Elementary classroom teachers typically identify language arts and math as the content areas in which they want co-teaching support. This can be problematic because most elementary classroom teachers prefer to teach language arts first thing in the morning. The solution to this dilemma is twofold. First, the number of personnel available to co-teach must be increased by utilizing all available personnel (e.g., Title I, special education, gifted and talented, librarian teachers, and English-language instructors; bilingual teachers, related service providers, school counselors; paraprofessionals; students) to co-teach during language arts and math classes. Second, if the number of personnel is still insufficient to allow co-teaching to occur at the same time in various classrooms, administrators develop a schedule that rotates language arts or math instructional time throughout the day, thereby allowing the necessary support to occur during the instructional time identified as most important by the classroom teachers. Some schools change the order of rotation each marking period, allowing all personnel to teach language arts during their preferred time of day during at least one marking period of the school year.

Resource Allocation at the Middle and High School Levels

There is no one way to do most anything in education, including constructing co-teaching configurations. All of the scheduling examples described in this section are meant to illustrate that there is no single correct way to allocate resources for co-teaching. Every solution has advantages and disadvantages. It is up to the teachers and administrators to think creatively, be inventive, take a risk, try new and different things, form unconventional partnerships, and trust their intuition in order to conceive of solutions that will be advantageous to their students.

Traditional Structure Scheduling

In middle and high schools that structure the day into 40- to 50-minute blocks, special educators may co-teach daily in four of six instructional periods and provide direct tutorial services and/or do paperwork and attend meetings for the remaining two periods of the school day.

Interdisciplinary Content Scheduling

Many middle-level and high school administrators have encouraged the formation of interdisciplinary teams (i.e., math, science, social studies, language arts) and designed master schedules that provide two planning periods per day. One planning period is set aside for common planning time among all team members, including the support personnel assigned to that team (e.g., Title I reading teacher, speech and language therapist, instructor of English learners), and the other planning period is used for individual or co-teaching team planning.

Natural Proportion Scheduling

Some middle and high schools have chosen to distribute all students heterogeneously across all subjects and grade levels and rely on regularly scheduled consultation and some co-teaching to support the students and general education classroom teachers. A major concern with this approach is that individual student needs may not be met and the co-teaching relationships may not evolve.

Differing Levels of Support Scheduling

There are at least three approaches for scheduling differing levels of co-teaching support at the middle and high school levels. For illustrative purposes for the first two approaches, each of the first two scheduling scenarios below assumes that there are six sections of a particular core curriculum area (e.g., biology) available at any grade level. These scheduling scenarios would work in schools structured into traditional 40- to 50-minute blocks as well as schools employing extended block scheduling or a combination of both approaches.

In the first scenario, students who are eligible for special education and require co-teaching support are placed in two of the six classes in which co-teaching will occur. Students with IEPs requiring consultation and part-time co-teaching support from a professional or paraprofessional are placed in one of two other classes in which consultation time between general education and special education teachers will occur weekly and basic skills or paraprofessional personnel will provide part-time co-teaching support. The remaining students with disabilities who require minimal accommodations and modifications are placed in the remaining two classes, where the classroom teacher assumes responsibility for implementing and monitoring the effectiveness of the accommodations and maintaining communication with the special educator.

In the second scenario of differentiated support, two classroom teachers of the same grade level or content area team up with a special educator and a special education paraprofessional. The students eligible for special education are divided evenly across the two classrooms, and the team determines when the special educator will co-teach with the classroom teacher. While the special educator is in one of the two classes, the paraprofessional works in the other class, providing support to the other classroom teacher and the students eligible for special education. Students who require basic skills or English language support are evenly divided among two of the other four content classes, and other support personnel (e.g., Title I personnel, teachers of English learners, reading specialists, curriculum consultants) provide co-teaching support to those classes. In this scheduling scenario, the remaining two sections do not have students eligible for special education or other categorical support programs. School personnel implementing this approach monitor the percentage of students eligible for special education who are placed in the co-taught classes to avoid violating the principle of natural proportion discussed earlier.

The third scenario, implemented in an Albuquerque, New Mexico, middle school, employs three different options to support students with disabilities in inclusive classrooms. In the first support option, teachers who are dually certified as general and special educators are assigned to be the sole instructor of record for heterogeneous classrooms that include several students with disabilities and that has an overall smaller class size (e.g., 19 vs. 26). These teachers assumed all special education paperwork and case management responsibilities for their students eligible for special education as well as the instructional responsibilities for all of the students in their classes. These teachers have two daily planning periods, one for typical general education teacher responsibilities and the other for executing special education responsibilities such as conducting special education assessments and IEP meetings, meeting with and supervising paraprofessionals, and completing special education paperwork. In the second support option, students with disabilities are supported in co-taught classrooms in which a general educator is paired with and supported by a special education professional or paraprofessional. In the third support option, only students with mild disabilities are placed with a general education teacher, who receives at least weekly scheduled collaborative consultation planning and brainstorming meetings with one of the school's special education faculty with the title and role of Inclusion Facilitator. At these collaborative consultation meetings, the classroom teacher and Inclusion Facilitator discuss the progress of and plan differentiation strategies for students with disabilities as well as support strategies for all of the students assigned to the general educators' classrooms.

Scheduling Everyone for Co-Teaching Over Time

Many schools have made a conscious decision to rotate, over time, co-teaching responsibilities across all personnel. For example, given the six sections of a particular core content area used in the scheduling scenarios just described, the two content area classroom teachers assigned to co-teaching would rotate every 2 years, resulting in all classroom teachers having 2 years of co-teaching responsibilities and experience over a 6-year period.

Department, Grade-Level, or Content-Emphasis Scheduling

Some schools have chosen to assign special educators to departments; some have chosen to assign them to grade levels. Some schools assign special educators to co-teach in the two primary areas of special education eligibility (language arts and math) because these are the subjects in which students generally need support and are two of the typical high-stakes assessment areas. In these schools, if co-teaching is needed in science or social studies, a paraprofessional is assigned (and supervised) as the co-teacher.

Scheduling General Educators to Co-Teach

Across the nation, many other creative and novel co-teaching structures have been successfully implemented. In one Pennsylvania middle school, the special educators co-teach in science and social studies and provide consultation in math and language arts. It was decided that the best way to support the students in this school who were eligible for special education in math and language arts was to have two general education "content experts" co-teach. Math and language arts teachers teach alone for three of their four 1.5-hour extended block periods. Teachers have staggered preparation periods, during which the first half is used for planning and the second half is dedicated to co-teaching with another same-content teacher, helping students apply information taught in the first half of the period. This co-teaching support is reciprocated during one of each teacher's three instructional periods. The teachers enjoy this unique collaborative arrangement, and the students are succeeding. It should be noted that the school administration implemented the general educator co-teaching structure only after they had co-taught at least 2 years with special education "access experts" and had participated in professional development on co-teaching, differentiated instruction, and inclusive education.

Forming Outside Partnerships to Access Resources to Support Co-Teaching

Developing partnerships with personnel in state departments of education, faculty of institutions of higher education, and staff in other school districts with a similar interest in co-teaching is another way to gain much-needed human, political, and fiscal resources. State department of education personnel may provide fiscal incentives or regulatory relief for innovations. They may provide valuable public relations support, articulating in circulars, publications, and public presentations the need for co-teaching. Higher education–school district collaboration offers mutual benefits to both organizations. Together, the two organizations can design and solicit state or federal support for model demonstrations; arrange for valuable internship experiences for students in teacher-preparation programs; conduct research to document the challenges, solutions, and impacts of co-teaching practices; or deliver coursework to help develop the new roles or skills necessary for co-teaching. Finally, schools with a common vision of co-teaching should join forces to share or exchange resources, including personnel (e.g., reciprocal inservice presenters, joint hiring of a specialist in augmentative communication); resolve barriers to change; form coalitions to advocate change in outdated teacher-preparation programs and state-level funding policies; and celebrate successes together.

■ GETTING STARTED: PLANNING AND TAKING ACTION

If co-teaching is to become an integral part of the school culture, the administrative leaders must have an action plan for building consensus for the vision, helping staff members acquire competence, providing meaningful incentives, and allocating the necessary resources. Action planning means attending to all of these variables and being thoughtful and communicative about the process of change—how, with whom, and in what sequence the steps or stages of change are formulated, communicated, and set into motion. Action plans for co-teaching require the right mix of planning versus action and the continual involvement of the many people affected by the change. Resource K is an Action Plan Template that administrators can use to ensure that all planned activities are delineated and articulated to those who are involved in creating and executing the plan. A sample 1-year plan for establishing co-teaching in a school district is presented in Table 10.3 to show how each activity is delineated, timelines are set, success is measured, and actual outcomes of the activity are noted. We highly recommend that leaders who initiate any change, including co-teaching, use this or a similar planning format to inform and hold accountable those engaged in the change process.

Benefits of Involvement and Communication in Planning

Engaging people in action planning for co-teaching is important for at least two reasons. First, participatory planning promotes individuals' personal ownership of the coming changes. Second, it helps prepare people for change by getting them to believe that change really will occur. Planning is the alarm signaling to everyone that things will no longer be the same. For planning to accomplish this, administrators need to be up front and effective communicators who can articulate the desired future and get people to see clearly how it can be achieved and what part each person will play.

An integral part of action planning is regular and continuous evaluation. What is worthy of evaluation? Clearly, in the case of co-teaching, we want to know whether students and staff benefit from this organizational and instructional arrangement. We also want to know about affective and process variables such as educators' feelings at various points during the change process. Both outcome and affective process evaluations provide change agents the information needed to adjust the action plan or undertake new actions to deal with concerns, failures, and successes.

Working With the Unwilling

Obviously, the best-case scenario is that school personnel choose to co-teach rather than do it simply because they're required to. Likewise, co-teaching may initially work best if the partners not only choose to co-teach but also are able to choose the colleague(s) with whom they will co-teach. However, this is not always possible. Sometimes administrators have to assign staff to co-teach. Collaboration in planning and teaching cannot be viewed as a voluntary activity. For educators to think that they have a choice as to whether to collaborate is similar to a team of health care professionals perceiving that they have a choice as to whether to collaborate in performing an operation, following the patient's progress, and providing follow-up care. Students and families have a right to expect educators to collaborate in planning and teaching, and educators have a professional, legal, and ethical responsibility to do so.

Administrators need to understand that a teacher's initial reluctance to co-teach is not necessarily a permanent barrier to implementing co-teaching or any other innovation. McLaughlin (1991) found that teachers' commitment to an innovation comes only after they have acquired initial competence in the new skills necessary to implement the innovation. The key is for administrators to support school personnel in implementing co-teaching so that they acquire the skills and feel successful. Administrators can take actions to expand the number of personnel willing and able to co-teach. Table 10.1, shown earlier in this chapter, describes the levels of support to students—from classroom peer support and specialist consultation to full-time staff support—that an administrator can facilitate. Table 10.2 suggests other administrative actions, such as creating a master schedule that includes time for co-teachers to meet.

Another strategy for assisting personnel in overcoming their initial reluctance is to highlight how co-teaching can help teachers meet their own basic psychological needs (see Chapter 12). Administrators also report being able to overcome resistance from some staff members by clarifying teaching personnel's legal responsibilities for educating students with disabilities in the least restrictive environment by providing any necessary supplemental supports, aids, and services (e.g., co-teaching) identified by the IEP team within general education classrooms.

Schools initiating co-teaching often start small, with teachers who volunteer to try co-teaching as a pilot project. As explained in Figure 7.2 in Chapter 7, co-teachers may need various levels of support to co-teach successfully, depending on their competence and willingness to co-teach. Administrators need to assess the support needs of beginning co-teachers and provide that support, whether it is training, incentives (e.g., common meeting time), coaching and mentoring, or opportunities for reflective analysis for improvement. Pilot projects can then be extended to other

Table 10.2 Administrator Actions to Promote Co-Teaching

✓ Publicly articulate the rationale for co-teaching.

✓ Redefine staff roles (i.e., in the job description of classroom teachers and support personnel) so that all are expected to participate in collaborative planning and teaching.

✓ Assess the staff's need for collaboration (e.g., With whom do I need to collaborate to adapt instruction successfully? From which colleagues can I acquire skills through modeling and coaching?).

✓ Create a master schedule that allows for collaboration (e.g., common planning and lunch periods).

✓ Change length of the workday or school year (e.g., provide teachers with 220-day instead of 185-day contracts; early dismissal of students).

✓ Establish professional support groups to help staff learn about and begin to practice co-teaching.

✓ Provide time for co-teachers to meet by relieving them from noninstructional duties that other staff members who are not co-teaching are required to perform (e.g., bus duty, lunchroom supervision).

✓ Provide training in collaborative planning and creative problem solving via courses and workshops, mentoring and peer coaching systems, job shadowing, clinical supervision, and/or the pairing of new co-teaching teams with veteran co-teaching teams.

✓ Educate school and community members about the accomplishments of collaborative planning and teaching teams.

✓ Periodically provide additional time for co-teaching teams to meet (e.g., hire substitutes, use inservice time, provide release time).

✓ Provide incentives for co-teaching (e.g., recognize co-teaching teams' accomplishments, offer additional training, provide release time for co-teaching teams to observe one another teaching, attend conferences, and make presentations about their accomplishments).

✓ Inspect staff's use of provided planning time to assure it is used constructively to collaboratively plan for meeting the needs of students.

teachers and classrooms as the word gets out about the successes and benefits for students and teachers.

Put It in Writing

People do best if their decisions are put into some systematic written format (action plan) that specifies in some detail who will do what, by when, and to meet what criterion. Therefore, we encourage administrators to work with general education teachers, categorical support personnel, paraprofessionals, and others to develop a written plan that addresses actions that will be taken to (1) build support for the vision of co-teaching; (2) develop educators' skills and confidence to be co-teachers; (3) create meaningful incentives for co-teachers; and (4) reorganize, schedule, and expand human and other resources for co-teaching. Table 10.3 shows a completed action plan for a local school district that has dedicated itself to establishing co-teaching as a district-wide practice to promote differentiated instruction for the success of all students. The action-planning template that school personnel can use to plan and then fully embark on a co-teaching journey is presented in as Resource K.

SUMMARY ■

Reengineering educational practices can be a complex and seemingly overwhelming proposition. Yet an increasing number of communities are making the choice to implement co-teaching approaches with integrity and quality. The good news is that we now know some things about how to facilitate change so that co-teaching becomes part of the daily schooling routine. We know, for example, that schools have cultures and that to actualize a new vision of schooling and schooling practices, a new culture must come to replace the old one. We know that change inevitably creates cognitive and interpersonal conflict that can be managed through perspective taking, effective communication, collaboration, conflict resolution, creative problem solving, and the acquisition of shared understandings through professional development and conversation. We know that for fundamental change to occur, the roles, rules, relationships, and responsibilities for everyone (students included) will be redefined; hierarchical power relationships have to be altered so that everyone affected by the impending change has a voice and a role in decision making. We know that change is not necessarily progress; only close attention to valued outcomes will tell us if change equals progress. We know that action planning is important and that resources, incentives, and skill building make a difference. We know that commitment to a change often does not occur until people have developed skills and gained experience with the change. Finally, we know that effective school organizations can be crafted, and they are crafted by individuals—individuals who choose to ensure the success of all students by being courageous and engaged in a school community during the change process.

Table 10.3 Sample One-Year Action Plan

	Activities	Success Measure	Responsible Person(s)	Date	Outcomes
	• Major Activities • Chronological Order • Preparation Steps • Implementation Steps	"We will know we are successful if . . ." • What is measured? • Who will measure? • When to measure?			
Building Consensus for a Vision of Co-Teaching	At the beginning of the new school year, tell teachers that the district will implement a co-teaching approach at each site in 1 year's time. Explain that this year the approach will be piloted with volunteers at each site during the second semester.	Message communicated at August inservice	Dr. Nash (superintendent)	August 23 3-hour inservice provided	Message communicated verbally and in writing at August 23 meeting
Skill Development	Provide district-wide inservice on rationales for and approaches to co-teaching for all administrative, general special education, related services, and other support program personnel and paraprofessionals.	Presenter hired	Ms. Dome (Director of Instructional Services and Staff Development)	Hire speaker by July 1	Speaker hired July 15
		Books purchased	Ms. Dome	October 5	3-hour inservice provided
	Purchase co-teaching books for pilot team.	Training occurs	Ms. Dome	July 1	Books purchased June 15 and arrived on June 30
	Set up book study groups in each building.	Book study groups established at each site	Building principals	September 15	Groups established in five of seven sites by target date and in other two by September 30

	Activities	Success Measure	Responsible Person(s)	Date	Outcomes
Incentives	Arrange for visitation to neighboring schools to see examples of co-teaching	Visits occur	Building principals and Ms. Dome	September, October, November	Each site sent teams to observe veteran co-teaching teams in other schools. Fifteen visitations to area schools occurred over 3 months.
	Arrange for substitute coverage once a month to allow piloting co-teachers to plan during the school day.	Substitutes hired, and teachers meet	Building principals and pilot co-teaching teams at each building site	Monthly October through June	Substitute coverage provided monthly for all teams except in December, when subs were not available for three teams; these teams were given substitute coverage for an additional planning meeting in January or February.
	Co-teachers re-create co-taught lessons for faculty colleagues to participate in as if they were students in these classes.	Co-teachers teach lessons to colleagues	Ms. Dome, building principals, and pilot co-teaching teams	March 15	Occurred at all school sites on March 15
Resources	Identify pilot co-teachers for first year of implementation.	A minimum of five co-teaching teams recruited at each building site	Building principals	September 15	Five teams recruited at all but one site, where four were recruited
	Develop a master schedule that allows for common planning and teaching time for the pilot co-teaching partnerships.	Master schedule completed	Building principals and guidance counselors	December 10	Target met
	Identify new co-teachers for second year of implementation.	A minimum of five additional co-teaching teams recruited at each building site	Building principals	March 20	Target achieved at all building sites

FREQUENTLY ASKED QUESTIONS

The following questions are ones that administrators and teachers often ask when co-teaching is being considered as an initiative or when they have not experienced administrative support.

1. My teachers complain about all the initiatives we "throw" at them. We are asking them to employ research-based strategies, differentiate instruction, and include students with disabilities in general education classes and curriculum. I am concerned that my teachers will be overwhelmed if I also ask them to co-teach. Isn't there a limit to the number of new things to which I can ask my teachers to commit?

Without a doubt, numerous initiatives are being introduced in schools today. We acknowledge that many of our teacher and administrator colleagues feel overwhelmed. We know teachers do not burn out from too much work; they burn out from a lack of support. Providing the training and other logistical support described in this chapter can help teachers feel less overwhelmed and more supported as they broaden their repertoires to include new skills and strategies.

Our work with successful educational leaders has taught us that teachers can be motivated to take on a new initiative such as co-teaching if they are given the information to show how the initiative connects to the overall mission of the school and how the initiative is connected to what they already are doing. It is interesting to note that co-teaching has been shown to be an important vehicle for teachers to deliver the very initiatives you mentioned (i.e., research-based strategies, differentiated instruction, inclusive education). Once teachers have this information, they will be able to see how co-teaching links with, supports, and makes more efficient the implementation of other best-practice initiatives. This can motivate teachers to take on co-teaching as part of their collaborative teaching repertoire.

2. I don't have administrative support where I work. We have received no training on how to co-teach and we don't have common planning time. Very few of the classroom teachers are interested in co-teaching. I am a special educator and believe co-teaching is a valuable practice that will allow my students to succeed in general education classrooms. But I am only one person working in a bureaucracy. What can one person do?

While we firmly believe that it is an administrative responsibility to provide time for co-teachers to meet and plan and to arrange for professional development to support co-teaching teams in acquiring new skills and becoming proficient in their use, we recognize that not all teachers are fortunate enough to work in a school system that provides these types of administrative support.

We know teachers like you who have designed and employed a variety of strategies to promote co-teaching in their school. Perhaps some of the actions they have taken could work for you:

- Share this chapter with an administrator. Ask him or her to read it so that you can sit down together to discuss how the strategies outlined in the chapter might be adjusted to fit your school situation.
- Locate training on co-teaching in your area. Find someone—a teaching colleague and/or an administrator—to go with you.
- With an administrator and/or a general education colleague, visit co-taught classes in another school.
- Start a book study of this co-teaching book with colleagues who agree to read about and try using the four co-teaching approaches described in it.
- Talk with someone from your central office (e.g., special education director, curriculum coordinator), and advocate that your school purchase the media kit (Villa, Thousand, and Nevin 2008) to accompany this book and use the suggestions in the kit's facilitator's guide to design training in co-teaching for yourself and others.

- Begin small, wherever and whenever you can. Find a general education colleague who is willing to experiment in co-teaching with you. Remember that whatever small steps you take, you are making a positive difference for yourself, a colleague, and students you teach. Over time, others will notice the success of your co-teaching and perhaps be motivated to try it as well.

3. Does every child eligible for special education need to be placed in a co-taught classroom?

No, every child eligible for special education does not need to be placed in a co-taught classroom. The Individualized Education Program (IEP) team for every child is ultimately responsible for determining whether the child will be placed in a co-taught classroom. It would be nice if every student could be placed in co-taught classrooms, but few schools have the resources available to provide co-teaching in all classrooms. If there are limited resources (e.g., personnel to co-teach), then individuals charged with scheduling (e.g., administrators, guidance counselors, special educators) need to be strategic in determining which students are scheduled in co-taught classrooms. They need to capitalize on the wide range of available personnel who can co-teach with general education classroom teachers (e.g., Title I personnel, related service providers, paraprofessionals, English language learning specialists, special educators, literacy coaches, teacher librarians, gifted and talented educators, and students themselves. See Tables 10.1 and 10.2 in this chapter, Chapter 8 for details about the role of paraprofessionals as co-teachers, and Chapter 9 for the role of students as co-teachers.

4. Will co-teaching eliminate pullout?

Co-teaching should greatly reduce the number of minutes a child with special needs is out of the classroom for specially designed instruction (known as the pullout model). In planning for reducing time away from the general education curriculum and instruction, we ask IEP team members to discuss how to differentiate their instruction in the co-taught classroom by using the methods and strategies that may be transferable from the specialized setting. We remember that special education is a service, not a place. Bringing supports and services such as co-teaching to students within the general education classroom is a practice that helps school personnel meet two legal requirements of IDEIA—educating students with disabilities in the least restrictive environment and providing students with disabilities maximum access to their nondisabled peers.

Nevertheless, many students may require additional support for learning outside of the general education classroom. Some schools use their RTI system to provide additional supplemental and/or intensive support to students who benefit from this level of intervention. Other schools implement Tier II (supplemental) and Tier III (intensive) level supports to students within the classroom by utilizing parallel co-teaching approaches (see Chapter 6 for details).

Co-Teaching in Teacher-Preparation Clinical Practice

11

Jacqueline Thousand with Elizabeth Garza, Patricia Stall, and Jodi Robledo

Topics Included in This Chapter:

❖ Why is co-teaching in clinical practice needed?

❖ What is co-teaching in clinical practice and how is it different from traditional clinical practice?

❖ How can teacher candidates and cooperating teachers be prepared for co-teaching clinical practice?

❖ What are changes in the roles of teacher candidates, cooperating teachers, and clinical supervisors when using co-teaching in clinical practice?

❖ What are the research outcomes of co-teaching in clinical practice?

❖ What do cooperating teachers, candidates, and supervisors say about co-teaching in clinical practice?

It has been emphasized throughout this book that all educators who are employed to work with students in today's schools are expected to teach with one another and collaboratively plan and problem solve with colleagues to differentiate instruction for their increasingly diverse student populations (Villa and Thousand 2011). In what ways might we prepare our new teacher candidates to have both the disposition and the background knowledge and skill to engage in quality co-teaching partnerships? Why is a new approach to clinical practice needed?

WHY CO-TEACHING IN CLINICAL PRACTICE? ■

Many teachers are reluctant to mentor a student teacher because of this era of high-stakes testing, especially given the requirement to leave the classroom during the student teacher's solo teaching time (Ellis and Bogle 2008).

In addition, many teachers are now participating in schools that have adopted a response-to-intervention approach (see Chapter 2) in which the core instructional program is enhanced to accelerate student learning. They are required to differentiate instruction to meet diverse needs of learners.

Co-teaching has been shown to be an effective strategy for increasing student achievement (see Chapter 2) by partnering teachers with different expertise (e.g., special educator and general educator). Bacharach, Washut Heck, and Dahlberg (2010) of St. Cloud University in Minnesota showed that co-teaching during clinical practice helped close the achievement gap for English language learners, students with disabilities, and the general student population overall. Nevertheless, as Bacharach and colleagues point out, teacher-preparation programs continue to structure the clinical practice experience *after* completing all coursework and featuring 1 to 2 weeks of *solo teaching*. This practice has been recognized as an undesirable and unsuccessful induction approach (Darling-Hammond and Bransford 2005) and has prompted a national push to enhance school and teacher-preparation-program collaborative partnerships for teacher induction that are "fully grounded in clinical practice" (National Council for Accreditation of Teacher Education 2010, p. 2). Given this reform initiative in combination with the documented academic and other benefits of the St. Cloud University co-teaching model of clinical practice on student performance, schools and colleges of education across the nation are piloting transformations of their clinical practice paradigms through the application of co-teaching practice and principles (e.g., McGrath 2012).

■ WHAT IS CO-TEACHING IN CLINICAL PRACTICE? HOW IS IT DIFFERENT FROM TRADITIONAL CLINICAL PRACTICE?

Clinical practice or student teaching is an expected and essential dimension of any teacher-preparation program, with the overarching objective of providing teacher candidates with the modeling and guided practice to demonstrate their abilities to translate educational theory into actual practice with real students in real classroom settings. A co-teaching clinical practice approach departs from the traditional approach in which after some period of observation, the candidates take over all classroom duties with little guidance or intervention from the cooperating teacher. Bacharach and colleagues (2010) aptly characterize this *solo teaching* experience in which the cooperating teacher steps aside as a "'sink or swim' approach [in which] a teacher candidate either survived or failed on his or her own" (p. 4).

As a reader of this text, you already know that co-teaching involves two or more people sharing responsibility for all of the students assigned to them for instruction. In the case of clinical practice or student teaching, the co-teachers are the teacher candidate and the cooperating teacher. As co-teachers, they have an ongoing and evolving relationship throughout the duration of the clinical partnership, which might be several weeks, a semester, or an entire year. In co-teaching clinical practice, the cooperating teacher gradually releases classroom responsibilities to the teacher candidate. As partners, they engage in ongoing planning for and practice of co-teaching variations in which both collaboratively teach and assess all students throughout the clinical experience.

The co-teaching clinical practice approach described in this chapter relies on the four co-teaching approaches (i.e., supportive, parallel, complementary, and team) and the collaboration and planning structures and tools described in previous chapters of this book. This co-teaching clinical approach and tools have been piloted by a large clinical practice team of faculty, teacher candidates, and local teachers affiliated with the School of Education in the College of Education, Health, and Human Services at California State University San Marcos (CSUSM). They are under ongoing revision and refinement. We offer them as suggested processes and tools for your own efforts to induct new educators into the field and welcome hearing from you about your own innovations or variations on the use of these processes and instruments. Teacher induction through co-teaching is in its infancy, so borrow and modify liberally as we jointly make our baby steps forward!

PREPARATION AND INTRODUCTION OF THE CO-TEACHING CLINICAL PRACTICE PLAYERS

To what extent are teacher candidates, cooperating teachers, university supervisors, teacher-preparation program faculty, school site administrators, school district induction program coordinators, and/or students prepared to know what to expect in clinical practice? In many cases, there is little to no preparation for some or all of these stakeholders. In contrast, in a co-teaching clinical practice approach, it is essential that, at a minimum, the required and essential players in clinical teams—the candidate, the cooperating teacher, and the evaluating supervisor—receive a baseline of information and training. For the CSUSM pilot initiative, not only were these triads provided instruction and coaching, but the school site principals, program course instructors, on-site liaisons (i.e., site teachers who provide daily and weekly "touch-in" support to the credential candidates) are invited to and, in fact, have routinely attended professional development that provides direct instruction in, modeling of (via DVD demonstrations of co-teachers in action), and guided practice in at least the following topics that are described throughout this text:

1. The research base for co-teaching (see Chapter 2 for the history and research base for co-teaching)

2. The four approaches to co-teaching—supportive, complementary, parallel, and team (see Chapter 3 for the basic definitions of each approach)

3. What each of the approaches looks and sounds like in action (see Chapters 4–7)

4. Cautions for the use of each approach (see Chapters 4–7 for detailed descriptions of each co-teaching approach and cautions in using the approaches)

5. Issues all new co-teaching teams must address, including identification of planning time, establishing norms or ground rules for communication, and clarifying discipline and classroom management procedures (see Table 3.3 of Chapter 3 for Co-Teaching Issues for Discussion and Planning)

It is ideal if the candidate–cooperating teacher–supervisor triad receives training in the above content simultaneously as a team to facilitate conversations as a team. Topics should include "getting to know you" and logistical issues such as when to schedule regular planning meetings, when the university supervisors will observe planning and teaching, and how and when lessons will be debriefed. We acknowledge that this is not possible for many triads due to conflicting work schedules, training opportunity conflicts, or structure of the training program delivery. What we have learned is that as long as all parties can (a) acquire and share the common co-teaching concepts and language with which to speak about their co-teaching experiences, (b) get to know each other and decide on logistical issues, and (c) access support materials (e.g., the training materials, supervision forms, clinical community resource website), these key stakeholders have the basic essential information to converse about and describe their actions and relationships. For example, the authors recently overheard a teacher candidate effectively communicate about co-teaching with his cooperating teacher with whom he had not had simultaneous training: "So, when you take the lead in whole-class direct instruction, I could take the supportive co-teacher role and collect data on student engagement through a 'management by walking around' check-in with table groups to see that individual students are attending and taking notes."

■ COMMUNICATION AND PLANNING

Often in clinical practice arrangements that do not follow a co-teaching approach, little time or focus is directed toward relationship building or collaborative planning of instruction. In contrast, in co-teaching clinical practice, conversation and planning are deliberate, frequent, and initiated from the start of the relationship. Part of the initial training is expressly designed to prompt critical conversations about everything from time for planning to logistics such as how the teacher candidate will be introduced to and addressed by the students. Table 3.3 of Chapter 3 offers a comprehensive list of issues co-teachers discuss and resolve. One role of the university supervisor in co-teaching clinical practice is to support both the teacher candidate and the cooperating teacher through these conversations, especially when it is the first time that the cooperating teacher as well as the candidate have had to negotiate agreements about certain topics such as joint planning time (see Table 12.1 in Chapter 12 for suggested strategies for expanding time for planning) and the role of the cooperating teacher when the teacher candidate is in the lead in a *supportive* or *complementary* co-teaching lesson arrangement.

In the authors' view, whenever two or more people are in a classroom interacting with students, co-teaching is occurring, whether it is planned or not. To optimize the effectiveness of teacher–student interacting, teacher candidates and cooperating teachers plan in advance by deciding "if one of us is doing this" then "the other person could be doing this" (Murawski and Dieker 2004). This requires joint time for planning lessons and the flow of the day and strategies for efficiently using that time. To support this planning, we offer two tools. Table 11.1, lists concrete suggestions for how co-teachers can differentiate and coordinate their actions during a supportive, parallel, complementary, or team co-teaching lesson. This table provides space for co-teachers to brainstorm ways in which "If one of us is doing this . . . the other could be doing this . . ." This format allows co-teachers to discuss and agree upon how they will work out their division of labor during instruction and also practice labeling their co-teaching arrangement as supportive, parallel, complementary, or team co-teaching.

Table 11.1   Role Differentiation: If one is . . . then the other is . . .

Co-Teaching Approach	If one of us is . . .	The other could be . . .
Supportive	Providing direct instruction to whole class	Circulating, providing one-on-one support as needed
	Leading an activity	Circulating, checking for comprehension
	Providing large-group instruction	Circulating, using proximity control for behavior management
Parallel	Prepping half of the class for one side of a debate	Prepping the other half for the opposing side of the debate
	Reteaching or preteaching with a small group	Monitoring large group as they work on practice materials
	Facilitating stations or groups	Facilitating stations or groups
Complementary	Giving instructions orally	Writing down instructions on board
	Lecturing	Modeling note taking on the board/overhead
	Explaining new concept	Conducting role play or modeling concept
Team	Considering differentiation, modification, and enrichment needs	Considering differentiation, modification, and enrichment needs
	Guiding students through odd steps of a procedure	Guiding students through even steps of a procedure

Source: Adapted from Murawski, W., and L. Dieker. 2004. Tips and strategies for co-teaching at the secondary level. *Teaching Exceptional Children 36*(5): 53–58.

The second tool that clinical practice co-teachers have found useful is the Co-Teaching Differentiation Lesson Planning Matrix shown in Table 11.2 and as Resource Q and illustrated in Tables 11.3 and 11.4. Clinical supervisors of credential candidates in co-teaching clinical placements have noticed that co-teachers tend to plan their collaboration for a school day by first thinking about each time block of the day and the content and curriculum objectives that typically are addressed in that block, then discussing how they will coordinate their actions through co-teaching. The Co-Teaching Differentiation Lesson Planning Matrix planning tool acknowledges this planning process and offers a structure for guiding conversations about what the cooperating teacher and the teacher candidate will be doing in each time block, which co-teaching approach(es) their actions represent, and, perhaps most important, how the co-teaching arrangement(s) they select support the differentiated instructional needs of the students in the classroom. The matrix explicitly includes a discussion on differentiating instruction, with the column titled, "What are differentiated instructional needs of our students?" This question allows co-teachers to consider and discuss the needs of students as the basis for decisions about their co-teaching arrangements. Table 11.3 shows how a fourth grade co-teaching team used the matrix to organize its morning co-teaching blocks and structure supportive, parallel, and complementary co-teaching approaches to address student needs. Table 11.4 shows an example of how the cooperating teacher and teacher candidate in a first- and second-grade combination bilingual classroom used the matrix to structure their co-teaching with their bilingual and struggling first and second graders in mind.

■ GRADUAL AND SYSTEMATIC RELEASE OF RESPONSIBILITY IN CO-TEACHING CLINICAL PRACTICE

The goal of clinical practice is to support each teacher candidate in demonstrating competent, independent teaching performance that meets professional and state teaching performance expectations and standards. A unique feature of co-teaching clinical practice is the ongoing collaborative planning, teaching, and reflection that occur between the teacher candidate and the cooperating teacher, with coaching support from the clinical supervisor. This is in contrast to a non–co-teaching model in which the cooperating teachers often have only their own past clinical practice experience to guide them in determining their role as a coach or collaborator with the teacher candidate. And that past experience often is the *sink-or-swim* experience of *solo* teaching, with the cooperating teacher leaving classroom responsibilities fully to the teacher candidate to negotiate on his or her own.

Co-teaching clinical practice, then, provides a teacher candidate the opportunity to demonstrate increasing instructional competence and independence through a gradual release or shift of responsibility from the cooperating teacher to the teacher candidate. Within a co-teaching clinical practice approach, it is this shift of responsibility of *who takes the lead in the collaborative*

Table 11.2   Co-Teaching Differentiation Lesson Planning Matrix

When co-teachers plan for instruction for each block of instructional time, they also plan the co-teaching approaches they will use based on the differentiation needs of their students. This graphic organizer is a tool designed to *facilitate the planning conversation* for co-teaching. Writing in the graphic organizer is *optional.* The tool prompts co-teachers to:

1. identify what and how content is being taught in each instructional block

2. identify differentiation needs of students

3. identify the co-teaching approach(es) that best allow for instruction and differentiation

4. describe what the actions of each co-teacher will be when executing instruction and the co-teaching approach

For each time block, what/how are we teaching?	What are differentiated instructional needs of our students?	Which co-teaching approach(es) will we use?	COOPERATING TEACHER What will I do? (If one is doing this . . .)	TEACHER CANDIDATE What will I do? (The other is doing this . . .)
		Supportive Parallel Complementary Team		
		Supportive Parallel Complementary Team		
		Supportive Parallel Complementary Team		
		Supportive Parallel Complementary Team		
		Supportive Parallel Complementary Team		
		Supportive Parallel Complementary Team		

Table 11.3 Co-Teaching Differentiation Lesson Planning Matrix—Fourth-Grade Example

For each time block, what/how are we teaching?	What are differentiated instructional needs of our students?	Which co-teaching approach(es) will we use?	COOPERATING TEACHER What will I do? (If one is doing this . . .)	TEACHER CANDIDATE What will I do? (The other is doing this . . .)
Review math homework	Several students are easily distracted; several students need further clarification on math procedures and concepts.	*Supportive* Parallel Complementary Team	I am leading. I go over the answers for the math homework and clarify concepts and procedures as needed.	I am supporting. I make sure children are listening and "tutor" and redirect as needed to be sure questions are answered.
Math mini-lesson: multiplying fractions	Four students in the class need visual and concrete representations, (i.e., manipulatives) to construct their understanding.	Supportive Parallel *Complementary* Team	I am leading. I teach the mini-lesson on the concept and skills of multiplying fractions.	I am complementing. I provide illustrations and fraction models while my co-teacher is teaching the concept/skills.
Differentiated guided practice of fraction multiplication	Students have different levels of support needs, so homogeneous small-group work with manipulatives provides targeted support to students with needs.	Supportive *Parallel* Complementary Team	I work with a group of struggling students who need pizza pie manipulatives to practice multiplying fractions.	I work with and monitor the rest of the groupings of students who are ready to use drawings, paper, and pencil to multiply fractions.
Reading fluency using iPods	Students benefit from close monitoring in order to note any student struggling with the iPod recording process or with evaluation of their recording.	*Supportive* Parallel Complementary Team	I am leading. I facilitate students reading the section of text into their iPods and then evaluating their fluency based on our criteria.	I am supporting. I listen in as they read/record and support those struggling. I make sure they use each criterion when they are prompted to evaluate.

Table 11.4   Co-Teaching Differentiation Lesson Planning Matrix—First-/Second-Grade Combination Bilingual Classroom Example

For each time block, what/how are we teaching?	What are differentiated instructional needs of our students?	Which co-teaching approach(es) will we use?	COOPERATING TEACHER What will I do? (If one is doing this . . .)	TEACHER CANDIDATE What will I do? (The other is doing this . . .)
Daily language warm-up	First graders and identified students do not know how to fix mistakes and need extra support and more teacher–student interaction.	Supportive *Parallel* Complementary Team	I meet with a small group of students, reteaching how to "fix" mistakes, and provide additional support and prompting.	I monitor and tutor the majority of the students engaged in the daily language activity.
Fluency development	A group struggles in fluency and needs more teacher–student interaction.	Supportive *Parallel* Complementary Team	I monitor and tutor the majority of the students engaged in fluency activity.	I meet with struggling students to clarify meaning and prompt phrasing to support their fluency development.
Calendar and mathematics	Most of the students struggle with concept of number sequence, such as number before or after.	Supportive Parallel *Complementary* Team	I complement with visual/motion/examples of numbers coming before and after the day's date.	I lead the calendar activities.
Preparation for spring high-stakes assessments	Students are learning the English vocabulary for concepts learned in Spanish and need more teacher–student interaction and teacher support.	Supportive *Parallel* Complementary Team	Station #1: I teach concept 1 to small groups as they rotate to my station.	Station #2: I teach concept 2 to small groups as they rotate to my station.
RTI and EL differentiation block	Students are at different reading skill levels. Homogeneous groups for guided reading.	Supportive *Parallel* Complementary Team	I teach one guided reading-level group.	I teach one guided reading-level group using "En el bosque."
Writing	First graders struggle with writing complete sentences. Nine students need intensive support.	*Supportive* Parallel *Complementary* Team	I lead, teaching the writing lesson.	I *complement* with reminders of related strategies learned in Spanish, such as filling in sentence frames. I *support* individual students.

work (i.e., from cooperating teacher to teacher candidate) that best describes the trajectory toward competent independent teacher candidate performance.

The Table 11.5 Suggested Timeline for the Systematic Release of Responsibility in Co-Teaching Clinical Practice suggests a progression or shift in the roles of a teacher candidate and his or her cooperating teacher in (a) planning and reflection and (b) instruction from the beginning to the end of a co-teaching clinical practice experience. Note the complementary role of the cooperating teacher in the process of gradually releasing planning, teaching, and reflection leadership responsibilities to the teacher candidate. The *beginning* of clinical practice is characterized by the *cooperating teacher* taking a lead in the collaborative planning, teaching, and reflection processes across four phases—beginning, early, middle, and end—of clinical practice. The *end* of clinical practice is characterized by the *teacher candidate* taking the lead in each of the dimensions (i.e., planning, instruction, reflection) of the recursive instructional cycle. It is recommended that not only the teacher candidate, the cooperating teachers, and clinical supervisor become familiar with and discuss how they plan to execute the timeline suggested in Table 11.5, but all of those involved with the teacher candidate (e.g., the site administrators and formal or informal on-site clinical practice liaisons, grade-level or department chairs) become familiar with this suggested timeline so they too may prompt and support the teacher candidate's movement toward independently demonstrating competence in teaching performance.

A major debate, particularly among cooperating teachers and clinical supervisors, is whether, in a co-teaching clinical practice approach, teacher candidates should be held accountable for planning and delivering instruction alone. The argument for solo teaching goes like this: "Most teachers today still have to plan and teach by themselves, so we have to make sure that this candidate can do this without the cooperating teacher's 'wind beneath his/her wings' during planning or teaching." Clearly, all teacher candidates must have opportunities to demonstrate that they can individually plan for and instruct and manage a classroom of students. However, in co-teaching clinical practice, when a teacher candidate is expected to lead both the planning and the instruction with minimal input from the cooperating teacher, that candidate will have had a well-supported, well-modeled, and well-guided set of previous collaborative planning and teaching experiences to draw on. Further, during the time that the teacher candidate takes the full lead in planning and instruction, the cooperating teacher is free to remain in the classroom. The cooperating teacher might take on a role similar to that of a clinical supervisor. Using the *supportive* co-teaching approach, the cooperating teacher may observe and script the teacher candidate's performance for discussion in a follow-up meeting in which they reflect collaboratively on the lesson. The cooperating teacher can also engage in other supportive, parallel, or complementary roles under the direction of the teacher candidate.

■ CHANGES IN THE ROLE OF THE CLINICAL SUPERVISOR

In a co-teaching clinical practice paradigm, the clinical supervisor becomes much more of a coach than an evaluator of teacher candidate

Table 11.5 Suggested Timeline for the Systematic Release of Responsibility in Co-Teaching Clinical Practice

Timeline	Cooperating Teacher (CT) Actions	Teacher Candidate (TC) Actions
Beginning of Clinical Practice	**Planning and Reflection** CT leads planning and reflection conversations in all areas of instruction. **Instruction and Instructional Role(s)** CT takes the lead *Supportive:* CT in lead role *Parallel:* CT teaches own plans *Complementary:* CT leads *Team:* Likely not yet employed	**Planning and Reflection** TC actively participates in all planning and reflection conversations. **Instruction and Instructional Role(s)** TC follows lead of CT *Supportive:* TC in support role *Parallel:* TC teaches CT plans *Complementary:* TC complements, as directed *Team:* Likely not yet employed
Early in Clinical Practice	**Planning and Reflection** CT leads and prompts TC contributions to planning and reflection conversations. **Instruction and Instructional Role(s)** CT leads most of the time. *Supportive:* CT leads and supports *Parallel:* CT teaches own plans *Complementary:* CT usually leads *Team:* CT prompts TC role	**Planning and Reflection** TC begins leading at least one part of the planning conversations in one or more areas of instruction and contributes to reflection conversations. **Instruction and Instructional Role(s)** TC begins taking the lead periodically. *Supportive:* TC supports, may lead *Parallel:* TC sometimes designs and teaches own plans *Complementary:* TC complements with guidance, as needed *Team:* TC teaches with guidance
Middle of Clinical Practice	**Planning and Reflection** CT and TC share leadership of planning and reflection conversations. **Instruction and Instructional Role(s)** The CT equally shares taking the lead in the co-teaching approaches. *Supportive:* CT in lead and support roles *Parallel:* CT teaches own plans for groups *Complementary:* CT leads, complements *Team:* CT and TC jointly instruct	**Planning and Reflection** TC and CT share leadership of planning and reflection conversations. **Instruction and Instructional Role(s)** The TC equally shares taking the lead in the co-teaching approaches. *Supportive:* TC in lead and support roles *Parallel:* TC designs and teaches own plans for groups *Complementary:* TC leads, complements *Team:* CT and TC jointly instruct
End of Clinical Practice	**Planning and Reflection** CT participates in planning and reflection conversations. May lead some. **Instruction and Instructional Role(s)** The CT follows the TC's lead (or shares the lead, in team co-teaching). *Supportive:* CT supports *Parallel:* CT teaches own group(s) *Complementary:* CT complements *Team:* CT and TC jointly instruct	**Planning and Reflection** TC leads most or all planning and reflection conversations. **Instruction and Instructional Role(s)** The TC takes the lead (or shares the lead, in team co-teaching) in co-teaching roles. *Supportive:* TC in lead role *Parallel:* TC teaches own plans/ groups *Complementary:* TC leads *Team:* CT and TC jointly instruct

performance. Teacher candidates and cooperating teachers are more likely to move forward in their conversations about execution of the four co-teaching approaches if the teacher candidate is both prompted and held accountable through supervisory observations, regular face-to-face or online conversations about co-teaching experiences, and weekly tracking of the co-teaching approaches that are being used over time.

One essential teaching performance expectation is that of instructional planning, which, in the words of the California Commission on Teacher Credentialing (2008), encompasses "understand[ing] the purposes, strengths and limitations of a variety of instructional strategies" and the ability to "select or adapt instructional strategies, grouping strategies, and instructional material to meet student learning goals and needs" and "improve . . . successive uses of . . . strategies based upon experience and reflection" (p. A-14). If instructional planning and reflection on instruction to inform future planning are expected performances for earning a teaching credential, then both are worthy of observation and coaching. In co-teaching clinical practice, clinical supervisors observe not only the delivery of lessons—the execution phase of the instructional cycle—but also the planning and reflective debriefing conversations between the teacher candidate and the cooperating teacher (Murawski and Lochner 2011). As Table 11.5 highlights, the person taking the lead in these conversations is expected to shift over the course of a clinical practice experience, with the teacher candidate increasingly taking the initiative to lead instruction. One of the roles of the clinical supervisor, then, is to observe and offer comment on these planning and debriefing sessions. Table 11.6 offers a Co-Teaching Observation of Planning and Debriefing Reflection observation form that the clinical supervisor can use to provide feedback and coaching to the teacher candidate about their planning and reflective conversations. This tool is designed to assist the teacher candidate in setting goals for being proactive in the *planning* portion of the co-teaching partnership.

To further prompt and support teacher candidates to plan and reflect upon the co-teaching aspect of their clinical practice, clinical supervisors can request candidates to complete the Co-Teaching Clinical Practice Weekly Reflection form presented in Table 11.7. This form asks candidates to note their use of any of the four co-teaching approaches and indicate requests for an observation of their planning or delivery of a co-taught lesson. Clinical supervisors request that candidates complete this form at the end of the week and e-mail or otherwise deliver it to them. This weekly monitoring form allows a supervisor to both track a candidate's overall perceived progress in the clinical experience and hold the candidate accountable for transitioning to the lead role in planning and delivery of co-taught lessons. Teacher candidates might also be asked to complete the Co-Teaching Tracking Form initially presented in Chapter 3 in Table 3.2. Table 11.8 shows a completed form for a teacher candidate in the early weeks of clinical practice in a middle–level sixth-grade classroom.

To facilitate positive reflective conversations, clinical supervisors sometimes ask teacher candidates to use something like the "Report Card" Conversation Starter for Reflection and Debriefing shown in Table 11.9 in order to prompt teacher candidates to (a) provide their cooperating

Table 11.6   Co-Teaching Observation of Planning and Debriefing Reflection

Teacher Candidate _____ Date _____ Visit # _____

Phase of Clinical Practice: Beginning   Early   Middle   End   Solo   (Circle one)

Teacher Candidate: __ Participates   or   __ Leads conversations   (Check one)

Planning: Cooperating Teacher Actions	Planning: Teacher Candidate Actions
Reflection: Cooperating Teacher Actions	Reflection: Teacher Candidate Actions

Teacher Candidate Goals for Next Observation:

Table 11.7 Co-Teaching Clinical Practice Weekly Reflection

Return via e-mail by Tuesday of the next week.

Name: _____ Week: _____ Date: _____

1. When was an affirming or "aha" moment in my teaching this week? When did I feel most confident and competent with my skills?

2. What was my biggest challenge this week? When did I feel disconnected or discouraged?

3. If I could repeat this week, what would I do differently based on the learning and responses of my students?

4. What am I most proud of this week based on the learning and responses of my students?

5. Which co-teaching approaches did my Cooperating Teacher (CT) and I use this week?

____ **Supportive**	____ I led	____ CT led	
____ **Parallel**	____ I led planning	____ We jointly planned	____ My CT planned
____ **Complementary**	____ I led, my CT complemented	____ My CT led, I complemented	
____ **Team**	____ Guided by CT	____ We jointly planned & delivered instruction	

Questions I have; help I would like: _____

Requested focus of next observation. (Be sure to have a lesson plan available.)

_____ Co-teaching planning &/or implementation _____ Questioning strategies

_____ Classroom management/discipline _____ Differentiation of instruction

_____ Use of technology in instruction and/or in the hands of students

_____ Other _____

Table 11.8   Co-Teaching Tracking Form for a Teacher Candidate in Early Clinical Practice

Week of: November 1st

	Supportive	Parallel	Complementary	Team	Notes
Monday	Opening Class Meeting	Literacy intervention groups	Health lesson	Health lesson was team planned	
Tuesday	Opening Class Meeting; math block closure	Literacy intervention groups	Science lab		New science unit will be team planned & delivered
Wednesday	Opening Class Meeting; math block closure	Math intervention groups	Physical education demonstration of cooperative game	Physical education lesson was team planned	
Thursday	Opening Class Meeting; introduction of new social studies unit	Literacy intervention groups	Science lab		
Friday	Introduction of new social studies unit, Pt. 2	Literacy intervention groups	Opening Circle		Class Meeting will be led by Teacher Candidate next week
Notes and Plans for Next Week	The goal is that by the end of next week, I will lead both the planning and instruction for the Class Meeting and I will take over the lead in planning health and physical education lessons.				

Use this tool to monitor, plan, and document your co-teaching experiences.

Supportive—One co-teacher takes the lead instructional role, and the others rotate among the students providing support. The co-teacher(s) taking the supportive role watches or listens as students work together, stepping in to provide assistance when necessary, while the other co-teacher continues to direct the lesson. The roles of lead and supportive co-teacher can be alternated.

Parallel—Two or more people work with or monitor different groups of students at the same time in different sections of the classroom. Co-teachers may rotate among the groups; and, sometimes there may be one group of students that works without a co-teacher for at least part of the time.

Complementary—All co-teachers have a role teaching the whole group. One may introduce the new academic content while the other makes it more accessible through complementary instruction (e.g., modeling how to take notes, using different examples or analogies, paraphrasing, creating visuals).

Team—Co-teachers equitably share responsibility for that which one teacher otherwise would have performed alone, namely, planning, teaching, and assessing the instruction of all assigned students. Co-teachers are comfortable using and do use each co-teaching approach based on the needs of students and the demands of the lesson.

Table 11.9   The "Report Card" Conversation Starter for Reflection and Debriefing

Report
Card
♥♥♥♥♥♥
Love   **A+**
Kindness **A+**
Friendship **A+**

Report
Card
♥♥♥♥♥♥
Love   **A+**
Kindness **A+**
Friendship **A+**

Report Card

(A Conversation Starter for Reflecting and Debriefing)

Name of Co-Teacher(s):

"Some things I learned/noticed from planning with and observing you are . . ."

"Some questions I have are . . ."

"Some things we might consider for our next lesson(s) are . . ."

Initials: _____   _____   Date: _____

teachers with praise and positive feedback about what was learned from observing and co-teaching with the cooperating teacher and (b) question their cooperating teachers about the rationale for their observed instructional or classroom management decisions. The report card can create an opening for a teacher candidate to take the lead in suggesting ways in which to improve his or her own or the partnership's instruction in the future.

RESEACH PROMISE, ■
OUTCOMES, AND TESTIMONIALS

What Does the Research Say?

The research on clinical co-teaching models is limited to a handful of studies such as Bacharach and colleagues 2010; Larson and Goebel 2008; Nevin, Cohen, and Marshall 2007; and Swain, Nordness, and Leader-Janssen 2012. Research findings are summarized in terms of academic benefits and changes in perceptions of efficacy in use of instructional strategies.

Academic Benefits. Increased student achievement on standardized math and literacy achievement tests was reported for teacher candidates who were in a co-teaching clinical practice in contrast to student achievement with teacher candidates prepared in the traditional way (Bacharach et al. 2010). For example, in co-taught classrooms, 65% of students eligible for free and reduced lunch and 74% of students eligible for special education achieved proficiency in reading as compared to 53% in classrooms with no student teacher or ones without co-teaching being practiced in clinical practice. For English learners, nearly 45% achieved proficiency vs. 26%—31% in comparison to classrooms without co-teaching. An advantage they noted is that co-teaching in student teaching provides two professionally prepared teachers in the classroom for longer periods of time, leading to increased achievement gains. Students in co-taught classrooms also identified benefits including getting help and feedback more quickly and fewer disruptions due to routine tasks such as passing out papers or student behavior.

Changes in Perceptions of Efficacy in Use of Instructional Strategies Due to Direct Instruction on Strategies. Changes in classroom strategies were identified by Nevin and colleagues (2007) in a comprehensive study of 271 teacher candidates who were assigned to classrooms in a multiculturally diverse urban school system in which teachers were using co-teaching strategies to include students with disabilities. To prepare them for co-teaching, student teachers were required to participate in a 1-day hands-on seminar on inclusive instructional strategies such as peer tutoring, cooperative group learning, and quick cooperative structures such as *think-pair-share*. Evaluation results showed candidates highly rating the following two statements: "I can use different classroom routines to help meet diverse needs of my learners" and "I know how to use flexible grouping when I teach my lessons." Similar changes in teacher efficacy also were reported when teacher candidates completed a co-teaching clinical experience as part of a professional development school–university partnership (Larson and Goebel 2008).

What Do Candidates and Cooperating Teachers Say About Co-Teaching Clinical Practice?

During and after implementing a pilot program to assess the feasibility of a co-teaching clinical practice approach (Stall, Thousand, Garza, Robledo, and Rich 2012; Stall, Thousand, Garza, Robledo, and Rich 2013; Thousand 2012) collated and analyzed feedback on the experiences of cooperating teachers, teacher candidates, supervisors, school site administrators, and teacher education faculty. From their reflections, three strong themes emerged.

Theme 1: Shared Language About Co-Teaching

Teacher candidates, cooperating teachers, and clinical supervisors overwhelmingly indicated their appreciation of having a new, shared language and schema about collaborative planning and teaching and methods for high-quality co-teaching. Candidates, cooperating teachers, and supervisors had all participated in common professional development in which this language was introduced and they also had tools such as the Co-Teaching Differentiation Lesson Planning Matrix (shown in Tables 11.2, 11.3, and 11.4 and as Resource Q) to assist them in having conversations about their co-teaching role.

This shared language allows co-teachers to *talk* about their partnerships and plan for their roles and relationships in their lessons. As one teacher candidate noted, "One thing that co-teaching taught me is talking about what I am doing. Writing it down is one thing, but talking and getting another perspective was very helpful." Having a shared language allows co-teachers to jointly *think* and encode this thinking into a shared *understanding* of what they want to do with their students. This shared understanding not only allows the co-teachers to co-teach the lesson but also prepares them to be *flexible* to adjust their instruction "in the moment," based on observations of student performance.

Example. Consider the case of the clinical co-teaching partners who, in their planning, decided to use the complementary co-teaching approach to introduce a new math concept. As they delivered the lesson, they observed that several students did not seem to *get it*. Because they had a shared understanding of the purpose of the lesson (i.e., establishing all students' understanding of a new math procedure), it was natural for them to confer to make a quick, on-the-spot decision to shift from a complementary to a parallel co-teaching structure for a brief block of time. The split-class and supplementary co-teaching approach allowed one co-teacher (e.g., the cooperating teacher) to provide immediate supplemental instruction to the identified students while the other co-teacher (e.g., the teacher candidate) guided the remaining students through practice applications of the newly introduced procedure.

Theme 2: Efficacy in Overall Instruction and Differentiating Instruction

Teacher candidates and cooperating teachers overwhelmingly expressed that the overall quality of instruction in co-teaching was superior to either of them teaching alone. They emphasized the importance of increased opportunities to differentiate instruction. This allowed the co-teachers to increase student access to and performance in the core curriculum in their mixed-ability classrooms that included large numbers of English learners and students eligible for special education or other learning support services (e.g., Title I reading and mathematics). The increased ability to differentiate is due, in part, to the increased number of instructors in the classroom. However, to an even greater extent, it is likely due to the exchange of ideas, knowledge, and skills that resulted from co-teachers' regularly and deliberately planning not only for their co-teaching roles but also for the differentiation needs of their students, prompted by such aids as the Teaching Differentiation Lesson Planning Matrix and the clinical supervisor's observations of planning using the Co-Teaching Observation of Planning and Debriefing Reflection (in Table 11.6). Stated another way, the perceived increased capacity to differentiate instruction likely was due to the co-teachers' *acting* on the identified differentiation needs through the co-teaching arrangements they decided to use throughout the day.

Examples. Participants described their increased efficacy in various ways. One co-teaching partnership described how they were able to provide language models for their English learners through their regular ongoing *think-alouds.* A cooperating teacher noted how it became natural to jump in to clarify or explain in different ways, proudly describing how her teacher candidate would "enter in and rephrase, giving a suggestion so that students really connected with the concept." Another cooperating teacher noted that "when there are two teachers, it keeps the students' attention longer. We could role-play adult conversations and step in when one teacher seemed stuck." Others described increased use of differentiated supports such as visual supports. Acknowledging the *time for planning* demand of co-teaching, another cooperating teacher commented on the positive synergistic outcome of having a partner with whom to reflect and brainstorm, stating, "We reflected and planned extensively based on what we were seeing, combining our ideas. It took a lot longer, but it was meaningful time."

In a clinical co-teaching partnership, the cooperating teacher is, in most cases, more of the content expert. However, in some instances, a teacher candidate has expertise that allows for enhanced instruction and learning.

Example. One elementary cooperating teacher, acknowledging that the teacher candidate, with her current training in differentiation, had more knowledge than herself about strategies for working with different levels of English learners, turned over the lead for differentiation of instruction for those students to the candidate. In a high school setting, one cooperating teacher described teaching a unit on marine biology. The teacher candidate had actually been a marine biologist and was more of the content expert. The teacher candidate naturally took the lead while the cooperating teacher took more of the supportive or complementary co-teaching roles. In both cases, the co-teaching allowed for the cooperating teachers to expand and deepen their own content knowledge while simultaneously benefiting their students by giving them access to the knowledge of a content expert.

Theme 3: Confidence and Competence Building Through Planful Gradual Release of Responsibility

Participants appreciated the planful way that responsibility for planning and teaching was gradually released from the cooperating teacher to the teacher candidate as a consequence of their ongoing planning conversations prompted by the suggested timeline for systematic release of responsibility offered in Table 11.5. This is in contrast to being thrown into solo teaching without the support of planned transitions in leadership roles in instruction and planning.

In conversations that reflect this theme, numerous teacher candidates expressed the anxiety of pressure associated with planning on their own in a non-co-teaching situation. In one case, the teacher candidate described being "paralyzed by fear" and almost dropping out of his preparation program. However, the situation may have been as much situational as related to non-co-teaching. Nevertheless, the *gradual-release* nature of a co-teaching approach to clinical practice seems to make for better planning and delivery of lessons.

Examples. This gradual-release phenomenon is illustrated by a teacher candidate in his comparison of co-teaching and non–co-teaching clinical experiences. "Last semester [in non–co-teaching], I would plan for the whole week. I had really long lesson plans. I thought in theory they were cool, but in execution it didn't work as well. You had to adjust. Co-teaching allows for us to discuss and see what we need to do before and even during the lesson." Another teacher candidate noted, "I was shown the ropes more with co-teaching. I don't like to get thrown into things. I had more confidence through the support of my cooperating teacher and the smooth transition to my own teaching." Yet another candidate described the co-teaching transfer of responsibility as "like having a safety net."

FREQUENTLY ASKED QUESTIONS

Aside from the question about solo teaching already addressed in the chapter text, the topic people ask about the most when they are considering the use of co-teaching in clinical practice has to do with time.

1. Won't potential cooperating teachers decline having a teacher candidate in the classroom once they realize how much more time it will take to plan and debrief instruction with a candidate in a co-teaching clinical practice approach?

We know that the one resource that teachers have the least of is time for planning and that planning for co-teaching with a teacher candidate requires even more of that precious commodity. In fact, the number-one identified challenge for any co-teaching team, whether grade-level co-teachers, general and special education co-teaching partners, teachers supported by paraprofessional co-teachers, classroom teachers co-teaching with high school students, or teacher candidates and cooperating teacher partners, is finding enough time to plan. As with any co-teaching team, candidates and their cooperating teachers have had to be creative and flexible in using the time allotted for planning and finding or expanding new time to plan. In addition to the suggested ideas for expanding time for planning ideas offered in Table 12.1 of Chapter 12, co-teachers in clinical practice have utilized shared interests, existing collaborative structures in the school day and week, and technology to get their planning (and reflection) accomplished. For example, many of the schools in which co-teaching clinical practice is occurring also have such teacher and student support structures as Professional Learning Community blocks each week, in which teachers talk about individual students, groups of students (English learners, students performing "below basic" performance levels in reading and/or mathematics). Many schools already have built into their school day Tier II intervention blocks, in which interventions are already structured and require less planning because the research-based instructional strategies are already planned and organized.

One of the first things that co-teaching clinical practice partners are asked to do in their initial training is to share with one another their personal strengths, interests, and something the other might find surprising. Sometimes in these conversations clinical practice partners discover shared interests that also accommodate time for planning.

Examples. One co-teaching partnership discovered that they both walked 45 minutes every morning prior to school and decided that they would walk together 2 or 3 days a week while they simultaneously talked about and planned their lessons. This idea to talk while walking came from their shared knowledge of the "Talk Walk" quick cooperative learning structure that suggests that the physical movement involved in the problem-solving conversation "increases free thinking, creativity, and expression" (Villa, Thousand, and Nevin 2010, 31). Another shared running as a passion and used their daily jogs for the same purpose. Others have carpooled and used that time for planning. Many use technology to supplement their face-to-face time by (a) sending daily e-mail messages with lesson plans, PowerPoint presentations, and adapted materials attached; (b) video conferencing via Skype (see www.skype.com) or FaceTime on their iPads or iPhones; or (c) creating and sharing their work online at sites such as Google Docs (see https://docs.google.com/).

2. It makes sense that, over time, credentialed teachers (e.g., same-grade, same-content, complementary-expertise teachers such as general and special educators) can evolve in their partnerships to truly being team co-teachers in planning and instruction. However, given the short time a teacher candidate and cooperating teacher have together, is it possible for a teacher candidate and a cooperating teacher to actually go beyond the supportive, parallel, and complementary co-teaching approaches and become team co-teachers?

(Continued)

(Continued)

This question, in part, is about having the time to develop a deep partnership, as is suggested in the answer to the question posed in Chapter 7: "How long will it take for co-teaching teams to evolve to the team co-teaching stage?" We acknowledge that it does take time to build trust, communication, and collaborative problem-solving relationships for a clinical partnership to be truly equal in the shared responsibility for planning and instruction. This question also is very much about recognizing the reality that, in most cases, there will be a content-knowledge and instructional-authority discrepancy between the seasoned and experienced cooperating teachers and the novice teacher candidates, particularly when they first come together. This same authority discrepancy usually does not exist between co-teachers who hold valid credentials and have an ongoing professional relationship as colleagues at a school site. By virtue of the fact that a teacher candidate has a *learner* rather than a *collegial* relationship with his or her cooperating teacher and clinical supervisor, it is difficult to imagine a teacher candidate developing the level of content and pedagogical expertise and authority to be on equal footing in planning and teaching with the credentialed cooperating teacher. That said, we have observed co-teaching clinical practice partners get to the place of being able to dance the tango of team co-teaching, anticipating one another's moves, sharing the instructional stage, and being flexible in adjusting their lessons and roles as co-teachers as they diagnose student progress in the moment. What helps to make this happen? The answer is, "Likely, a combination of factors!"

One factor involves setting the expectations and coaching the teacher candidate to be proactive, observant, and inquisitive. The clinical supervisor and cooperating teacher can prime these dispositions and behaviors in several ways. For example, if you look back at the Report Card conversation starters offered in Table 11.9, you will see that the sentence starters prompt teacher candidates to observe and note exemplary practices of their cooperating teachers and to be inquisitive by asking questions of their cooperating teachers about *what* the instruction practices they are observing represent in terms of effective pedagogy, *how* these practices are planned and structured, and *why* these practices are selected for use with the class or particular students. Ground rules can be established to clarify that it is the teacher candidate's responsibility to take action from day one to proactively study the curriculum and classroom management demands of the placement (e.g., take home and study the grade-level curriculum guides) and solicit suggestions for improving their own teaching. It is important for teacher candidates to remind themselves that becoming a competent and confident educator is not a destination but an ongoing journey that requires the dispositions and the practice of inquiry and wonder.

Another factor that likely contributes to co-teaching teams achieving the equitable collaborative team teaching instructional arrangement in a clinical practice situation has to do with *role release* or *role exchange,* the release of planning and instructional tasks and methods usually performed by the cooperating teacher to the teacher candidate. As recommended in Chapter 6, role release is more likely to occur smoothly and naturally when it is systematically planned (see Table 11.5 for a suggested timeline for systematic release of responsibility). This, of course, requires that the cooperating teacher has both the disposition and a strategic plan (as suggested in Table 11.5) to *let go* and gradually increase the teacher candidate's roles and responsibilities so as to become an equal and equitable team co-teacher in planning and instruction. As suggested earlier, cooperating teachers can be supported through this *letting-go* process if site administrators, clinical supervisors, and grade-level or department chairs communicate their understanding of and agreement with this letting-go process to achieve a team teaching partnership at least for certain lessons or portions of the day.

Does a clinical practice co-teaching team need to have had a team co-teaching experience by the end of a clinical practice experience? We would say that the answer to this question is "No." Can a clinical practice co-teaching team become genuine team co-teachers? Certainly! We have seen it happen time and time again, particularly when both partners have had previous experience with co-teaching (e.g., at least one previous co-teaching partnership) and when both perceive that they have permission and encouragement to take the risk and attempt to dance this tango.

Meshing Planning With Co-Teaching

12

Topics Included in This Chapter:

❖ Planning for starting out as co-teachers
❖ Finding and creating time for ongoing planning and reflection
❖ Effective and efficient use of planning time
❖ Lesson planning as co-teachers
❖ Planning for professional growth and future partnerships
❖ Frequently asked question

Failing to plan is a plan to fail.

People usually do not plan to fail; they simply sometimes fail to plan adequately, which results in a failed or less-than-effective effort. This holds as true with co-teaching partners as with co-workers in any other organization in which there is a desired collaborative outcome or product. In a co-teaching partnership, the desired outcome is the implementation of a co-taught differentiated lesson that results in student learning.

What, then, must be considered and addressed for co-teachers to plan to teach effectively, to mesh teaching and planning effectively? First, there is a set of planning considerations involved in getting a co-teaching relationship up and running. Second, there is the challenge of finding and creating time to meet and plan. Third, there are tools to ensure that the time spent planning is, in fact, effective and efficient. Fourth, co-teachers need a lesson plan format that they can understand, implement, and use to communicate their teaching actions to one another. A final area of planning concerns how co-teachers plan for their own professional growth and for continuation, expansion, or other future changes in their partnerships.

PLANNING FOR STARTING OUT AS CO-TEACHERS

Even if you have been in a co-teaching relationship before, as a co-teacher in a *new* co-teaching relationship, you begin all over again in getting started. If you have the opportunity to choose your co-teaching partners, you need to invite them into the co-teaching relationship. You need to be clear about your rationale and objectives for co-teaching so that you can communicate this information to your partner(s), your administrator(s), your students' parents, and the students themselves. It is also necessary so that you can motivate and assess yourself against the objectives you have set for your co-teaching efforts.

In terms of up-front planning, you need to determine with your co-teachers a specific time to sit down and address the role and responsibility issues identified in Chapter 3 (Tables 3.2 and 3.3). Specifically, you need to discuss and agree on how, where, when, and how often you will meet to plan. You will need to discuss the strengths each of you brings to the team as well as any fears or concerns that you have about co-teaching. You will need to decide on global issues regarding how you will get to know the learning characteristics of the students, what content you will teach, the instructional procedures you will and will not use, and the ways in which you will assess student learning. You will have to agree on which of the four types of co-teaching partnerships you will start using and when you will expand your repertoire to include all of the approaches. You will need to decide how discipline will be handled in the classroom and how communication with families, administrators, and others will occur. There are many logistical questions as well, from how student and teacher spaces will be arranged to how you will refer to each other in front of students to how decisions will be made when there is disagreement among co-teachers.

■ FINDING AND CREATING TIME FOR ONGOING PLANNING AND REFLECTION

As stated earlier in this book, although many incentives are unique to individuals, one incentive is common to and highly valued by everyone engaged in education: time—time for planning and shared reflection. "The time necessary to examine, reflect on, amend, and redesign programs is not auxiliary to teaching responsibilities—nor is it 'released time' from them. It is absolutely central to such responsibilities, and essential to making school succeed" (Raywid 1993, 34).

Time is a finite resource. Its use must be planned and allocated efficaciously because it is the basic dimension through which co-teachers' work can be constructed and evaluated. Time often defines the possibilities and limitations of co-teachers' ability to successfully perform and deliver in the classroom. Table 12.1 highlights ways in which some schools can and have attempted to meet the time challenges that all co-teachers will face throughout their partnerships. The Frequently Asked Questions at the end of the previous chapter, Chapter 11, also offer examples of ways in which teachers have used shared interests, existing collaborative structures in the school day or week (e.g., existing Professional Learning Community meetings), and technology (e.g., e-mail, Skype) to find time for planning.

■ EFFECTIVE AND EFFICIENT USE OF PLANNING TIME

In addition to the challenge of finding time to plan, co-teachers often are confronted with the challenge of using effectively what little time they

Table 12.1   Strategies for Expanding Time for Planning

Borrowed Time
1. Rearrange the school day so there is a 50- to 60-minute block of time before or after school for co-teachers to plan.
2. Lengthen the school day for students by 15 to 30 minutes on 4 days, allowing for early student dismissal on the fifth, thus gaining a long (i.e., 1- to 2-hour) time block for co-teachers to meet.
Common Time
3. Ask co-teachers to identify when during the day and week they prefer to plan and redesign the master schedule to accommodate this with a block for common preparation time.
Tiered Time
4. Layer preparation time with existing functions such as lunch and recess.
Rescheduled Time
5. Use staff development days for co-teachers to do more long-range planning.
6. Use faculty meeting time to problem solve common co-teaching issues of either immediate or long-range importance.
7. Build into the school schedule at least one co-teacher planning day per marking period or month.
8. Build in time for more intensive co-teacher planning sessions by lengthening the school year for teachers but not for students, or shortening the school year for students but not teachers.
Released Time
9. Go to year-round schooling with 3-week breaks every quarter; devote four or five of the 3-week intersession days to co-teacher planning as professional development days.
Freed-Up Time
10. Institute a community-service component to the curriculum; when students are in the community (e.g., Thursday afternoon), co-teachers meet to plan.
11. Schedule "specials" (e.g., art, music, physical education), clubs, and tutorials during the same time blocks (e.g., first and second period) so that co-teachers have at least that extra time block to plan.
12. Engage parents and community members in conducting half-day or full-day exploratory, craft, hobby (e.g., gourmet cooking, puppetry, photography), theater, or other experiential programs to free up time for co-teachers to plan.
13. Partner with colleges and universities; have their faculty teach in the school, provide demonstrations, or conduct university-campus experiences to free up time for co-teachers to plan.
Purchased Time
14. Hire permanent substitutes to free up co-teachers to plan during the day rather than before or after school.
15. Compensate co-teachers for spending vacation or holiday time planning with pay or compensatory time during noninstructional school-year days.
Found Time
16. Strategically use serendipitous times that occasionally occur (e.g., snow day, student assembly) to plan.
New Time
17. Discuss with the school administration ways to provide co-teachers with incentives that would encourage the use of their own time to plan.

actually create, expand, rearrange, or find. Often it is not how much time is finally set aside for planning but how that resource is used. The real issue is not just adding or manipulating time but changing the fundamental way that teachers do business when they do sit down face to face to plan.

Co-teaching planning meetings are more likely to be both effective and efficient when co-teachers consistently use a structured agenda to guide their conversations. Co-teachers have found the Co-Teaching Planning Meeting Agenda Format that is presented in Resource L to be useful in helping them get to all of their discussion topics in a timely and efficient way. This meeting format ensures that the five elements of the cooperative process that are present when co-teachers engage in co-teaching are also present when co-teachers meet to plan (Thousand and Villa 2000). Table 12.2 shows how the elementary co-teaching team featured in this book used the Co-Teaching Planning Meeting Agenda Format to plan the language arts lesson that used differentiated learning stations. You will find this lesson described in Chapter 5; the plan for this lesson is shown in Resource D.

An element of the cooperative process is face-to-face interaction. This element is prompted and recognized with the "public" recording of who is present, late, and absent from the meeting. Positive interdependence is also structured when leadership is distributed through rotating roles. Roles may be task related (e.g., timekeeper, recorder) or relationship oriented (e.g., encourager, observer). As Table 12.2 indicates, roles are assigned in advance of the next meeting. This ensures that each person has the materials needed to carry out his or her role (e.g., the timekeeper has a watch or timer, the recorder has chart paper and markers or a computer to record minutes). Assigning roles in advance also prompts co-teachers to rotate roles and thus create a sense of distributed responsibility and positive interdependence.

The Co-Teaching Planning Meeting Agenda increases co-teachers' accountability for task completion and use of interpersonal skills through the monitoring and group processing of task and relationship behaviors. This occurs both midway through and at the end of the meeting. By prompting the assignment of action items to individual team members and the setting of due dates in the Minutes of Outcomes section of the worksheet, the agenda further develops co-teachers' accountability for completing the actions to which they commit. Finally, the building of the next meeting's agenda ensures that co-teachers will come together again face to face to do more planning.

Co-teachers can also make planning meetings more efficient by "doing their homework" in advance. For example, in one high school in which the authors have provided training and coaching, on Wednesdays, subject matter co-teachers draft plans for the coming week and e-mail them to their co-teaching partners (e.g., the special educator, the English language support teacher), who review them and come up with suggested adaptations in materials, assessments, instruction processes, or goals for particular students or the entire class. On Fridays, co-teachers meet to finalize the next week's plans. This advance work allows the co-teachers to be both well informed and efficient in their limited face-to-face planning time.

Table 12.2   Elementary Team's Use of Co-Teaching Planning Meeting Agenda Format

People Present	Absentees	Others Who Need to Know
Ms. Gilpatrick, classroom teacher	None	No one
Ms. Nugent, speech and language therapist		
Ms. Hernandez, paraprofessional		
Roles	This meeting	Next meeting
Timekeeper	Ms. Nugent	Ms. Hernandez
Recorder	Ms. Gilpatrick	Ms. Nugent
Other		

Agenda	
Agenda Items	**Time Limit**
1. Review agenda and positive comments	5 minutes
2. Identify objectives and standards	3 minutes
3. Identify student learning preferences and needed supports	5 minutes
4. Brainstorm number and types of stations	7 minutes
5. Identify necessary materials	5 minutes
6. Discuss assessment of student progress	5 minutes
6. Complete Co-Teaching Lesson Plan	20 minutes
7. Processing of task and relationships	5 minutes

Minutes of Outcomes		
Action Items	**Persons Responsible**	**By When?**
1. The way we will communicate outcomes to absent members and others	N/A	
2. Division of labor	Refer to lesson plan	

Agenda Building for Next Meeting		
Date: Following day	Time: 7:45 am	Location: Ms. Gilpatrick's room

Expected agenda items
1. Review previous day's lessons
2. Brainstorm and make any necessary adjustments

■ LESSON PLANNING AS CO-TEACHERS

Figure 12.1 presents a suggested Co-Teaching Daily Lesson Plan Format that we have found to be effective in constructing co-taught lessons (Thousand, Liston, and Nevin 2006). This template is also included as a reproducible template in Resource B. The plan prompts co-teachers to think about the essential elements of any good lesson plan, such as the content objectives, the curriculum standard(s) addressed in the lesson, the materials needed by each partner, how student learning will be assessed, and any accommodations or modifications that might be needed for particular students. Note that co-teachers are prompted to go to Resource A: A Checklist of Sample Supplemental Supports, Aids, and Services. This helps spark ideas for individual supports that will be the least intrusive, only as special as necessary, and the most natural to the context of the classroom.

Because this is a lesson plan for two or more co-teachers, it prompts co-teachers to deliberately consider the following:

1. Which of the four types of co-teaching arrangements will the team be using?

2. How will the room be arranged so that each co-teacher has the needed space to deliver instruction? Will instruction be delivered by one or more co-teachers in another space outside of the classroom, such as a learning center or the school library, for all or part of the lesson?

3. Exactly what will each co-teacher be doing before, during, and after the lesson?

Collaboratively deciding how to answer these three questions ensures that all partners in the co-teaching venture are clear about their own and each other's instructional roles and responsibilities.

The final question in the lesson plan is the following: Where, when, and how do co-teachers debrief and evaluate the outcomes of the lesson? This question is designed to prompt co-teachers to engage fully and systematically in the recursive *plan-teach-reflect* cycle that promotes not only co-teachers' communication with one another but also the overall quality of their instruction.

To show how easy it is to use the Co-Teaching Daily Lesson Plan Format with the supportive, parallel, complementary, and team-teaching co-teaching approaches, we have translated one team scenario from each of Chapters 4 through 7 into a lesson plan and included them as Resources C through F. Resource C shows the high school supportive co-teaching example from Chapter 4. Resources D and F translate the elementary team scenarios from Chapters 5 and 7 to illustrate parallel and team-teaching co-teaching approaches. The middle-level team scenario from Chapter 6 is used in Resource E to show a complementary co-teaching lesson plan. Resource G features the lesson plan for the paraprofessional as a co-teacher featured in Chapter 8. Resource H illustrates students as co-teachers by translating the lesson for the third-grade mathematics reciprocal peer-tutoring scenario from Chapter 9.

Figure 12.1 Co-Teaching Daily Lesson Plan Format

Date: _____

Co-Teachers: _____
(Names)
_____

Content Area(s):

Lesson Objectives:

Language Objectives:

Content Standards Addressed:

Underline the Co-Teaching Approach(es) Used:

Supportive   Parallel   Complementary   Team Teaching

What is the *room arrangement?* Will other spaces outside of the classroom be used? (Draw a picture of the room arrangement.)

What *materials* do the co-teachers and/or students need?

How is student *learning assessed* by the co-teachers?

What specific supports, aids, or services do *select students* need? (See Resource A for suggestions.)

(Continued)

Figure 12.1 (Continued)

What does each co-teacher do before, during, and after the lesson?

Co-Teacher Name:			
What are the specific tasks that I do BEFORE the lesson?			
What are the specific tasks that I do DURING the lesson?			
What are the specific tasks that I do AFTER the lesson?			

Where, when, and how do co-teachers debrief and evaluate the outcomes of the lesson?

168

We recommend that, before looking at each lesson plan, you review the scenario on which it is based to familiarize yourself with the team members and the overall flow of the lesson. We found the lesson plan format easy to use to describe each co-teacher's responsibilities, clarify the expected student outcomes, note any needed adjustments for particular students, and ensure co-teacher communication.

PLANNING FOR PROFESSIONAL GROWTH AND FUTURE PARTNERSHIPS

Anyone who has been involved in teaching for any length of time has heard people talk about the importance of educators being reflective practitioners. Reflective practitioners strive to improve their teaching by gathering data on the effectiveness of their instruction through examining student performance and soliciting feedback on their instructional performance from other instructors and from students themselves. Reflective practitioners think about these data and feedback to make better instructional decisions in future lessons or to arrange for additional training, coaching, or mentoring. People who co-teach are in an ideal situation to spur their own professional growth through dialogue with their co-teachers. They can ask teammates to observe and provide direct feedback, and they can set joint professional goals and receive support and encouragement from their partners.

Co-teachers can also reach outside of their co-teaching team and ask others who have expertise in an area in which improvement is desired to observe, mentor, or more formally provide instruction in that area of expertise. Co-teachers can take workshops, seminars, or courses together to learn and practice jointly innovations that the team considers important to use with their students, including improving the quality with which they use each of the four co-teaching approaches described in this book.

It is important for co-teachers to know what the desired co-teaching behaviors are so that they are able to self-assess and reflect on the degree or quality with which they engaged in these behaviors. For this purpose, we have created a self-assessment in the form of a checklist consisting of 34 items, titled "Are We Really Co-Teachers? (see Resource M). This checklist can be reproduced and used in a number of ways to promote team members' professional development. Each co-teacher can rate the co-teaching partnership individually on the 34 items and then compare *Yes* and *No* assessments. Doing so provides team members with a starting point for discussion about the strengths of the partnership thus far and enables them to target areas for improvement. The team can also complete the assessment jointly. Rather than coming to consensus on an item, we suggest that the team use a different approach to self-rating. We suggest the rule that every member must definitively agree to the *Yes* rating. If any team member is unsure that a *Yes* rating is merited, then the score must remain *No.* This reduces the temptation to pressure a person with a differing perception to give in for the sake of consensus and, instead, encourages a real dialogue about differing perspectives, perceptions, and experiences of co-teaching team members. Others who are not on the team but who are

Table 12.3   Self-Assessment: Are We Really Co-Teachers?

Directions: Check Yes or No to each of the following statements to determine your co-teaching score at this point in time.

Yes	No	In our co-teaching partnership:
X		1. We decide which co-teaching approach we are going to use in a lesson based on the benefits to the students and the co-teachers.
X		2. We share ideas, information, and materials.
X		3. We identify the resources and talents of the co-teachers.
X		4. We teach different groups of students at the same time.
	X	5. We are aware of what one another is doing even when we are not directly in one another's presence.
X		6. We share responsibility for deciding what to teach.
X		7. We agree on the curriculum standards that will be addressed in a lesson.
X		8. We share responsibility for deciding how to teach.
X		9. We share responsibility for deciding who teaches what part of a lesson.
X		10. We are flexible and make changes as needed during a lesson.
X		11. We identify student strengths and needs.
X		12. We share responsibility for differentiating instruction.
	X	13. We include other people when their expertise or experience is needed.
X		14. We share responsibility for how student learning is assessed.
X		15. We can show that students are learning when we co-teach.

	Yes	No
16. We agree on discipline procedures and jointly carry them out.	X	
17. We give feedback to one another on what goes on in the classroom.	X	
18. We make improvements in our lessons based on what happens.	X	
19. We communicate freely our concerns.	X	
20. We have a process for resolving our disagreements and use it when faced with problems and conflicts.	X	
21. We celebrate the process of co-teaching and the outcomes and successes.	X	
22. We have fun with the students and each other when we co-teach.	X	
23. We have regularly scheduled times to meet and discuss our work.	X	
24. We use our meeting time productively.	X	
25. We can effectively co-teach even when we don't have time to plan.		X
26. We explain the benefits of co-teaching to the students and their families.	X	
27. We model collaboration and teamwork for our students.	X	
28. We are each viewed by our students as their teacher.	X	
29. We include students in the co-teaching role.		X
30. We depend on one another to follow through on tasks and responsibilities.	X	
31. We seek and enjoy additional training to make our co-teaching better.	X	
32. We are mentors to others who want to co-teach.		X
33. We can use a variety of co-teaching approaches (i.e., supportive, parallel, complementary, team teaching)	X	
34. We communicate our need for logistical support and resources to our administrators.	X	

TOTAL YES: 29 NO: 5

requested to respond or who have a responsibility to observe the co-teachers can use the checklist to provide constructive feedback, which can lead to professional reflection and team-member growth. The completed Are We Really Co-Teachers? self-assessment shown in Table 12.3 is an example of the results of a principal's observations of a mature co-teaching team, which has many strengths and just a few areas for targeted growth.

FREQUENTLY ASKED QUESTION

1. My co-teacher and I co-teach two class periods together. We have a common planning time, but we also have many other responsibilities and demands placed on our time. How important is common planning time to the success of our co-teaching team?

Educators today face many tasks and demands that compete for their time. In essence, they are asked to run and reinvent schools at the same time. Our experience has taught us that purposeful planning is essential to the development of a highly effective co-teaching team. While there are exceptions, co-teachers who regularly co-plan seem to be the ones who are able to broaden their repertoire to include all four of the co-teaching approaches. Those who do not set aside time to plan end up planning on the spot and, as a result, tend to primarily employ the supportive co-teaching approach. While a supportive co-teaching approach has benefits, it is not always the most effective use of professional expertise to support diverse students.

We suggest that you and your co-teaching partner discuss the various demands, including co-teaching, with which you are charged and prioritize them in order of importance. Also determine which of these responsibilities the two of you must absolutely address jointly and which you could do on your own. We also suggest that, at least initially, you and your co-teacher commit to meeting at least twice a week for at least 30 minutes to discuss students, design lessons, and divide up tasks to be completed before, during, and after the two classes that you co-teach. We encourage you to reflect on your co-teaching team's effectiveness when you do spend time planning as compared to when you do not. Were you more flexible and responsive to student needs and differences? Did you feel more comfortable and competent? Did you have more fun? Did you go beyond supportive co-teaching and use parallel, complementary, and/or team-teaching co-teaching approaches in your lessons?

From Surviving to Thriving

Tips for Getting Along With Your Co-Teachers

13

Topics Included in This Chapter:

- ❖ Advice from co-teachers
- ❖ Keeping communication alive
- ❖ Becoming culturally competent co-teachers
- ❖ Understanding the developmental nature of co-teaching relationships
- ❖ Managing conflict
- ❖ Tips for dealing with challenging and unproductive behavior
- ❖ Tips for avoiding potential problems

In this chapter, we discuss how you can thrive as a co-teacher. We begin by sharing some advice from co-teachers. Then we explain the communication skills and psychological supports that may help you move beyond survival mode, especially when experiencing the conflicts that co-teachers typically face. We emphasize that understanding the developmental nature of co-teaching relationships can help resolve conflicts. Finally, we offer practical tips for avoiding potential problems.

ADVICE FROM CO-TEACHERS ■

R. Whitehouse, a member of a first-grade teaching team, explained the following:

> Co-teaching can be viewed as the vehicle for teaching professionals the social skills of openness and honesty in communication, flexibility, compromise, and acceptance of difference. Because we stress the importance of feeling that we do not always need to be perfect, that we can make mistakes in front of one another, it's OK to fail now. I'm more likely to try new things. It's easier to try new things if you have someone to take the risk with—someone to laugh with.

A student co-teacher wrote,

> I learned to lose my shyness and let the story I was reading aloud to my partner come to life through me. I enjoyed making voices and facial

expressions, but most of all, I enjoyed the acceptance [of my partners]. . . .
I became a more patient person. . . . [My partners] taught me to be outgo-
ing and always try new things. Once I actually danced in the middle of
the group as we were playing a game. I would never have guessed I would
be brave enough to do that in front of people. Yet it was all because I was
a co-teacher.

A co-teacher member of a multicultural teaching team wrote,

I have really changed. I teach in a completely different way. I am no
longer so threatened by difference. When I admit I do not understand
a particular perspective, my [co-teachers] actually try to help me
understand.

A high school co-teacher of students learning English explained,

I have always considered myself a good teacher, but with the changes that
I have made in an effort to be more responsive, I am now becoming my
best.

Finally, a junior high school science co-teacher and her special education co-teacher wrote,

We also became comfortable talking about our interpersonal interactions
and our progress as co-teachers. Although at times these discussions were
difficult, they yielded tremendous results for us. We both are better teach-
ers as a result of these open and honest discussions.

■ KEEPING COMMUNICATION ALIVE

A common characteristic that shows up in these comments from co-teachers
is that they have discovered that the underlying keys to success are the
three Cs of co-teaching: communicate, communicate a different way, and
communicate again! This is similar to the idea contained in the adage, "If
at first you don't succeed, try, try again." The more flexible and versatile
your communication skills, the more likely you are to communicate
successfully with your co-teachers. There are three strategies in particular
that co-teachers can use to communicate more effectively: helping to meet
each other's psychological needs, adjusting to each other's learning styles,
and coaxing each other out of distress patterns.

First, use your communication skills creatively to help meet the basic
psychological needs of yourself and your fellow co-teachers. Recall that,
previously in Chapter 2, you learned of Glasser's (1999) belief that people
choose to do what they do because it satisfies one or more of the five basic
human needs: survival, power over or control of one's life, freedom and
choice, a sense of belonging, and fun. By communicating your respect and
appreciation for your co-teachers' personal commitment or work accomplishments, you help them meet their needs for survival and power. By
working in a co-teacher relationship and enjoying the give and take, you
and your co-teachers may experience a sense of belonging and freedom

from isolation by having others with whom to share the responsibility for accomplishing the challenging tasks of teaching in classrooms of diverse students. It can be fun to problem solve creatively and to engage in stimulating adult dialogue and social interactions, especially when your co-teachers acknowledge the humor and enthusiasm that each brings to the partnership.

Second, successful co-teachers know they are more effective communicators when they use words their partners understand, pay attention to their partners' preferred learning styles (e.g., visual, auditory, kinesthetic), and change the tone of voice and gestures they use when speaking. Co-teachers can strengthen their communications by using predicates (verbs, adverbs, and adjectives to describe a subject) that reflect their listeners' visual, auditory, or kinesthetic learning styles and preferences. As defined by the communication framework known as *neurolinguistic programming* (NLP), predicates are used to identify which representational system a person prefers to use in processing communication—visual, auditory, or kinesthetic. Co-teachers who use visual predicates such as "Do you see what I mean?" are more likely to connect with their partners who have a visual learning style. Co-teachers who use auditory predicates such as "Does that sound right to you?" are more likely to be heard by their partners who prefer an auditory learning style. Similarly, when co-teachers use kinesthetic predicates such as "Will you put me in touch with your ideas about what we're doing?" they are more likely to get action from their partners with a kinesthetic learning style.

A third strategy co-teachers can use to communicate more effectively is to practice the skill of the *process communication model* (PCM). PCM research suggests that communication mismatches abound in American schools (Bradley, Pauley, and Pauley 2006; Kahler 1982; Pauley, Bradley, and Pauley 2002; Pauley and Pauley 2009). Mismatches between co-teacher personality types can result in the failure to connect and collaborate effectively with one another. PCM identifies six personality types (i.e., reactor/feeler, workaholic/thinker, persister/believer, dreamer/imaginer, rebel/funster, promoter/doer) based on individual behavior patterns, needs, motivators, and perceptions. Each person possesses a personality structure comprising these six personality types, with relative strengths differing from one person to the next. No one type or personality is better or more successful than another. Although everyone has all six, each person typically is able to communicate easily with two or three but struggles with the other three or four. Co-teachers whose most well-developed personality types match tend to do well communicating with each other. Those who have personality structures that differ can be expected to have difficulty communicating unless they become familiar with the needs, motivations, and perceptions associated with their own strongest personality types and the needs, motivations, and perceptions associated with their partners' strongest personality types. Keefe, Moore, and Duff (2004) corroborate the premises of PCM in their study of creating and maintaining co-teacher relationships. They found that effective co-teachers must know not only their students and their content but also themselves and their co-teacher partners.

PCM can create a more supportive and responsive classroom and working relationship with co-teachers who are the most difficult to reach. When co-teachers match their communication patterns to meet the communication preferences and personality types of their partners, they can experience increased achievement and satisfaction in what they are doing both individually and jointly. In other words, if we want our co-teachers to listen to what we are saying, we need to speak their language. In fact, PCM can create a more supportive and responsive relationship with co-teachers who are the most difficult to reach.

Co-teachers must address multiple issues related to assessment, accountability, lack of time for planning or even taking care of personal needs, dealing with challenging students and families, individualizing instruction for a wide range of diverse students, and lack of praise and recognition (Pauley et al. 2002; Pauley et al. 2009). When co-teachers have their psychological needs met on a daily basis and help meet their partners' needs as well, they are more likely to thrive despite these multiple stressors. For example, co-teachers who have a preference for perceiving the world through feelings may overadapt by continuously trying to please others when they are distressed; then they may make mistakes and lack assertiveness. The result may be that they are rejected by their co-teachers. When these co-teachers are appreciated for who they are and provided with sensory stimulation (e.g., flowers, scented candles), however, their distress patterns may disappear. Similarly, co-teachers with a preference for perceiving the world through ideas may overthink for their co-teacher partners, overcontrol and criticize their co-teachers' thinking skills, and, finally, reject their co-teachers. When their psychological need for recognition of their work is met, they are less likely to criticize others.

Some co-teachers perceive the world through their opinions and convictions. Their distress patterns move from focusing on what their partners are doing wrong to pushing their beliefs and preaching and then to forsaking their partners as having no commitment. When their psychological needs are met through recognition of their work and opinions, they are much less likely to show these distress patterns. Some co-teachers have a need for solitude, and when that need is not met, their distress pattern moves from being inattentive to their partners to passively waiting or avoiding their partners to being left out of activities altogether.

Co-teachers who thrive on fun activities will try hard to do what is asked of them and then begin blaming things, situations, or their co-teachers for what goes wrong, and finally they will become vengeful. When their psychological need for fun and their strong likes and dislikes are acknowledged, they are more likely to not become distressed or engage in disruptive behaviors. Co-teachers who have a strong preference for risk taking and excitement may expect their partners to fend for themselves when they are in distress, then may manipulate and create negative drama among the co-teaching team members, finally abandoning their partners. To keep them out of distress, co-teachers can help these people fulfill their psychological need for excitement by making deals with them, setting them up to be in the limelight, and asking them to promote the co-teaching agenda with the administration.

It should be emphasized that everyone moves in and out of distress many times a day. Knowing your own distress patterns can support you in getting your own psychological needs met. The bottom line is that when co-teachers perceive so-called disruptive or challenging behaviors as signals of distress, helping colleagues meet their psychological needs becomes a key to successful communication.

BECOMING CULTURALLY ■
COMPETENT CO-TEACHERS

"Our worldviews are shaped by our cultural and family attachments. Each of us drags around a cultural tail a thousand years long, as well as our more personal family tail."

(Brokenleg 1998, 130)

To what extent can co-teachers who are culturally, racially, ethnically, or linguistically different from one another and their students identify their own cultural tails and understand and respectfully interact with their co-teachers and students who may have very different cultural and family tails? How can co-teachers gain cultural competence and avoid intercultural communication difficulties known as cross-cultural collisions? Why are these questions of importance in co-teaching?

First, the questions are important because co-teachers often are partnered precisely because of their differences, at least their differences in professional preparation and expertise. For example, special educators, teachers of English learners, and teachers of students with gifts and talents are often partnered with general educators in order to better include and meaningfully instruct students who are perceived as having learning, language, and other differences. In fact, students in our classrooms reflect increasing diversity along multiple dimensions (e.g., race, culture, ethnicity, heritages that reflect multiple cultures, gender preferences and sexual orientation, religious practices), while the majority of K–12 teachers are monolingual and white. According to the report compiled by Davis (2008), of the approximately 79.9 million students in grades preK through 12, the majority of students were non-Hispanic white (59%), followed by Hispanic students (18%), black students (15%), and Asian students (5%). In contrast, comparative statistics (http://nces.ed.gov/programs/coe/tables/table-tsp-1.asp) show that the majority of full-time K–12 teachers are monolingual Caucasians. Moreover, students with disabilities from culturally and linguistically diverse families increased from 33% in 1992 to 46.7% in 2001 (U.S. Department of Education, 2001). Paige (2004) emphasizes these demographics among the 6.4 million students (13.4%) who are served in programs for students with disabilities. In other words, we can say with confidence that diversity in America's classrooms is here to stay.

What can we learn from the research about being culturally responsive and responsible that might instruct co-teachers who do not share the same race, ethnic, cultural, or linguistic background? In a study of two culturally linguistically diverse schools in California, Santamaria (2009) showed how combining differentiated instruction for culturally and linguistically diverse learners and culturally responsive teaching empowered learners to make dramatic achievement gains. In a study of culturally diverse novice and veteran teachers, Gudwin and Salazar-Wallace (2009) explained how they relied upon pedagogies such as cooperative learning, the use of multiple modes of representing information and the setting of high expectations to develop effective cross-cultural communication patterns and reduce marginalization and isolation of their culturally diverse beginning special educators and their mentors. Daunic, Correa, and Reyes-Blancs (2004) described how culturally responsive pedagogy such as that just noted can influence the way teachers think about their students' backgrounds, ability to extend students' thinking, and respectfulness or fairness. Co-teachers also can take advantage of the abilities of their bilingual paraprofessionals to serve as cultural ambassadors, interpreting for them the cultural norms of the members of their community and bridging the home–school communication gap (Wenger, Lubbes, Lazo, Azcarraga, Sharp, and Ernst-Slavit 2004).

Co-teachers can gain skills to identify their own unconscious assumptions, beliefs, subjectivities, and positions (e.g., "I am a general educator, not a special educator" or "I am a special educator, not a bilingual educator.") that can influence interactions with others from different cultures. For example, we can learn how whiteness and white privilege influence curriculum, pedagogy, and policies that marginalize the diverse students we teach. Teachers (including co-teachers) are directed to the work of multicultural critics, such as Steinberg (2009), who challenge traditional representation of multicultural education as a collection of distinct entities such as disability, race, and social class and help us identify our assumptions and, thus, break the unspoken code of silence about discussing our respective diversities.

In summary, there is no definitive answer to the question, "How do co-teachers from diverse cultures negotiate their differences in culturally responsive and respectful ways?" There is a research basis for collaboration between general and special educators in multicultural classrooms (e.g., Nevin, Harris, and Correa 2001) but none that could be found on the dynamics between other diverse co-teachers. In other words, co-teachers who come from culturally and linguistically diverse heritages need to invent ways of working together that emphasize the strengths they bring from their unique heritages, languages, and knowledge bases. Becoming culturally competent means becoming deliberate about gaining a deeper understanding of how one's own "cultural tail" (Brokenleg 1998) might influence differences that arise as the co-teachers go through the stages of relationship development.

■ UNDERSTANDING THE DEVELOPMENTAL NATURE OF CO-TEACHING RELATIONSHIPS

Most people learn to be competent in their group work as a direct result of actually working with other people. In addition, having the cognitive knowledge about the social psychology of how individuals behave when working as partners or groups can be helpful in understanding that co-teacher relationships go through various stages of development. Knowing that people in co-teaching relationships go through specific stages can help us choose to use specific interpersonal and communication skills that facilitate achievement of the goal and maintain a positive relationship.

As with the stages that members of groups experience, there are the four Fs that co-teachers pass through in the development of a co-teaching relationship: the forming stage, the functioning stage, the formulating stage, and the fermenting stage. Each stage can be experienced more successfully when co-teachers practice the collaboration skills associated with each stage. This is quite similar to how children feel when they first achieve a difficult task, such as climbing up and down stairs or riding a bicycle. They remember what it felt like to be unsure and incompetent before achieving mastery of the skill.

Many of the same feelings may be experienced when you begin to work as a member of a co-teaching team, even if you have worked as a co-teacher with others. When you are committed to an agreed-on goal and when you want to maintain positive relationships with your co-teachers (in case you ever have to work with them again!), however, it becomes particularly important to practice the specific interpersonal communication skills associated with each of the stages of group development. Because you and your co-teachers may take baby steps as you learn some of the skills, remember to give positive feedback on how well each other is doing. Some teams use these stages and skills as a checklist to measure their growth individually and as a team.

During the forming stage, the goal is to build a mutual and reciprocal relationship. The interpersonal skills that facilitate this goal include building trust, being on time, establishing goals, and setting norms (agreements) such as no put-downs and use of appropriate tone of voice to match co-teaching partners' communication styles.

During the functioning stage, co-teachers must come to an agreement about specifically how their co-teaching partnership will function. They decide how they will work together, specifying who will do what tasks and when. To facilitate this stage, communication and shared leadership skills are needed—clarifying or explaining one's views, coordinating tasks, paraphrasing others' views, and then checking for understanding of the decisions that have been made.

In the formulating stage, it is important to emphasize the task to be accomplished in the co-teacher relationship. During this stage, helpful collaboration skills that co-teachers should practice include decision making and creative problem solving. These skills refer to communication strategies such as stating the decision that needs to be made, thinking of new ways to include everyone in the decision, being willing to try something even though you aren't sure it will work, and being comfortable with taking risks.

The fermenting stage is when co-teacher team cohesiveness can reach its greatest potential. The skills of conflict management are important to facilitating the fermenting stage. Such skills include criticizing ideas, not people, differentiating opinions, asking for more information to understand someone else's ideas, and using creative problem-solving techniques.

We believe that understanding these stages can improve the outcomes and enjoyment of the teams in which you participate. First of all, please understand that it's up to you! Only you can change your behaviors, and by modeling some of the skills required at each stage of development, you can help your co-teachers achieve better results and experience more enjoyment from the partnership. As shown in Table 13.1, the checklist of skills associated with each of the four stages of development illustrates the many different ways you can advance both goal achievement and maintenance of positive relationships with co-teaching team members. This checklist is also provided as a reproducible resource, Resource N, for teams to use in assessing and tracking their interpersonal development.

Second, you can enlist the support of your co-teachers by asking for feedback on how well you are communicating and how well you are using the skills associated with each stage of the co-teacher relationship. When

Table 13.1   Checklist of Skills for the Stages of Co-Teacher Development

Skills for the Forming Stage

___ Use co-teachers' preferred names

___ Use no put-downs

___ Come to co-teacher meetings on time and stay for the entire time

___ Follow through on agreements (show I am trustworthy)

___ Acknowledge co-teachers for their follow-through

Skills for the Functioning Stage

___ State and restate the purpose of co-teaching

___ Set or call attention to the time limits

___ Suggest procedures for how to do the task effectively

___ Express support and acceptance verbally

___ Express support and acceptance nonverbally

___ Paraphrase and clarify

___ Energize co-teachers with humor, ideas, or enthusiasm

___ Describe feelings when appropriate

Skills for the Formulating Stage

___ Summarize what has been said

___ Seek accuracy by correcting or adding to the summary

___ Seek connections to other knowledge

___ Seek clever ways to remember ideas, facts, and decisions

___ Ask co-teachers to explain their reasoning

___ Ask co-teachers to plan aloud

Skills for the Fermenting Stage

___ Criticize ideas without criticizing people

___ Differentiate ideas when there is disagreement

___ Integrate different ideas into a single position

___ Probe by asking questions that lead to deeper understanding

___ Suggest new answers and ideas

___ Think of new ways to resolve differences of opinion

receiving feedback, it is important to listen and keep an open mind as you hear what your co-teachers are saying so that you can change your communication style or your actions to get the results you desire.

Third, you can practice and encourage your co-teachers to practice skills that you are not familiar with or comfortable in performing just yet. This takes a lot of courage; however, with a norm or expectation among co-teachers that feedback and corrective action are part of the relationship, practicing unfamiliar skills leads to increased success. To help guide your co-teaching partners, you might be interested in the definitions of various roles that help co-teachers go through the various stages of group development. Table 13.2 lists possible roles that co-teachers can practice to facilitate goal achievement. Table 13.3 lists the roles co-teachers can practice to maintain positive interpersonal relationships. Feel free to invent other roles, including those that are unique to the tasks your co-teachers need to achieve. Co-teachers can select two or three roles to practice during their planning time or while they communicate during their teaching time. For example, during the learning-stations lesson described in the elementary parallel teaching vignette (Chapter 5), Ms. Hernandez (the paraprofessional) was the timekeeper, Ms. Nugent (the speech and language therapist) was the recorder, and Ms. Gilpatrick (the classroom teacher) was the facilitator. Dave and Juan, the student co-teachers introduced in Chapter 9, reciprocally practiced two major roles: the relationship role of praiser and the task achievement role of checker.

Table 13.2   Roles That Facilitate Goal Achievement

Timekeeper

The timekeeper monitors the time, encourages co-teachers to stop at agreed-on times, and alerts co-teachers when it is approaching the end of the agreed-on time period. "We have 5 minutes left to finish."

Recorder

The recorder writes down the decisions made by the co-teachers and distributes copies to each present and absent co-teacher team member within 1 week's time.

Checker

The checker makes sure co-teachers understand discussion and decisions. "Can you explain how we arrived at this decision?"

Photocopier

The photocopier takes completed minutes from the recorder, copies them, and distributes them to absent and present co-teachers. Sometimes the photocopier makes copies of specific teaching/learning procedures so that all co-teachers can follow the same strategy.

"Yes, But . . ." Monitor

During brainstorming sessions, when all ideas are being recorded, the "yes, but . . ." monitor signals when judgmental or negative statements are made that might thwart the creative process and decrease the generation of ideas.

Others

To be added by you and your co-teachers.

Table 13.3 Roles That Maintain Positive Interpersonal Relationships

Facilitator

The facilitator encourages all co-teachers to participate and to carry out their roles. The facilitator summarizes outcomes of a discussion before moving on to a new topic and makes sure that co-teachers' needs are met by adding items as requested.

Praiser

The praiser lets co-teachers know when they are using collaborative skills that positively impact each other. The praiser is careful to make the praise sound and feel authentic and focused (e.g., "Thanks to [insert co-teacher's name] for keeping us focused on our tasks!") rather than general comments (e.g., "Good job!").

Prober

The prober makes sure all possibilities have been explored. "What else could we include?" "Are there any other ways we could do this?"

Jargon Buster

The jargon buster lets co-teachers know when they are using terms that not all those who are present may understand, such as acronyms, abbreviations, and so on. This is an especially important role when co-teachers include people from a specialty area that is not familiar to everyone. "Whoops—does everyone know what IEP means?"

Others

To be added by you and your co-teachers.

■ MANAGING CONFLICT

Johnson and Johnson (1991) are cooperative learning experts from the University of Minnesota who teach about the reality and value of conflict:

> Conflicts occur all the time. They are a natural, inevitable, potentially constructive, and normal part of school life. Students disagree over who to sit by at lunch, which game to play during recess, when to work and when to play, when to talk and when to listen, and who is going to pick the paper up off the floor. . . . Covert conflicts are ones where you and your classmates sit and fester about your perceived grievances. Covert conflicts have to be made overt and resolved. (p. 58)

In fact, the same is true of adults. Covert conflicts need to be made overt and resolved, or they will fester and destroy the potential for a positive co-teacher relationship. Conflict is a natural, ever-present part of co-teaching. Johnson and Johnson (1988) define conflicts in terms of actions that frequently prevent, block, or interfere with another person's attempts to achieve his or her goals. Knowing what kind of conflict you are having can help you select a conflict resolution strategy. Consider the following four types of conflict:

1. A controversy exists when a person's ideas or conclusions are incompatible with the ideas of another person, and an agreement must be reached.

2. A conceptual conflict occurs when a person has two incompatible ideas.

3. A conflict of interest exists when one person tries to achieve a goal and another person blocks it.

4. A developmental conflict occurs as part of normal social development, for example, when recurring incompatible actions arise between a child and an adult.

It can be helpful to understand the sources of conflict. As noted earlier, people thrive when their psychological needs are met. When there are limited resources, conflicts may arise when people become afraid that their needs will not be met. Schrumpf and Jansen (2002) suggest that some conflicts arise because of differing values and convictions. Concepts and beliefs about timeliness, equality, fairness, and honesty are culturally embedded. When these beliefs and concepts are clarified, co-teachers often can avoid conflicts among co-teaching partners.

There is a lot of research to support the notion that conflicts have value. For example, achievement, problem solving, positive social development, flexibility in the face of change, and the experience of fun all can be improved when a conflict is constructive (Johnson and Johnson 1988). You know that a conflict is constructive when a problem is solved, when the relationship among those involved is strengthened, and when the people involved increase their ability to resolve conflicts in the future. Ensuring that a conflict is constructive requires co-teachers to practice the task and relationship skills for the fermenting stage described in Table 13.1, think of new ways to resolve differences of opinion, differentiate your ideas when there is disagreement, and integrate different ideas into a single position. A good example of constructive conflict occurred between Mr. Silva (the middle-level science and math teacher) and Ms. Spaulding (the special educator) when they developed a creative way to use the Multiple Intelligences Pizza to teach Boyle's law (see Chapter 7). The co-teachers had to seek connections with MI theory to identify and then share their own MI strengths and suggest new ways to present the ideas and then integrate their ideas into a single lesson plan.

TIPS FOR DEALING WITH CHALLENGING AND UNPRODUCTIVE BEHAVIOR

We agree that few of us are ideal co-teachers all the time. Consequently, many people ask, "What do we do with co-teaching partners whose behavior is challenging or unproductive?" Some challenging behaviors that occur infrequently or in isolated situations can be ignored. Humor may provide another solution because it can be used to lightly call attention to the behavior. For example, Rich is a person who can talk on and on about any topic, often not allowing others to speak. One of his co-teachers often says with a smile, "Rich, I guess you are really excited about this topic. Let's check in with other teaching partners on our team to find out what they think." Another solution is to call attention to alternative desired behaviors. For example, Jacque frequently interrupts. During the regularly scheduled time to process, Ann notes how Jacque has waited for others to complete their statements to allow them to elaborate or piggyback on ideas, which results in even better ones. This encourages Jacque to do the same in subsequent meetings.

When a co-teacher's negative behavior becomes incessant and distracting, however, it may be necessary to confront the person directly. Confrontation is often uncomfortable for both the confronter and the confronted, yet it is necessary at times. If team members determine that the individual who is going to receive the negative feedback will respond positively, any team member may initiate the feedback process. If they believe the person will respond negatively, be embarrassed or angry, or that public feedback will escalate the person's behavior, a supervisor or one of the team members who has a positive relationship with the individual might offer the feedback in private. We have found it helpful to use a five-step procedure for confronting a person with regard to disruptive or challenging interactions:

1. Observe the person and the impact of his or her behavior on others.

2. Try to understand why the person may be persisting in the behavior.

3. Describe the behavior and its impact to the person by using nonjudgmental language (use "I" statements, not "you" statements).

4. Establish some rules for minimizing future undesired behavior and increasing alternative behaviors.

5. Turn the unfavorable behavior into a favorable one (e.g., assign an aggressor the role of devil's advocate for certain issues, ask the joker to open each meeting with a funny story, invite a dominator to take the role of encourager or equalizer, ask the person who often wanders off the topic to signal whenever anyone gets off track).

■ TIPS FOR AVOIDING POTENTIAL PROBLEMS

In our experience, when co-teachers practice the eight tips listed in Table 13.4, they can achieve more effective outcomes for their students, can feel happier about their work, and are more likely to work together in the future (Villa, Thousand, and Nevin 1999). Practicing these tips will help co-teachers be proactive and thus avoid many potential problems.

Know With Whom You Need to Co-Teach

Co-teaching partners need not be limited to other teachers. Your co-teachers can, and in many cases must, include students, parents, administrators,

Table 13.4 Practical Tips for Avoiding Potential Problems

1. Know with whom you need to co-teach.
2. Establish and clarify co-teaching goals to avoid hidden agendas.
3. Agree to use a common conceptual framework, language, and set of interpersonal skills.
4. Practice communication skills for successful co-teacher interactions—achieving the tasks and maintaining positive relationships.
5. Know how to facilitate a collaborative culture.
6. Recognize and respect differences in excellence and the multiple sources of motivation for co-teachers.
7. Expect to be responsible and to be held accountable.
8. Agree to reflective analysis of the co-teaching process, and celebrate often.

specialists, community members, and advocates. Consider these three guidelines for deciding who will be your co-teachers:

1. Include those whom decisions will affect.

2. Include those who have the needed expertise.

3. Include anyone who has an interest in participating.

To promote inventive and creative outside-the-box thinking and to capitalize on existing excitement and enthusiasm, think about working with people who may not be formally expected to participate with your co-teaching team.

Establish and Clarify Co-Teaching Goals to Avoid Hidden Agendas

A planned method of developing and articulating goals for the co-teachers decreases much of the anxiety of not knowing what is expected. Creating common goals also encourages positive interdependence. An essential component of goal setting is for each co-teacher to say what he or she needs from the other co-teachers. When such needs are not recognized, there is a real possibility that co-teachers may come to think of others' goals and needs as hidden agendas.

Agree to Use a Common Conceptual Framework, Language, and Set of Interpersonal Skills

More effective co-teaching outcomes occur when co-teachers use a common language to share meaning and avoid or demystify jargon. Participation in staff development and other training activities can support the development of a common conceptual framework. (See Chapter 10 for more details about staff development.)

Co-teachers can establish ground rules for how they will operate. For example, a ground rule might be that it is OK to ask questions when something is not understood. Per Table 12.3, one co-teacher could play the role of jargon buster, a person who asks others for clarification when terms are used that not everyone may understand.

Sometimes co-teachers agree to participate in inservice workshops or mentoring to acquire and master interpersonal and communication strategies and skills. Other co-teachers may agree to receive training in a particular problem-solving process to deal with conflict and then share the process with other co-teachers. Through such reciprocity, all members of the co-teaching team improve their skills.

Practice Communication Skills for Successful Co-Teacher Interactions

Co-teachers have an array of interpersonal skills (e.g., trust building, communication, creative problem solving, conflict resolution) to practice. Skills for helping co-teachers achieve their mutual goals and for maintaining relationships must be consciously practiced. Be sure that absent co-teachers receive the minutes or notes of meetings. Build in time to reflect on how well co-teachers are interacting, and then make adjustments as needed. Clarify lines of accountability by stating who will do what, setting deadlines, and building in celebrations for the small successes that occur every day.

Know How to Facilitate a Collaborative Culture

The education profession is well versed in the *lone arranger* way of doing business—one teacher is expected to teach a class of 30 students without support from or communication with others. The notion that the so-called self-contained classroom and the lone teacher can somehow meet the ever-increasing needs of a diverse student body is a myth. Only through sharing ideas, materials, resources, and expertise do teachers develop, survive, and thrive.

To facilitate the change to a collaborative culture, co-teachers must bring to consciousness their unconscious beliefs. An example of an unconscious belief is the following: "If I have to have a co-teacher to succeed, then I must be a less-than-adequate teacher." New traditions and celebrations that reflect the values of cooperation must replace old traditions. For example, instead of celebrating a teacher-of-the-year award, add a co-teacher team award. Include co-teaching and collaboration as expected roles in every job description.

Recognize and Respect Differences and Multiple Sources of Motivation

Co-teacher teams improve their effectiveness when the individuals improve. Make sure incentives are varied enough to meet individual preferences. Create flexible scheduling that encourages co-teachers to use their time to meet and plan as well as debrief and problem solve. Seek and use training opportunities for learning new ways to co-teach. Set up site-visit opportunities to observe other co-teachers and interview them to find out their secrets of successful co-teaching.

Expect to Be Responsible and to Be Held Accountable

Effective co-teachers act responsibly. They follow through on what they agree to do. They show up for meetings on time. They consciously practice effective communication skills. They support and facilitate the participation of their co-teacher partners. They celebrate individual and team successes. They expect to be held accountable, and they hold their co-teachers accountable in return.

Agree to Reflective Analysis, and Celebrate Often

Create a tool to measure the changes you and your co-teacher partners experience as a result of your partnership. Consider Table 12.3, the Are We Really Co-Teachers? self-assessment, as one way to assess your development. Keep a journal of your feelings, thoughts, and observations. When co-teachers use some form of reflective analysis, they typically become more empowered to celebrate their current levels of co-teaching skills and to set goals for continued improvement. Yes, it takes time to learn the interpersonal and thinking skills needed for effective co-teaching, but the results are worth it. Celebrate often!

In Chapter 14, Nancy Keller and Lia Cravedi describe the development of their co-teaching relationship. They illustrate each of the eight tips for avoiding potential problems that are offered in Table 13.4 of this chapter. The tips are highlighted in set-aside boxes throughout their story.

Developing a Shared Voice Through Co-Teaching

Nancy Keller and Lia Cravedi

14

NANCY'S VOICE ■

Several years of working as a middle-level science teacher in an inclusive school district gave me the opportunity to experience how co-teaching with teachers from other content areas and with special educators can help children of varying abilities participate meaningfully in regular classrooms. I must confess that I was initially uneasy about the inclusion in my classroom of students with physical, academic, and social challenges. My teacher-preparation program, although excellent at the time, did not include practical experiences in inclusive educational settings. Today, my understanding of how we can educate all students together has broadened. I realize that my initial concerns about inclusive education had to do with the unknown and with not being able to visualize how it might work.

LIA'S VOICE ■

Before I began co-teaching with regular educators, I had worked for years as a special educator in pullout resource rooms and separate special education classrooms. Although I was uncomfortable with sorting students by perceived ability, teaching them in isolation, and then hoping they would be able to apply this learning in a new context, this was not an uncommon practice at the time. My contact with general educators was limited to saying "Hello" to each other as I pulled my students from their classes.

Co-teaching addressed my dilemmas and ended my social and professional isolation. Co-teaching with Nancy convinced both of us that when teachers have adequate support and the opportunity to share their respective expertise, a rich educational experience can be created that benefits all students.

■ OUR VOICE

What you will hear in the following pages is our shared voice, our description of how our co-teaching partnership evolved over the 2 years we taught together. We hope that what we learned will be helpful to you in your co-teaching endeavors. The school district in which we co-taught together was one that underwent a dramatic, decade-long transformation from a district in which students with special needs were placed in special classes or bused outside of the district to a district in which all students were educated in general education classrooms, with co-teaching as a predominant student support mechanism.

The first step in the district's transformation was to close the on-site special classes and discontinue the practice of sending students out of the district. Although all students were now on campus and included in most general education classes, the benefits of inclusive education were not being fully realized. Specifically, the dropout rate of students with disabilities was still high (30%), and their absenteeism was a chronic problem. We were convinced that a primary reason these students were reluctant to continue their education was that they did not feel as if they really were a part of the school community. They were still frequently separated from their classmates when pulled from their general education classes to receive academic coursework in a resource room. We were faced with a serious challenge: In what ways could we structure a learning environment in which these students would want to participate? We had to look no further than our students and listen to what they were telling us: They wanted to learn alongside their friends, just as every other student wanted.

Now that we had embraced the concept of all students learning side by side, our administrator for special services decided that the general and special educators also needed to teach (and learn) side by side. He explained that with this co-teaching configuration, the differences in our general and special education teacher preparation would be an asset. For example, Nancy had been trained as a secondary science teacher, with little focus placed on making accommodations for students with learning differences. Lia, on the other hand, possessed these very skills—the ones Nancy lacked. By combining teaching skills, we complemented one other.

> **Tip 1** Know with whom you need to co-teach.

Unlike some teaching teams, we did not enter into our co-teaching relationship by choice. It was an administrative decision. In fact, we had not previously worked with each other. We are here to tell you that this does not have to spell doom for a team. Given time to meet, a framework such as the one we describe here, and attention to the collaborative teaming process, teachers can form an effective teaching partnership. This is what occurred for us.

■ OUR FIRST YEAR—DEVELOPING TRUST

There are several important aspects to the way we worked together. We have since learned to describe them as the essential ingredients of the cooperative process: face-to-face interaction through planning time, positive interdependence, individual accountability, and monitoring and processing of our achievements.

Face-to-Face Planning Time

Before we could stand together in front of our students and represent ourselves as a viable teaching team, we had to establish a weekly planning time. Prior to the start of the school year, we agreed to set aside one prep period per week for this to occur. Given that we did not know each other very well, we knew that without this initial investment of time, our co-teaching would not be successful. Therefore, this became our sacred time, time that would not be interrupted by the typical demands that teachers face. Although it was just the two of us, we set an agenda, took minutes, and assigned tasks to be completed later (e.g., prepare worksheets, make copies, talk to a student, grade papers). Without investing adequate time to plan, we can almost guarantee, a co-teaching team will not reach its potential. Notes in the mailbox and planning on the run cannot build solid, trusting relationships.

> **Tip 2** Establish and clarify co-teaching goals to avoid hidden agendas.

> **Tip 4** Practice communication skills for successful co-teacher interactions.

> **Tip 5** Know how to facilitate a collaborative culture.

Positive Interdependence

Setting Mutual Goals

Much of our weekly planning time was driven by the mission that we and our school district had adopted, namely, that all students were to receive instruction in the general education classroom. To accomplish this mission, Nancy wanted to learn how to differentiate curriculum and instruction. Lia wanted to ensure that all the students for whom she coordinated services would be successful in general education classrooms. In retrospect, we now see that establishing a common purpose and setting clear goals provided a meaningful context in which to work. Once determined, a mission can guide a team in decision making, prompting team members to ask, "Is what we are doing congruent with our mission?" For example, given our mission of maintaining students in the regular classroom, the choice to remove a student from that environment became a choice of last resort because such an action was not in sync with our mission.

> **Tip 2** Establish and clarify co-teaching goals to avoid hidden agendas.

In addition, our individual professional goals became a yardstick by which to measure our growth as teachers. Did Nancy learn how to differentiate curriculum and instruction? How successful was Lia at structuring for student success?

Defining Roles

Something that wasn't discussed during the year but that both of us assumed from the beginning was that Nancy would be responsible for delivering the content and Lia would play the supportive co-teacher role (see Chapter 4 for details about the supportive co-teaching approach). This assumption, although conventional (teacher and teacher assistant), provided the basis for dividing our labor. This meant that Nancy took on the tasks related to what would be taught and how (i.e., identify the content to be covered; set objectives and do the majority of lesson planning, teaching, and evaluating). Lia supported this instruction through her skilled classroom and student management, verbally and physically prompting students to focus on the instruction, checking for student understanding, and intervening when off-task behavior occurred. When defining roles, it is critical to consider what the students need as well as what expertise each co-teacher brings to a situation. Redefining roles requires setting aside egos. For Lia, being an assistant to another teacher may not have been a glamorous job, but it was exactly what the students needed in order to engage and learn.

Individual Accountability

Once our roles were defined, trust was further built by following through on our commitments. Lia promised Nancy that she would co-teach for a minimum of one period per day, 4 days per week. Nancy depended on Lia to be there; had Lia not been dependable, Nancy would not have trusted that what had been planned would be realized. Conversely, if Nancy did not clearly plan the objectives for the science lessons, Lia would have felt let down. She would not have known how to support the students in Nancy's classes. The glue to this co-teaching relationship was individual accountability. We recommend that co-teachers apply this glue liberally!

Monitoring and Processing of Accomplishments

In our first year working together, we kept our reflections and processing within the noncontroversial realm of how the students were doing. We avoided conversations regarding our performance as teachers. Although Nancy's goal was to improve skills in differentiation and instruction, she did not seek feedback from Lia in this area, fearing that she would be criticized instead of supported in Lia's evaluations. It wasn't until Lia suggested that we take a district-sponsored course together to focus on our co-teaching that Nancy felt she could trust Lia to offer feedback. Receiving feedback and reflection on one's own work can be a scary proposition. It takes trust, and that is what we developed, first and foremost, in our first year.

■ OUR SECOND YEAR—SUSTAINING TRUST

We were fortunate to be able to work together for a second year. Our school district is often fluid when it comes to scheduling and partnering personnel from year to year. When we requested that we remain partners, our administrators listened and granted us a second year to develop continuity as a team. We were deliberate about attending to the same collaborative ingredients (i.e., face-to-face planning time, positive interdependence, individual accountability, monitoring and processing of accomplishments) that had allowed us to succeed as a co-teaching team in our first year.

Face-to-Face Planning Time

Co-teaching teams that have been together for a while can easily be lulled into complacency about planning. After all, team members are familiar with each other, and a routine has been established. Much can be lost, however, if planning (in terms of instructional integrity and quality) is incidental. As in our first year, planning time remained key to our success.

A big challenge in our second year was to move beyond our routine—that is, to use the lessons learned from the previous year as a starting point for refinement and improvement. Because we believed the adage that two heads are better than one, we knew that adequate planning time needed to remain part of the routine, even if it sometimes seemed as if the lessons could write themselves and the classroom could run itself. We found it helpful to use a structured planning meeting format (much like the one in Table 13.2 of Chapter 13) to guide us when we met face to face. We found we made much more efficient use of the little planning time available to us when we had an agenda and time frames to keep us focused.

> **Tip 3** Agree to use a common conceptual framework, language, and set of interpersonal skills.

> **Tip 5** Know how to facilitate a collaborative culture.

> **Tip 7** Expect to be responsible and to be held accountable.

> **Tip 8** Agree to reflective analysis of the co-teaching process, and celebrate often.

Positive Interdependence

In our second year, we established positive interdependence in new ways that resulted in an enhancement of our feeling that we were in this together. We revisited our goals, redefined our roles, and refined the monitoring of our progress so as to be more accountable for our individual and collective tasks.

Revisiting Goals

Although we were in our second year, we remained aware of our goal—ensuring that all students received instruction in general education—and continued to work toward it. In our first year, we had set broad goals, such as learning to differentiate instruction and adequately support students in general education classes. By our second year, we knew that there were several specific skills and strategies that we needed to master. We targeted the following as professional development areas: (1) positive discipline and behavior supports, (2) principles of effective instruction, and (3) the use of a universal design approach to planning that systematically considered our students' learning characteristics (This preceded the planning of content, instructional processes, and products of a lesson or unit (Thousand, Villa, and Nevin, 2007). Participation in a district-sponsored course, which we took together, facilitated our professional goal setting. For us, this course was one concrete way that our school district supported us as a teaching team. In many ways, our studying and learning together enhanced our "all for one and one for all" ethic and encouraged us to revisit and redefine not only our goals but our co-teaching roles as well.

Redefining Roles

Just as our goals became more interdependent, so did our roles. In our first year, we defined our roles along the boundaries of our relative expertise—Lia was the special educator, and Nancy was the science teacher. During our second year, we both saw ourselves as teachers of children, not as different types of teachers for different types of children. This change of perspective significantly changed the roles we played when co-teaching. Now both of us were responsible for developing lesson objectives, evaluating student progress, conferencing with parents, managing student behavior, and covering the logistics (e.g., making copies, preparing worksheets, setting up labs). We jointly shared all of the responsibilities a regular classroom teacher would normally have. We learned about the importance of redefining roles throughout a co-teaching partnership so that we could evolve into what, by our second year, could truly be called a teaching team (see Chapter 7 for more details about the team-teaching approach to co-teaching).

Individual Accountability

Even in the second year, accountability continued to be the glue that held our relationship together. For example, each of us had come to expect that the other would follow through on her responsibilities, as demon-

Tip 8 Agree to reflective analysis of the co-teaching process, and celebrate often.

strated during the first year. At this point, it may have been easy for either of us to have occasionally neglected our commitments, thinking that the other could handle it or would understand. Given the skills we had acquired, either one of us probably could have handled it and likely would have understood, but the other person's accountability to our teaching team would have begun to erode. The challenge for established teaching teams is to not take each other for granted, but to maintain a high level of mutual support.

Monitoring and Processing of Accomplishments

Tip 3 Agree to use a common conceptual framework, language, and set of interpersonal skills.

Tip 8 Agree to reflective analysis of the co-teaching process, and celebrate often.

In our second year of working together, we continued to reflect on student performance, considering this a critical and safe topic. Because we had developed a high level of trust and because we now shared a common language of instruction gained from the course we took together, we were now able to discuss our own and each other's teaching methods as well. We became comfortable talking about our interpersonal actions and our progress as co-teachers. Although at times these discussions were difficult, they yielded tremendous results for us. We are both better teachers as a result of these open and honest discussions.

■ FINAL REFLECTIONS

When school districts give general and special educators the opportunity to share their respective expertise by working as co-teachers, a rich and often remarkable educational experience for all students can emerge. In our 2 years as an evolving teaching team, we experienced for ourselves how students of all perceived abilities can learn and reach their potential together, in the same class, avoiding the stigma associated with being pulled out of the classroom for specialized instruction. Co-teachers benefit as well. Their social networks within the school community grow. They no longer experience teaching as the isolated profession, as they jointly experience the joy and fun of a student's success or a great co-taught lesson. Finally, co-teachers' perspectives evolve, as ours did, from a *yours-versus-mine* view of students, curriculum, and instruction to a *we-and-ours* view of everything about good schooling.

Tip 6 Recognize and respect differences and multiple sources of motivation.

Resources

Resource A Checklist of Sample Supplemental Supports, Aids, and Services

Directions:

When considering the need for personalized supports, aids, or services for a student, use this checklist to help identify which supports will be the least intrusive, only as special as necessary, and the most natural to the context of the classroom.

Environmental

___ Preferential seating

___ Planned seating

___ Bus __ Classroom __ Lunchroom __ Auditorium __ Other _____

___ Alter physical room arrangement (Specify: _____)

___ Use study carrels or quiet areas

___ Define area concretely (e.g., carpet squares, tape on floor, rug area)

___ Reduce/minimize distractions

___ Visual __ Spatial __ Auditory __ Movement

___ Teach positive rules for use of space

Pacing of Instruction

___ Extend time requirements

___ Vary activity often

___ Allow breaks

___ Omit assignments requiring copying in timed situations

___ Send additional copy of the text home for summer preview

___ Provide home set of materials for preview or review

Presentation of Subject Matter

___ Teach to the student's learning style/strength intelligences

___ Verbal/Linguistic __ Logical/Mathematical __ Visual/Spatial __ Naturalist

___ Bodily/Kinesthetic __ Musical __ Interpersonal __ Intrapersonal

___ Use active, experiential learning

___ Use specialized curriculum

___ Record class lectures and discussions to replay later

___ Use American Sign Language and/or total communication

___ Provide prewritten notes, an outline, or an organizer (e.g., mind map)

___ Provide copy of classmate's notes (e.g., use NCR paper, photocopy)

___ Use functional and meaningful application of academic skills

___ Present demonstrations and models

___ Use manipulatives and real objects in mathematics

___ Highlight critical information or main ideas

___ Preteach vocabulary

___ Make and use vocabulary files or provide vocabulary lists

___ Reduce the language level of the reading assignment

___ Use facilitated communication

___ Use visual organizers/sequences

___ Use paired reading/writing

___ Reduce seat time in class or activities

___ Use diaries or learning logs

___ Reword/rephrase instructions and questions

___ Preview and review major concepts in primary language

Materials

___ Limit amount of material on a page

___ Record texts and other class materials

___ Use study guides and advanced organizers

___ Use supplementary materials

___ Provide note-taking assistance

___ Copy class notes

___ Scan tests and class notes into computer

___ Use large print

___ Use braille material

___ Use communication book or board

___ Provide assistive technology and software (e.g., Intelli-Talk)

Specialized Equipment or Procedure

___ Wheelchair	___ Walker
___ Standing board	___ Positioning
___ Computer	___ Computer software
___ Electronic typewriter	___ Video/DVD
___ Modified keyboard	___ Voice synthesizer
___ Switches	___ Augmentative communication device
___ Catheterization	___ Suctioning
___ Braces	___ Restroom equipment

___ Customized mealtime utensils, plates, cups, and other materials

Assignment Modification

___ Give directions in small, distinct steps (written/picture/verbal)

___ Use written backup for oral directions

(Continued)

___ Use pictures as supplement to oral directions

___ Lower difficulty level ___ Raise difficulty level

___ Shorten assignments ___ Reduce paper-and-pencil tasks

___ Read or record directions to the student(s)

___ Give extra cues or prompts

___ Allow student to record or type assignments

___ Adapt worksheets and packets

___ Use compensatory procedures by providing alternate assignments when demands of class conflict with student capabilities

___ Ignore spelling errors/sloppy work ___ Ignore penmanship

___ Develop alternative rubrics

Self-Management/Follow-Through

___ Provide pictorial or written daily or weekly schedule

___ Provide student calendars

___ Check often for understanding/review

___ Request parent reinforcement

___ Have student repeat directions

___ Teach study skills

___ Use binders to organize material

___ Design/write/use long-term assignment timelines

___ Review and practice in real situations

___ Plan for generalization by teaching skill in several environments

Testing Adaptations

___ Provide oral instructions and/or read test questions

___ Use pictorial instructions/questions

___ Read test to student

___ Preview language of test questions

___ Ask questions that have applications in real setting

___ Administer test individually

___ Use short answer ___ Use multiple choice ___ Shorten length

___ Extend time frame ___ Use open-note/open-book tests

___ Modify format to reduce visual complexity or confusion

Social Interaction Support

___ Use natural peer supports and multiple, rotating peers

___ Use peer advocacy

___ Use cooperative group learning

___ Institute peer tutoring

___ Structure opportunities for social interaction (e.g., Circle of Friends)

___ Focus on social process rather than the end product

___ Structure shared experiences in school and extracurricular activities

___ Teach friendship, sharing, and negotiation skills to classmates

___ Teach social communication skills

___ Greetings ___ Conversation ___ Turn Taking ___ Sharing

___ Negotiation ___ Other _____

Level of Staff Support (Consider after considering previous categories)

___ Consultation

___ Stop-in support (one to three times per week)

___ Part-time daily support

___ Team teaching (parallel, supportive, complementary, or co-teaching)

___ Daily in-class staff support

___ Total staff support (staff are in close proximity)

___ One-on-one assistance

___ Specialized personnel support (If indicated, identify time needed.)

Support	*Time Needed*
___ Instructional support assistant	_____
___ Health care assistant	_____
___ Behavior assistant	_____
___ Signing assistant	_____
___ Nursing	_____
___ Occupational therapy	_____
___ Physical therapy	_____
___ Speech and language therapist	_____
___ Augmentative communication specialist	_____
___ Transportation	_____
___ Counseling	_____
___ Adaptive physical education	_____
___ Transition planning	_____
___ Orientation/mobility	_____
___ Career counseling	_____

Resource B Co-Teaching Daily Lesson Plan Format

Date: _____

Content Area(s): _____

Co-Teachers: _____
(Names) _____

Lesson Objectives:

Language Objectives:

Content Standards Addressed:

Underline the Co-Teaching Model(s) Used:

Supportive   Parallel   Complementary   Team

What is the *room arrangement?* Will other spaces outside of the classroom be used? (Draw a picture of the room arrangement.)

What *materials* do the co-teachers and/or students need?

How is student *learning assessed* by co-teachers?

What specific supports, aids, or services do *select students* need? (See Resource A for suggestions.)

(Continued)

What does each co-teacher do before, during, and after the lesson?

Co-Teacher Name			
What are the specific tasks that I do BEFORE the lesson?			
What are the specific tasks that I do DURING the lesson?			
What are the specific tasks that I do AFTER the lesson?			

Where, when, and how do co-teachers debrief and evaluate the outcomes of the lesson?

Resource C High School Supportive Co-Teaching Lesson Plan

Date: Three-day lesson

Co-Teachers: Mr. Woo, H.S. Social Studies Teacher
(Names)

Mr. Viana, Special Educator

Content Area(s): U.S. history

Lesson Objectives:

Academic objectives:

Working in groups of three with a variety of resource materials regarding the constitutional powers of the three branches of the U.S. federal government, members of each triad become "expert" in the powers of one of the three branches of government. (Days 1 and 2)

Given six scenarios regarding the constitutional powers of the three branches of government, members of triads comprising one expert for each of the three branches of government (a) share information learned in expert groups about each branch of government and (b) correctly decide on and agree to the responsibilities of each branch of government in each scenario (for a total of 18 decisions) for a minimum of 15 of 18 decisions (80% accuracy). (Day 3)

Social objectives:

While working in two different cooperative groups of three (i.e., expert group, jigsaw group of experts), students demonstrate the small-group social skills of sharing information, active listening, equal participation, and reaching consensus as evidenced by anecdotal observational notes collected by the co-teachers. (Days 1, 2, and 3)

Language objectives:

Provided with varied materials and partner and group work, students read information, write notes, and speak with and listen to peers to teach one another about the responsibilities of the branch of government.

Content Standards Addressed:

Social Studies Standard 12.1.5 Describe the systems of separated and shared powers, the role of organized interests (Federalist Paper Number 10), checks and balances (Federalist Paper Number 51), the importance of an independent judiciary (Federalist Paper Number 78), enumerated powers, rule of law, federalism, and civilian control of the military.[1]

Underline the Co-Teaching Approach(es) Used:

<u>Supportive</u>   Parallel   Complementary   Team

What is the *room arrangement*? Will other spaces outside of the classroom be used?

Student desks are arranged facing each other in groups of three. Because of a strategic teacher decision regarding a particular student, one group has four members. Students also access the library media center for resources, as needed.

What *materials* do the co-teachers and/or students need?

U.S. history textbooks, news magazines, other related print materials, and videos; Internet access; a task instruction sheet for each expert group; a task instruction sheet for each jigsaw group.

How is student *learning assessed* by co-teachers?

Mr. Woo examines the 18 jigsaw team responses for correctness. Both co-teachers observe student groups and note examples of the use of the targeted small-group interpersonal skills identified above as social objectives.

What specific supports, aids, or services do *select students* need?

Certain students are strategically placed in groups with supportive peers and assigned roles that they can perform (e.g., assign timekeeper role to student who has difficulty performing secondary-level reading and writing tasks). One student is seated in a group of four rather than three in order to benefit from the academic modeling of an additional peer.

(Continued)

What does each co-teacher do before, during, and after the lesson?

Co-Teacher Name	Mr. Woo, Social Studies Teacher	Mr. Viana, Special Educator
What are the specific tasks that I do BEFORE the lesson?	• Meet and plan • Clarify co-teaching responsibilities • Decide which co-teacher monitors which groups • Develop and copy a task list for the students	• Meet and plan • Clarify responsibilities • Divide class into three predetermined "expert" (i.e., legislative, executive, judicial branch) groups • Identify specific complementary roles within groups (especially for students who struggle with learning)
What are the specific tasks that I do DURING the lesson?	• Introduce the lesson and explain the academic and social objectives • Explain the criteria for success and emphasize that students have a common goal and individual roles and are individually held accountable • Assign students to each of the three expert groups created by Mr. Viana • Assign group roles • Monitor time and student academic and social skill performance in the groups	• Adjust group membership if necessary (e.g., due to absences) • Pass out materials to groups • Monitor student academic and social skill performance in the groups
What are the specific tasks that I do AFTER the lesson?	• Reflect on that day's lesson, and make any necessary modifications or adjustments for the following day(s) • Read and score Day 3 jigsaw group responses	• Share any relevant observations with Mr. Woo to assist him in making any modifications

Where, when, and how do co-teachers debrief and evaluate the outcomes of the lesson?

We will meet each day for a couple of moments following that day's lesson to share observations about what worked well and what, if anything, needs to be changed for the next day. We will touch base briefly right before class each day to review any modifications to the plan developed by Mr. Woo and to clarify our responsibilities.

Resource D Elementary Parallel Co-Teaching Lesson Plan

Date: One lesson period   **Co-Teachers:** Ms. Gilpatrick, classroom teacher   Ms. Nugent, speech and language therapist
                                          (Names)

                                    Ms. Hernandez, paraprofessional

Content Area(s): Language arts

Lesson Objectives:

Working with classmates at four differentiated learning stations, students identify, create, and form sentences using compound words with instructor guidance and feedback.

Language Objectives:

Students silently and orally read, orally state, and write compound words and sentences, including compound words.

Content Standards Addressed:

Vocabulary Acquisition and Use L.2.4: Determine or clarify the meaning of unknown and multiple-meaning words and phrases based on grade 2 reading and content, choosing flexibly from an array of strategies. . . . L.2.4.d Use knowledge of the meaning of individual words to predict the meaning of compound words (e.g., *birdhouse, lighthouse, housefly; bookshelf, notebook, bookmark*).[2]

Underline the Co-Teaching Approach(es) Used:

Supportive   Parallel (Primarily used)   Complementary   Team (Used to introduce lesson)

What is the *room arrangement*? Will other spaces outside of the classroom be used?

There are four stations. Two stations are carpeted areas, a third is a kidney-shaped table with chairs, and the fourth is a bank of five laptop computers.

(Continued)

What *materials* do the co-teachers and/or students need?

Each of four stations requires different sets of materials as described below:

Materials for Station 1	Materials for Station 2	Materials for Station 3	Materials for Station 4
Four identical sets of simple words (i.e., three sets for pairs of students and one set for the teacher) written on flashcards that can be combined to form compound words	Sets of three worksheets providing practice at creating compound words for each student	Large whiteboard with markers	Five computers with two student chairs at each computer
Timer	Whiteboard	Several big books	
	Teacher data sheet on which to record level of support required by each student	12 erasable markers	
		Three marker erasers	
		150 8 × 2-inch strips of paper (cut from regular paper)	

How is student learning assessed by co-teachers?

Station 1 (Ms. Hernandez)	Station 2 (Ms. Nugent)	Station 3 (Ms. Gilpatrick)	Station 4 (No co-teacher)
Engage in direct observation of student performance, and take notes regarding students who have difficulty.	Collect data on each student's level of independence and need for adult or peer support.	Engage in direct observation of student performance.	Students work independently.
Share data with the classroom teacher.	Share data with the classroom teacher.		Co-teacher examines computer printouts of sentences created by student pairs.

What specific supports, aids, or services do *select students* need?

The student with autism is strategically partnered with a classmate who is especially skilled at imitating instructors' modeling of tasks. Otherwise, no specific supports are needed, given the intensity of teacher modeling, guided practice, and monitoring at each station.

What does each co-teacher do before, during, and after the lesson?

Co-Teacher Name	Ms. Gilpatrick, classroom teacher	Ms. Nugent, speech and language therapist	Ms. Hernandez, paraprofessional
What are the specific tasks that I do BEFORE the lesson?	• Meet and plan activities during regular weekly meeting	• Meet and plan activities with Ms. Gilpatrick during regular weekly meeting • Meet with Ms. Hernandez during attendance to explain her station	• Brief on-the-spot at beginning of class during attendance regarding Station 1, which she will lead
What are the specific tasks that I do DURING the lesson?	• Large-group modeling of creation of compound words • Assign students to stations; explain independent task at Station 4 • Lead Station 3 • Signal time to switch stations • Be available to answer student questions at Station 4	• Large-group modeling of creation of compound words • Lead Station 2 • Complete data sheet regarding students' level of independence • Be available to answer student questions at Station 4	• Lead Station 1 • Available to answer student questions at Station 4
What are the specific tasks that I do AFTER the lesson?	• Examine student printouts from Station 4 • Review written data collected by Ms. Nugent • Consider Ms. Hernandez's observations and Ms. Nugent's data in planning next lesson	• Give Ms. Gilpatrick written data	• Verbally report observations to Ms. Gilpatrick

Where, when, and how do co-teachers debrief and evaluate the outcomes of the lesson?

Prior to the start of the next day's lesson, Ms. Gilpatrick shares with her co-teachers any adjustments to what they had planned, due to her review of student work and reports.

Date: <u>One class period</u>

Co-Teachers: <u>Ms. Kurtz, language arts teacher</u>
(Names) <u>Ms. Olvina, paraprofessional</u>

Content Area(s): <u>Language arts</u>

Lesson Objectives:
Given adult and student modeling of antonyms, synonyms, and homonyms and access to hard-copy and online resources, students construct and identify pairs of antonyms, synonyms, and homonyms through partner and group activities and games (i.e., Charades, Go Fish) within the time frames allocated by the teacher.

Language Objectives:
Students speak and write correct use of antonyms, homonyms, and synonyms.

Content Standards Addressed:
Vocabulary Acquisition and Use Language Standard L.7.5: Demonstrate understanding of figurative language, word relationships, and nuances in word meanings. L.7.5.b Use the relationship between particular words (e.g., synonyms/antonyms, analogy) to better understand each of the words.[3]

Underline the Co-Teaching Approach(es) Used:

Supportive   Parallel   <u>Complementary (Primarily Used)</u>   <u>Team (Used to introduce lesson)</u>

What is the *room arrangement*? Will other spaces outside of the classroom be used?
Traditional row seating with desks rearranged when needed for partner and group activities

What *materials* do the co-teachers and/or students need?
Dictionaries, thesauruses, a kitchen timer, a stack of starter words for co-teachers to use with groups, a stack of lined paper for students to use, a document projector, one or more computers with Internet access, five to six cans of 25 to 30 Popsicle sticks with different words written on each stick

How is student *learning assessed* by co-teachers?
1. Sample and assess accuracy of select student's oral examples of antonyms, synonyms, and homonyms.
2. Review accuracy of pair-generated lists of antonyms, synonyms, and homonyms.
3. Observe and write notes about student performance during Charades and Go Fish games.

What specific supports, aids, or services do *select students* need?
While instructors monitor student performance during the pair activity, both carry around a set of starter words to offer to pairs who are having difficulty coming up with antonyms, synonyms, and homonyms.

What does each co-teacher do before, during, and after the lesson?

Co-Teacher Name	Ms. Kurtz, language arts teacher	Ms. Olvina, paraprofessional
What are the specific tasks that I do BEFORE the lesson?	• Meet and plan the lesson with Ms. Olvina • Prepare materials for the lesson • Preassign students to pairs	• Meet and plan the lesson with Ms. Kurtz • Come prepared to act out charades of pairs of antonyms, synonyms, and homonyms
What are the specific tasks that I do DURING the lesson?	• Open lesson with examples of antonyms, synonyms, and homonyms • Select students to explain Charades and Go Fish • Solicit volunteers to model charade of antonym pair • Solicit volunteers to model charade of synonym pair • Solicit volunteers to model charade of homonym pair • Partner students for first activity and explain the activity • Monitor students during first activity • Form quads from pairs, explain Go Fish application activity • Set timer for second activity • Monitor second activity • Debrief second activity by soliciting examples from students • Debrief by sharing additional examples on overhead while monitoring • Provide closure with a "flash" round review	• Model charades of antonym pair • Model charades of synonym pair • Model charade of homonym pair • Display overhead of student partnerships • Monitor students during first activity • Collect work product at end of first activity • Monitor second activity • Debrief by sharing additional examples on overhead while monitoring • Lead second "flash" round review, following Ms. Kurtz's model
What are the specific tasks that I do AFTER the lesson?	• Given that there are no permanent student products to examine, no follow-up-tasks are planned or anticipated	• Given that there are no permanent student products to examine, no follow-up tasks are planned or anticipated

Where, when, and how do co-teachers debrief and evaluate the outcomes of the lesson?

After the lesson, we will set a time prior to the next day's lesson to meet to debrief and make any necessary adjustments.

211

Resource F   Elementary Team-Teaching Co-Teaching Lesson Plan

Date: One class meeting period

Co-Teachers: Ms. Gilpatrick, classroom teacher
(Names)

Ms. Nugent, speech and language therapist

Content Area(s): Reasoning

Lesson Objectives:

Given co-teacher guidance in using the steps of the SODAS problem-solving process, students will practice generating options and settling on a solution for a common playground problem.

Language Objectives:

Listens to peers and orally expresses ideas through oral generation of potential solutions to problems.

Content Standards Addressed:

Reasoning and Problem-Solving Standard 2.2: Students use reasoning strategies, knowledge, and common sense to solve complex problems related to all fields of knowledge.[4]

Underline the Co-Teaching Approach(es) Used:

Supportive   Parallel   Complementary   Team

What is the *room arrangement?* Will other spaces outside of the classroom be used?

Students are seated in a semicircle on the carpet facing their co-teachers, who use an overhead projector to display the SODAS steps and student responses on the wall.

What *materials* do the co-teachers and/or students need?

An overhead projector, overhead markers, transparencies of the SODAS format for recording student responses, and a box with a number of playground problem scenarios written on 3 × 5 index cards.

How is student *learning assessed* by co-teachers?

Co-teachers observe student engagement and participation at each step of the SODAS process.

What specific supports, aids, or services do *select students* need?

No additional supports, aids, or services are needed.

What does each co-teacher do before, during, and after the lesson?

Co-Teacher Name	Ms. Gilpatrick, classroom teacher	Ms. Nugent, speech and language therapist
What are the specific tasks that I do BEFORE the lesson?	• Meet beforehand to plan the weekly class meeting and agree on the problem-solving process (i.e., SODAS)	• Meet beforehand to plan the weekly class meeting and agree on the problem-solving process (i.e., SODAS) • Prepare playground problem scenarios and SODAS materials
What are the specific tasks that I do DURING the lesson?	1) Convene and clarify objective of the class meeting 3) Randomly select a problem from the problem-solving box 5) Call on student to identify the problem 7) Share responsibility calling on students to identify options 9) Discuss with Ms. Nugent disadvantages to Option 1, and record agreed-on disadvantages 11) Call on students to share disadvantages 13) Rotate roles of facilitator and recorder for remaining disadvantages 14) Model with Ms. Nugent a discussion of advantages of Option 1, and record the agreed-on advantages 15) Facilitate discussion of student-generated advantages 18) Tally student responses about worst disadvantages 19) Facilitate student discussion and identification of best advantages 21) Facilitate partner discussion and sharing of best solution(s) 24) Share an example of how she has used SODAS in her life	2) Ask students to identify the problem 4) Record problem situation on the overhead 6) Ask students to identify options for solving the problem 7) Share responsibility calling on students to identify options 8) Record student responses on the overhead 9) Discuss with Ms. Gilpatrick disadvantages of Option 1 10) Prompt students to discuss disadvantages of other options 12) Record student-generated disadvantages 13) Rotate roles of facilitator and recorder for remaining disadvantages 14) Model with Ms. Gilpatrick a discussion of advantages of Option 1 16) Record student-generated list of advantages for each option 17) Facilitate student discussion and identification of worst disadvantages 20) Tally student responses about best advantages 22) Tally students' best solution responses 23) Facilitate discussion about use of SODAS at school and home 25) Share an example of how she has used SODAS in her personal life, and tell students they will be using this process throughout the year
What are the specific tasks that I do AFTER the lesson?	• Meet to debrief the class meeting	• Meet to debrief the class meeting

Where, when, and how do co-teachers debrief and evaluate the outcomes of the lesson?

Do a quick check-in during our common lunch period.

Date: Three consecutive days

Co-Teachers: Mr. Jeffries, fourth-grade classroom teacher

(Names) Ms. Katz, paraprofessional

Content Area(s): Language arts

Lesson Objectives:

Given lecture, guided practice, and numerous examples, students develop their own stories with attention to character development and plot.

Language Objectives:

Speaking-Listening Standard 5.3: Summarize the points a speaker makes and explain how each claim is supported by reasons and evidence.[5]

Content Standards Addressed:

Writing Standard 5.3: Write narratives to develop real or imagined experiences or events using effective technique, descriptive details, and clear event sequences. 5.3.a. Orient the reader by establishing a situation and introducing a narrator and/or characters; organize an event sequence that unfolds naturally. 5.3.b. Use narrative techniques, such as dialogue, description, and pacing, to develop experiences and events or show the responses of characters to situations.[5]

Underline the Co-Teaching Approach(es) Used:

<u>Supportive</u>   <u>Parallel</u>   <u>Complementary</u>   Team Teaching

What is the *room arrangement*? Will other spaces outside of the classroom be used?

Students initially are seated in table arrangements of four. Following the opening of the lesson, students are assigned to one of three stations. Over the course of 3 days, all students rotate through all three stations.

What *materials* do the co-teachers and/or students need?

Co-teachers need a variety of books at different reading levels. They use computers, text-to-speech software, and Alpha Smart technology. Paper, colored markers, and paint also are collected.

How is student *learning assessed* by co-teachers?

Co-teachers assess student engagement, participation, knowledge, and products from each station. In addition, behavior checklists are used to assess behavior for Andreas and Wendy.

What specific supports, aids, or services do *select students* need?
No additional supports, aids, or services are needed.

What does each co-teacher do before, during, and after the lesson?

Co-Teacher Name	Mr. Jeffries, classroom teacher	Ms. Katz, paraprofessional
What are the specific tasks that I do BEFORE the lesson?	• Meet beforehand with Ms. Katz, Ms. Hoosokawa, the Title I teacher, the ESL teacher, and the gifted and talented consultant to select appropriate materials for diverse learners • Assign students to groups	• Meet beforehand with Mr. Jeffries, Ms. Hoosokawa, the Title I teacher, the ESL teacher, and the gifted and talented consultant to select appropriate materials for diverse learners • Assign students to groups
What are the specific tasks that I do DURING the lesson?	• Greet students as they enter • Open lesson with anticipatory set, minilecture, and reading • Prompt Wendy to solicit peer support before adult support • Day 1 and 2: Facilitate Station 1 (students all read the same book) • Day 3: Facilitate Station 3 (students write and illustrate their own stories) • Monitor Station 2 (independent station) • Check behavioral data and send home to Andreas's and Wendy's families	• Greet students as they enter • Add comments, ask questions, record, and illustrate while Mr. Jeffries leads discussion • Assign students to stations • Prompt Wendy to solicit peer support before adult support • Provide support to Andreas and Wendy, if needed • Day 1 and 2: Facilitate Station 3 (students write and illustrate their own stories) • Day 3: Facilitate Station 1 (students all read the same book) • Monitor Station 2 (independent station) • Record Andreas's and Wendy's behavioral data daily
What are the specific tasks that I do AFTER the lesson?	• Meet to debrief daily after the lessons • Select materials to include in student portfolios	• Meet to debrief daily after the lessons

Where, when, and how do co-teachers debrief and evaluate the outcomes of the lesson?

Mr. Jeffries and Ms. Katz meet to plan the next lesson sequence in a weekly 45-minute planning meeting.

Date: Daily 10-minute sessions

Co-Teachers: Elaine, third-grade classroom teacher; Laurie, special educator;
(Names)

Dave, third-grade student; Juan, third-grade student

Content Area(s): Third-grade math

Lesson Objectives:

Given six math facts per session (four known and two unknown or not yet mastered) and a 10-minute daily practice session with a peer tutor, students will participate in learning activities that match various learning styles (e.g., auditory, visual, kinesthetic) until mastery occurs.

Language Objectives:

Partners alternately speak to solve an operation and listen to their partner's solving of an operation.

Content Standards Addressed:

Mathematics, Operations and Algebraic Thinking Standard 3.0A Represent and solve problems involving multiplication and division . . . 3.4A Determine the unknown whole number in a multiplication or division equation relating three whole numbers. *For example, determine the unknown whole number that makes the equation true in each of the equations, $8 \times ? = 48, 5 = ?/3, 6 \times 6 = ?^6$.*

Underline the Co-Teaching Approach(es) Used:

Supportive   Parallel   Complementary   Team Teaching

What is the *room arrangement?* Will other spaces outside of the classroom be used?

Students sit at their desks or on the floor so that they are face to face in order to show the math facts in such way that each student can see the fact without seeing the answer printed on the back. They need room to lay out the flashcards for activities such as Concentration, Jump Rope Number Facts (they chant the fact as they jump rope), and Math Facts Raps (they develop raps based on the particular facts they are acquiring).

What *materials* do the co-teachers and/or students need?

Student co-teachers need their own stack of math facts, a checklist to record accuracy, a pencil, a graph to display the daily percentage or number correct, an oven timer to set the 10-minute time frame, and directions printed on 3 × 5 cards for the learning activities.

How is student learning assessed by co-teachers?

Student co-teachers match their partner's response to the answer on the back of the math fact flashcard. They give immediate correction for errors and/or immediate praise for correct responses. They check off the selected learning activities that were practiced each day.

What specific supports, aids, or services do select students need?

Select students (Dave and Juan) each have a learning contract that supports each of them to practice giving and receiving positive feedback (e.g., saying nice things, saying thank you).

What does each co-teacher do before, during, and after the lesson?

Co-Teacher Name	Elaine, third-grade classroom teacher	Laurie, special educator	Dave, third-grade student	Juan, third-grade student
What are the specific tasks that I do BEFORE the lesson?	• Make sure the oven timers are working and available • For a part of the student roster, check to make sure the sets of math cards include four known and two unknown facts	• For the other part of the student roster, check to make sure the sets of math cards include four known and two unknown facts	• Collect and bring to the session his set of math cards and the daily checklist to record progress	• Collect and bring to the session his set of math cards and the daily checklist to record progress
What are the specific tasks that I do DURING the lesson?	• Conduct on-the-spot monitoring of student co-teacher pairs	• Conduct on-the-spot monitoring of student co-teacher pairs	• Show math flashcard to partner • Model correct answer for the partner • Encourage partner to imitate the model • Praise and go on to next math fact • Encourage variety of learning activities	• Show math flashcard to partner • Model correct answer for the partner • Encourage partner to imitate the model • Praise and go on to next math fact • Encourage variety of learning activities
What are the specific tasks that I do AFTER the lesson?	• Spot check accuracy of records and graphs and, for Dave and Juan, the quality of their exchanges	• Spot check accuracy of records and graphs and, for Dave and Juan, the quality of their exchanges	• Enter number or percent correct on graph • Celebrate successes	• Enter number or percent correct on graph • Celebrate successes

Where, when, and how do co-teachers debrief and evaluate the outcomes of the lesson?

There are brief conferences with specific reciprocal co-teacher partners on a rotating basis—at least once a week to review portfolio of math facts acquired, check on the tutorial exchanges, problem solve, and celebrate.

Resource I   Levels of Student Support

- Classroom Companion—One or more classmates support another student's participation in academic or elective classes. Support may include helping with mobility to and from class, carrying or remembering materials, taking notes, assisting in task completion, facilitating communication, and being a role model for social/friendship interaction.

- Consultation—Support staff meet regularly with general education teacher to keep track of student progress, assess need for supplemental materials, problem solve, and maintain positive and open communication. Students know that they can stop in or request assistance from support staff on a specific assignment or for general support.

- Stop-In Support—Support staff observe students on a regular or periodic basis to determine possible needs, provide suggestions for curricular and instructional adaptations, and/or set up peer-support systems. They maintain open communication with the classroom teacher and the students.

- Part-Time Daily Support—Support staff provide support to students at a predetermined time, on a rotating basis, or for specific assignments or activities. They should maintain awareness of curriculum and assignments in order to encourage student productivity and provide additional tutorial or organizational support. Staff may also supply supplemental materials for classroom use.

- In-Class Co-Teaching Support—A support staff member (e.g., special educator) is partnered for co-teaching to assist all students by moving around the room and providing support as needed, teaching small groups, or complementing instruction. Support staff collaborate with the general education teacher to develop and plan for specific support strategies and student needs.

- Total Staff Support—A support staff member (e.g., paraprofessional) is assigned to support one or more target students, usually with significant academic or behavioral needs. Support staff may be in close proximity with the target student(s), facilitating interaction with classmates and the curriculum, and may assume responsibility for modifying, developing, or acquiring materials that support student engagement and success.

Resource J   Administrator Actions to Promote Co-Teaching

Directions: Check off the items that have been attended to or accomplished.

___ Publicly articulate the rationale for co-teaching.

___ Redefine staff roles (i.e., in the job description of classroom teachers and support personnel) so that all are expected to participate in collaborative planning and teaching.

___ Assess the staff's need for collaboration (e.g., With whom do I need to collaborate to successfully adapt instruction? From which colleagues can I acquire skills through modeling and coaching?).

___ Create a master schedule that allows for collaboration (e.g., common planning and lunch periods).

___ Change the length of the workday or school year (e.g., provide teachers with 220-day instead of 185-day contracts, early dismissal of students).

___ Establish professional support groups to help staff learn about and begin to practice co-teaching.

___ Provide time for co-teachers to meet by relieving them of noninstructional duties that other staff who are not co-teaching are required to perform (e.g., bus duty, lunchroom supervision).

___ Provide training in collaborative planning (e.g., courses and workshops, mentoring and peer coaching systems, job shadowing, clinical supervision, pairing of new co-teaching teams with veteran co-teaching teams).

___ Educate school and community members about the accomplishments of collaborative planning and teaching teams.

___ Periodically provide additional time for co-teaching teams to meet (e.g., hire substitutes, use inservice time, provide release time).

___ Provide incentives for co-teaching (e.g., recognize co-teaching teams' accomplishments; offer additional training; provide release time for co-teaching teams to observe one another teaching, attend conferences, and make presentations about their accomplishments).

Resource k Action Plan Template

	Activities • Major activities • Chronological order • Preparation steps • Implementation steps	Success Measure "We will know we are successful if . . . • What is measured? • Who will measure? • When to measure?	Responsible Person(s)	Date	Outcomes
Build Consensus for a Vision of Co-Teaching					
Skill Development					
Incentives					
Resources					

220

Resource L   Co-Teaching Planning Meeting Agenda Format

People Present	Absentees	Others Who Need to Know

Roles	This Meeting	Next Meeting
Timekeeper		
Recorder		
Other _____		

Agenda

Agenda Items	Time Limit
1. Review agenda and positive comments	5 minutes
2.	
3.	
4. Processing of task and relationships	5 minutes

Minutes of Outcomes

Action Items	Persons Responsible	By When
1. The way we will communicate outcomes to absent members and others		
2.		
3.		

Agenda Building for Next Meeting

Date: _____   Time: _____   Location: _____

Expected Agenda Items

1.

2.

3.

Resource M   Self-Assessment: Are We Really Co-Teachers?

Directions: Check *Yes* or *No* for statements to determine your co-teaching score at this point in time.

Yes	No	In our co-teaching partnership:
		1. We decide which co-teaching approach we are going to use in a lesson based on the benefits to the students and the co-teachers.
		2. We share ideas, information, and materials.
		3. We identify the resources and talents of the co-teachers.
		4. We teach different groups of students at the same time.
		5. We are aware of what one another is doing even when we are not directly in one another's presence.
		6. We share responsibility for deciding what to teach.
		7. We agree on the curriculum standards that will be addressed in a lesson.
		8. We share responsibility for deciding how to teach.
		9. We share responsibility for deciding who teaches what part of a lesson.
		10. We are flexible and make changes as needed during a lesson.
		11. We identify student strengths and needs.
		12. We share responsibility for differentiating instruction.
		13. We include other people when their expertise or experience is needed.
		14. We share responsibility for how student learning is assessed.
		15. We can show that students are learning when we co-teach.
		16. We agree on discipline procedures and jointly carry them out.
		17. We give feedback to one another on what goes on in the classroom.
		18. We make improvements in our lessons based on what happens.

Yes	No	In our co-teaching partnership:
		19. We communicate freely our concerns.
		20. We have a process for resolving our disagreements and use it when faced with problems and conflicts.
		21. We celebrate the process of co-teaching and the outcomes and successes.
		22. We have fun with the students and each other when we co-teach.
		23. We have regularly scheduled times to meet and discuss our work.
		24. We use our meeting time productively.
		25. We can effectively co-teach even when we don't have time to plan.
		26. We explain the benefits of co-teaching to the students and their families.
		27. We model collaboration and teamwork for our students.
		28. We are both viewed by our students as their teachers.
		29. We include students in the co-teaching role.
		30. We depend on one another to follow through on tasks and responsibilities.
		31. We seek and enjoy additional training to make our co-teaching better.
		32. We are mentors to others who want to co-teach.
		33. We can use a variety of co-teaching approaches (i.e., supportive, parallel, complementary, team)
		34. We communicate our need for logistical support and resources to our administrators.

TOTAL YES: _____ **NO:** _____

Resource N   Checklist of Skills for the Stages of Co-Teacher Development

Skills for the Forming Stage

_____ Use co-teachers' preferred names

_____ Use no put-downs

_____ Come to co-teacher meetings on time, and stay for the entire time

_____ Follow through on agreements (show I am trustworthy)

_____ Acknowledge co-teachers for their follow-through

Skills for the Functioning Stage

_____ State and restate the purpose of co-teaching

_____ Set or call attention to the time limits

_____ Suggest procedures for how to do the task effectively

_____ Express support and acceptance verbally

_____ Express support and acceptance nonverbally

_____ Paraphrase and clarify

_____ Energize co-teachers with humor, ideas, or enthusiasm

_____ Describe feelings when appropriate

Skills for the Formulating Stage

____ Summarize what has been said

____ Seek accuracy by correcting or adding to the summary

____ Seek connections to other knowledge

____ Seek clever ways to remember ideas, facts, and decisions

____ Ask co-teachers to explain their reasoning

____ Ask co-teachers to plan aloud

Skills for the Fermenting Stage

____ Criticize ideas without criticizing people

____ Differentiate ideas when there is disagreement

____ Integrate different ideas into a single position

____ Probe by asking questions that lead to deeper understanding

____ Suggest new answers and ideas

____ Think of new ways to resolve differences of opinion

Resource O   Instructional Observation Form

Instructor(s):	Observer:	Date:	Room #:	Period/Time:	Scheduled: ☐ Yes ☐ No
Grade:	Subject:	# of Students: present absent	# of SpEd:	# TAG:	# ELL:

Content

Instructional Objective/Learning Outcome(s):	
Language Objective: ☐ Reading ☐ Writing ☐ Speaking ☐ Listening	
Purpose Posted for Students to See ☐ Yes ☐ No	Objective Referenced ☐ Yes ☐ No
Differentiated Materials ☐ Yes ☐ No	

Product

☐ Yes	☐ No	Learning outcomes demonstrated in multiple ways
☐ Yes	☐ No	Learning outcomes measured in a variety of ways
☐ Yes	☐ No	Criteria for success explained

Process

Co-Teaching Approaches ☐ N/A ☐ Supportive ☐ Parallel ☐ Complementary ☐ Team	
Bell-to-Bell Instruction ☐ Yes ☐ No	Transition times are smooth ☐ Yes ☐ No
Think time provided ☐ Yes ☐ No ☐ N/A	Directions Clear ☐ Yes ☐ No ☐ Mostly
Checked for understanding of concepts/ principles/facts ☐ Yes ☐ No	Checked for understanding of directions ☐ Yes ☐ No
Active student engagement ☐ Low ☐ Medium ☐ High	
Teacher asks higher-level-thinking questions ☐ Yes ☐ No ☐ N/A	
Students ask higher-level-thinking questions ☐ Yes ☐ No ☐ N/A	
Called on learners who didn't volunteer ☐ Yes ☐ No ☐ N/A	

Utilized Think-Pair-Share and other quick cooperative structures ☐ Yes ☐ No	
Frequency ☐ Low ☐ Medium ☐ High	
☐ Formal ☐ Informal	

Students required to speak in complete sentences ☐ Yes ☐ No

Level of teacher talk ☐ Low ☐ Medium ☐ High

Level of student talk ☐ Low ☐ Medium ☐ High

Students engaged in academic dialogue ☐ Yes ☐ No

Level ☐ Low ☐ Medium ☐ High

Teacher(s) was/were in control of the classroom ☐ Yes ☐ No

Positive behavior support strategies employed ☐ Yes ☐ No

Degree used ☐ Low ☐ Medium ☐ High

Feeling Tone/Climate

☐ Positive ☐ Slightly Positive ☐ Neutral ☐ Slightly Negative ☐ Negative

Adapted lectures ☐ Yes ☐ No _____

Activity based ☐ Yes ☐ No _____

Simulation/role play ☐ Yes ☐ No _____

21st-century technology in the hands of teacher ☐ Yes ☐ No

21st-century technology in the hands of the students ☐ Yes ☐ No

Stations ☐ Yes ☐ No _____

Lecture/pencil-paper tasks ☐ Yes ☐ No _____

Whole group ☐ Yes ☐ No	Research-based strategies
Independent ☐ Yes ☐ No	☐ Yes ☐ No
Small group ☐ Yes ☐ No	Application of concepts from multiple intelligence theory
Partner work ☐ Yes ☐ No	☐ Yes ☐ No
Cooperative group learning ☐ Yes ☐ No	All students monitored through the lesson
Teacher-directed small groups ☐ Yes ☐ No	☐ Yes ☐ No
Instructional sequence	

Comments:

_____

_____

_____

Resource P Instructional Postconference Form

Name(s) _____ Date _____ Time _____

Teacher(s) identified "things that went well":	Teacher(s) identified "things that they would do differently":	Length of time co-teaching:
		Teacher-identified approaches used: Supportive Parallel Complementary Team
		Observer-identified approaches used: Supportive Parallel Complementary Team
		Planning Time
		Length: _____
		Frequency: _____

| Observer-identified *things that went well:* | Observer wonderings: |
| | |

Suggestions:

Teacher(s)-identified next steps / *takeaways:*

Resource Q Co-Teaching Tracking Form

Week of: _____

	Supportive	Parallel	Complementary	Team	Additional Notes
Monday					
Tuesday					
Wednesday					
Thursday					
Friday					
Notes and Plans for Next Week					

(Continued)

Use this tool to monitor, plan, and document your co-teaching experiences.

Supportive—One co-teacher takes the lead instructional role, and the others rotate among the students providing support. The co-teacher(s) taking the supportive role watches or listens as students work together, stepping in to provide assistance when necessary, while the other co-teacher continues to direct the lesson. The roles of lead and supportive co-teacher can be alternated.

Parallel—Two or more people work with or monitor different groups of students at the same time in different sections of the classroom. Co-teachers may rotate among the groups, and sometimes there may be one group of students that works without a co-teacher for at least part of the time.

Complementary—All co-teachers have a role teaching the whole group. One may introduce the new academic content while the other makes it more accessible through complementary instruction (e.g., modeling how to take notes using different examples or analogies, paraphrasing, creating visuals).

Team—Co-teachers equitably share responsibility for what one teacher otherwise would have performed alone, namely, planning, teaching, and assessing the instruction of all assigned students. Co-teachers are comfortable using and do use each co-teaching approach based on the needs of students and the demands of the lesson.

Resource R   Co-Teaching Differentiation Lesson Planning Matrix

When co-teachers plan for instruction for each block of instructional time, they also plan the co-teaching approaches they will use based on the differentiation needs of their students. This graphic organizer is a tool designed to *facilitate the planning conversation* for co-teaching. Writing in the graphic organizer is *optional*. The tool prompts co-teachers to:

1. identify what and how content is being taught in each instructional block

2. identify differentiation needs of students

3. identify the co-teaching approach(es) that best allow for instruction and differentiation

4. describe what the actions of each co-teacher will be when executing instruction and the co-teaching approach

For each time block, what/how are we teaching?	What are differentiated instructional needs of our students?	Which co-teaching approach(es) will we use?	COOPERATING TEACHER What will I do? (If one is doing this . . .)	TEACHER CANDIDATE What will I do? (The other is doing this . . .)
		Supportive Parallel Complementary Team		
		Supportive Parallel Complementary Team		
		Supportive Parallel Complementary Team		
		Supportive Parallel Complementary Team		
		Supportive Parallel Complementary Team		
		Supportive Parallel Complementary Team		

■ NOTES

1. California Grade 12 Principles of American Democracy Standard 12.1.5. Retrieved from http://www.cde.ca.gov/be/st/ss/.

2. *Common Core State Standards for English Language Arts & Literacy in History/ Social Studies, Science, and Technical Subjects* Grade 2 Vocabulary Acquisition and Use, Standard 4d. Retrieved from http://www.corestandards.org/the-standards.

3. *Common Core State Standards for English Language Arts & Literacy in History/ Social Studies, Science, and Technical Subjects* Grade 7 Vocabulary Acquisition and Use Language Standard. Retrieved from http://www.corestandards.org/the-standards.

4. *Vermont's Framework of Standards and Learning Opportunities (Fall, 2000),* Reasoning and Problem Solving Standard 2.2. Retrieved from http://education.vermont.gov/new/html/pubs/framework.html.

5. *Common Core State Standards for English Language Arts & Literacy in History/ Social Studies, Science, and Technical Subjects,* Grade 5 Speaking-Listening Standard 5.3 and Grade 5 Writing Standard 5.3, 5.3.a and 5.3.b. Retrieved from http://www.corestandards.org/the-standards.

6. *Common Core State Standards for Mathematics,* Grade 3 Operations and Algebraic Thinking Standard 3.4. Retrieved from http://www.corestandards.org/the-standards/mathematics/grade-3/operations-and-algebraic-thinking.

Glossary

active learning—This term refers to anything that involves students in doing things and thinking about the things they are doing. Active learning might include a spectrum of activities, from a modified lecture format to role playing, simulation, games, project work, cooperative problem solving, collaborative research, partner learning, service learning, and teaching others.

change agents—Change agents are those who direct reform efforts, such as a professional development director who guides inservice activities designed to help teachers learn how to co-teach effectively. Hall and Hord (2001) described six dimensions of a job description for change agents that emerged from several studies of change agents in action. The six dimensions are (1) developing, articulating, communicating a shared vision of change; (2) planning and providing resources; (3) supporting teachers' professional learning and development; (4) checking on progress in the use of the innovation; (5) providing ongoing assistance during implementation; and (6) creating a school context supportive of the innovation.

cooperative process—The cooperative process is an essential element of successful co-teaching and includes face-to-face interactions, positive interdependence, interpersonal skills, monitoring progress of the co-teachers, and individual accountability.

Common Core State Standards—Nearly all states have adopted the national Common Core State Standards, which can be found at http://www.corestandards.org. National core standards guide teachers to ensure that their students have knowledge and skills needed to be successful by providing clear goals for student learning (Wood, 2011).

complementary co-teaching—Complementary co-teaching is when co-teachers do something to enhance the instruction provided by the other co-teacher(s).

co-teaching—Co-teaching is two or more people sharing responsibility for teaching some or all of the students assigned to a classroom. It involves distribution of responsibility among people for planning, instruction, and evaluation for a classroom of students.

co-teaching clinical practice—Clinical practice or student teaching is an expected and essential dimension of any teacher preparation program, with the overarching objective of providing teacher candidates with the modeling and guided practice to demonstrate their abilities to translate educational theory into actual practice with real students in real classroom settings. Co-teaching is two or more people (i.e., cooperating teacher and credential candidate) sharing responsibility in planning for, teaching, and assessing the students assigned to them for instruction. Within a co-teaching clinical experience, the cooperating teacher gradually releases classroom responsibilities to the student teacher candidate. As partners, they engage in ongoing planning for and practice of co-teaching variations in which both collaboratively teach and assess all students throughout the clinical experience.

co-teaching lesson plan—A co-teaching lesson plan should include the essential elements of any good lesson plan, such as the content objectives, the curriculum standard(s) addressed in the lesson, the materials needed by each partner, how student learning will be assessed, and any accommodations or modifications that might be needed for particular students. In addition, the lesson plan specifies which of the four types of co-teaching arrangements the team will use, exactly what each individual co-teacher will be doing (before, during, and after the lesson), how the classroom will be arranged so each co-teacher has the space to deliver instruction, and whether instruction will be delivered by one or more co-teachers in another space outside of the classroom, such as the school library, for all or part of the lesson. Finally, the lesson plan explains where, when, and how co-teachers will debrief and evaluate the outcomes of the lesson. The lesson plan format should be set up in such a way that co-teachers can understand, implement, and use it to communicate their teaching actions to one another.

culturally responsive communication—Culturally responsive communication among co-teachers begins with having cultural competence or "the capacity to (1) value diversity, (2) conduct self-assessment, (3) manage the dynamics of difference, (4) adapt to diversity and the cultural contexts of the communities they serve" (Goode and Jackson, 2003, p. 2). An issue that co-teachers can address is "How we negotiate our differences in culturally responsive and respectful ways, especially if we do not share the same cultural heritage." This conversation can extend to being culturally responsive and responsible in interacting with children and their families.

DI—DI is an acronym for differentiated instruction. Differentiated instruction has been defined as a way for teachers to recognize and react responsively to their students' varying background knowledge, readiness, language, preferences in learning, and interests (Hall, 2002).

four approaches to co-teaching—The supplementary co-teaching approach, the parallel co-teaching approach, the complementary co-teaching approach, and team teaching.

ESEA—ESEA refers to the 2001 reauthorization of the Elementary and Secondary Education Act (ESEA; Pub. L. No. No. 107–110), commonly referred to as No Child Left Behind (NCLB). ESEA is the federal mandate for ensuring that schools and teachers are accountable for the academic progress of all students in public schools.

GATE—GATE is an acronym for gifted and talented education services that are often provided in resource rooms, separate schools, or by enhancing the general education curriculum.

IDEIA—The Individuals with Disabilities Education Improvement Act of 2004. This federal mandate empowers educators to provide services and supports within the least restrictive environment for all students with disabilities in order to provide access to the general education curriculum.

multiple intelligences—The theory of multiple intelligences (Gardner, 1983, 1997) poses the idea that there are at least eight (visual-spatial, musical, verbal-linguistic, logical-mathematical, interpersonal, intrapersonal, bodily-kinesthetic, and naturalistic) rather than only one type of intelligence. Teachers who embrace this theory stop asking, *"How smart is this student?"* and instead search for answers to the question, *"How is this student smart?"*

NCLB—See the definition of ESEA above.

paraprofessional—A paraprofessional is a school employee who delivers instructional and other support services to students and teachers and works under the supervision of professional staff who have the ultimate responsibility for the design, implementation, and evaluation of education and related services programs and student progress. A paraprofessional also may be referred to as a paraeducator, instructional aide or assistant, teacher's aide, or classroom aide or assistant.

process communication model—The process communication model (PCM) is based on the premise that people have a unique personality structure consisting of six types, with the relative strength of each type varying from person to person. When co-teachers practice the skills and strategies of the PCM, their communication can be enhanced, especially when interacting with those whose communication and personality preferences are quite different from their own (Kahler, 1982; Pauley, Bradley, and Pauley, 2002; Pauley and Pauley, 2009). PCM can create a more supportive and responsive classroom and working relationship with co-teachers who are the most difficult to reach.

RTI—RTI, an acronym for the response-to-intervention approach proposed in IDEIA 2004, allows for students to receive early intervention in general education as soon as it is detected that they are falling behind. Professional educators design and evaluate academic and behavioral interventions for students at increasing levels of intensity, depending on students' response (or lack of response) to the interventions. Graner, Faggella-Luby, and Fritschmann (2005) describe the RTI approach as having eight features: (1) high-quality classroom instruction, (2) research-based instruction, (3) classroom performance measures, (4) universal screening, (5) continuous progress monitoring, (6) research-based interventions, (7) progress monitoring during interventions, and (8) fidelity measures.

SODAS—SODAS is an acronym for the steps in a problem solving approach: *s*ituation, *o*ptions, *d*isadvantages, *a*dvantages, *s*olution.

speech and language therapists—Speech and language therapists often provide educational and therapeutic supports for students with special needs in communication and language.

stages of co-teacher development—As with the stages of group development, co-teachers should expect to experience and need different communication skills depending on whether they are just beginning (forming), deciding on how they'll work together (functioning), working through the problems they might face (formulating), or managing conflicts of ideas or procedures about what to emphasize or how to teach certain students (fermenting). The social interaction and communication skills they use at each of these stages will facilitate the development of their cohesiveness as a co-teaching team.

supportive co-teaching—Supportive co-teaching occurs when one teacher takes the lead instructional role and the other(s) rotate among the students providing support.

teaching—If you consult any dictionary, you will find a plethora of examples of the meanings that the English language attributes to the word *teaching*. For example, to teach is to impart knowledge or skills. To teach is to give instruction. To teach is to cause to learn by experience or example. To teach is to advocate or preach. On the other hand, to instruct or to tutor or to train or to educate implies methodological knowledge in addition to content knowledge.

team teaching—Team teaching occurs when two or more people do what the traditional teacher has always done—plan, teach, assess, and assume responsibility for all of the students in the classroom.

zone of proximal development—The zone of proximal development (ZPD) refers to an individual child's potential level of learning if helped by a teacher or peer. A ZPD is defined as a particular range of ability with and without assistance from a teacher or a more capable peer (Vygotsky, 1987). To scaffold students effectively within their ZPDs, a teacher should also have an awareness of the various roles students and teachers assume throughout the co-teaching process: teacher or peer models behavior for the student; student imitates the teacher's or peer's behavior; teacher or peer fades out instruction; student practices reciprocal teaching (scaffolding others) until the skill is mastered. Vygotsky emphasized that what children can do with the assistance of others is even more indicative of their mental development than what they can do alone.

References

PART I: INTRODUCTION TO CO-TEACHING ■

Chapter 1: What Is Co-Teaching?

Brandt, R. 1987. On cooperation in schools: A conversation with David and Roger Johnson. *Educational Leadership* 45(3): 14–19.

Devecchi, C., and A. Nevin. 2010. Leadership for inclusive schools and inclusive school leadership. In *Global perspectives on educational leadership reform: The development and preparation of leaders of learning and learners of leadership,* ed. Anthony H. Normore, Advances in Educational Administration, Volume 11, 211–241. Bingley, UK: Emerald Group Publishing Limited.

Fishbaugh, M. S. E. 2000. *The collaboration guide for early career educators.* Baltimore, MD: Paul H. Brookes Company.

Fishbaugh, M. S. E. 1997. *Models of collaboration.* Needham Heights, MA: Allyn & Bacon.

Friend, M., and L. Cook. 2009. *Interactions: Collaboration skills for school professionals.* 6th ed. Upper Saddle River, NJ: Prentice Hall.

Hehir, T., and L. Katzman. 2012. *Effective inclusive schools: Designing successful schoolwide programs.* Hoboken, NJ: Jossey-Bass.

Hourcade, J., and J. Bauwens. 2002. *Cooperative teaching: Rebuilding and sharing the schoolhouse.* Austin, TX: PRO-ED.

Idol, L., A. Nevin, and P. Paolucci-Whitcomb. 2000. *Collaborative consultation.* 3rd ed. Austin, TX: PRO-ED.

Johnson, D. W., and R. T. Johnson. 2009. An educational psychology success story: Social interdependence theory and cooperative learning. *Educational Researcher* 38(5): 365–379.

Johnson, D. W., and R. T. Johnson. 1999. *Learning together and alone: Cooperative, competitive, and individualistic learning.* 5th ed. Needham Heights, MA: Allyn & Bacon.

National Center for Educational Restructuring and Inclusion. 1995. *National study on inclusive education.* New York: City University of New York.

Skrtic, T. 1991. *Behind special education: A critical analysis of professional culture and school organization.* Denver, CO: Love.

Villa, R., and J. Thousand. 2004. *Creating an inclusive school.* 2nd ed. Alexandria, VA: Association for Supervision and Curriculum Development.

Villa, R. A., and J. Thousand. 2011. *RTI: Co-teaching & differentiated instruction.* Port Chester, NY: National Professional Resources, Inc.

Chapter 2: Why Co-Teach?
What History, Law, and Research Say

Arguelles, M. E., M. T. Hughes, and J. S. Schumm. 2000. Co-teaching: A different approach to co-teaching. *Principal* 79(4): 48, 50–51.

Bahamonde, C., and M. Friend. 1999. Teaching English language learners: A proposal for effective service delivery through collaboration and co-teaching. *Journal of Educational and Psychological Consultation* 10(1): 1–9.

Bauwens, J., J. J. Hourcade, and M. Friend. 1989. Cooperative teaching: A model for general and special education integration. *Remedial and Special Education* 10(2): 17–22.

Blackorby, J., M. Wagner, R. Camero, E. Davies, P. Levine, L. Newman, C. Marder, and C. Sumi. 2005. *Engagement, academics, social adjustments, and independence.* Palo Alto, CA: SRI.

Brisca-Vega, R., K. Brown, and D. Yasutake. 2011. Science achievement of students in co-taught inquiry-based classrooms. *Learning Disabilities: A Multidisciplinary Journal* 17(1): 23–31.

Caywood, K. D., and S. I. Fordyce. 2006. *Facilitation of language skills via co-teaching model to integrate children with autism.* Paper presented at the annual conference of the Teacher Education Division of the Council for Exceptional Children, San Diego, CA.

Compton, M. V., A. Stratton, A. Maier, C. Meyers, H. Scott, and T. Tomlinson. 1998. It takes two: Co-teaching for deaf and hard of hearing students in rural schools. In *Coming together: Preparing for rural special education in the 21st century,* ed. D. Montgomery, 204–9. (ERIC Document Reproduction Service No. ED417901)

Cramer, E., A. Liston, A. Nevin, and J. Thousand. 2010. Co-teaching in urban secondary school districts to meet the needs of all teachers and learners: Implications for teacher education reform. *International Journal of Whole Schooling* 6(2): 59–75.

Cramer, E. D., and A. I. Nevin. 2006. A mixed methodology analysis of co-teacher assessments: Implications for teacher education. *Teacher Education and Special Education* 30(1): 261–274.

Cramer, E., A. Nevin, L. Salazar, and K. Landa. 2006. Co-teaching in an urban, multicultural setting: Research report. *Florida Educational Leadership* 7(1): 43–50.

Dieker, L. 1998. Rationale for co-teaching. *Social Studies Review* 37(2): 62–65.

Dieker, L., and W. Murawski. 2003. Co-teaching at the secondary level: Unique issues, current trends, and suggestions for success. *High School Journal* 86(4): 1–13.

Dove, M., and A. Honigsfeld. 2010. ESL co-teaching and collaboration: Opportunities to develop teacher leadership and enhance student learning. *Teaching English to Speakers of Other Languages (TESOL) Journal* 1(1): 3–22.

Duke, D., B. Showers, and M. Imber. 1980. Teachers and shared decision making: The costs and benefits of involvement. *Educational Administration Quarterly* 16: 93–106.

Garrigan, C. M., and J. S. Thousand. 2005. The effects of co-teaching on student achievement in the reading domain. *New Hampshire Journal of Education* 8: 56–60.

Glasser, W. 1999. *Choice theory: A new psychology of personal freedom.* New York: Perennial.

Hourcade, J., and J. Bauwens. 2002. *Cooperative teaching: Rebuilding and sharing the schoolhouse.* Austin, TX: PRO-ED.

Johnson, D. W., and F. F. Johnson. 2005. *Joining together: Group theory and skills.* 9th ed. Needham Heights, MA: Allyn & Bacon.

Kluwin, T. N. 1999. Coteaching deaf and hearing students: Research on social integration. *American Annals of the Deaf* 144(4): 339–344.

Luckner, J. 1999. An examination of two co-teaching classrooms. *American Annals of the Deaf* 144(1): 24–34.

Magiera, K., C. Smith, N. Zigmond, and K. Gebauer. 2005. Benefits of co-teaching in secondary mathematics classes. *Teaching Exceptional Children* 37(3): 20–24.

Mahoney, M. 1997. Small victories in an inclusive classroom. *Educational Leadership* 54(7): 59–62.

Miller, A., Valasky, W., and P. Molloy. 1998. Learning together: The evolution of an inclusive class. *Active Learner: A Foxfire Journal for Teachers* 3(2): 14–16.

Nevin, A., J. Thousand, P. Paolucci-Whitcomb, and R. Villa. 1990. Collaborative consultation: Empowering public school personnel to provide heterogeneous schooling for all. *Journal of Educational and Psychological Consultation* 1(1): 41–67.

Pardini, P. (2006). One voice: Mainstream and ELL teachers work side-by-side in the classroom teaching language through content. *Journal of Staff Development* 27(4): 20–25.

Pugach, M., and L. Johnson. 1995. Unlocking expertise among classroom teachers through structured dialogue: Extending research on peer collaboration. *Exceptional Children* 62(2): 101–10.

Pugach, M., and J. Winn. 2011. Research on co-teaching and teaming: An untapped resource for induction. *Journal of Special Education Leadership* 24(1): 36–46.

Rice, D., and N. Zigmond. 2000. Co-teaching in secondary schools: Teacher reports of developments in Australian and American classrooms. *Learning Disabilities Research & Practice 15:* 190–97.

Salazar, L., and A. Nevin. 2005. Co-teachers in an urban multicultural school. *Florida Educational Leadership* 5(2): 15–20.

Santamaria, L., and J. Thousand. 2004. Collaboration, co-teaching, and differentiated instruction: A process-oriented approach to whole schooling. *International Journal of Whole Schooling* 1(1): 13–27.

Schwab Learning. 2003. Collaboratively speaking: A study on effective ways to teach children with learning differences in the general education classroom. *The Special EDge* 16(3): 1–4.

Scruggs, T. A., M. A. Mastropieri, and K. A. McDuffie. 2007. Co-teaching in inclusive classrooms: A metasynthesis of qualitative research. *Exceptional Children* 73(4): 392–416

Skrtic, T. 1987. The national inquiry into the future of education for students with special needs. *Counterpoint* 4(7): 6.

Thousand, J., A. Nevin, and W. Fox. 1987. Inservice training to support education of learners with severe handicaps in their local public schools. *Teacher Education and Special Education* 10(1): 4–14.

Thousand, J., R. Villa, and A. Nevin. 2007. Collaborative teaching: Critique of the scientific evidence. In *Handbook of special education research,* ed. L. Florian, 417–28. London: Sage.

Thousand, J., R. Villa, A. Nevin, and P. Paolucci-Whitcomb. 1995. A rationale and vision for collaborative consultation. In *Controversial issues confronting special education: Divergent perspectives,* 2nd ed., ed. W. Stainback and S. Stainback, 223–32. Baltimore: Paul H. Brookes.

Trent, S. 1998. False starts and other dilemmas of a secondary general education collaborative teacher: A case study. *Journal of Learning Disabilities 31:* 503–13.

U.S. Department of Education. 2010. *Twenty-ninth annual report to Congress on the implementation of the Individuals with Disabilities Education Act, 2007, vol. 1.* Washington, DC: United Sates Department of Education.

Van Garderen, D., M. Stormont, and N. Goel. 2012. Collaboration between general and special educators and student outcomes: A need for more research. *Psychology in the Schools* 49(5): 483–97.

Vaughn, S., B. E. Elbaum, J. S. Schumm, J.S., and M. T. Hughes. 1998. Social outcomes for students with and without learning disabilities in inclusive classrooms. *Journal of Learning Disabilities* 31(5): 428–436.

Villa, R., K. Braney, R. Haniford, B. Livingston, C. Meyer, R. Hamasaki, and R. Fernandez. 2012, February. *Inclusive practices in Boulder Valley School District: All means all—session 3: Systems perspective—building principals.* Paper presented at the

2012 PEAK Parent Center Conference of Inclusive Education: Opening Doors to Curriculum, Classmates, and Community, Denver, CO.

Villa, R., and J. Thousand. 2004. *Creating an inclusive school.* 2nd ed. Alexandria, VA: Association for Supervision and Curriculum Development.

Villa, R. A., and J. Thousand. 2011. *RTI: Co-teaching & differentiated instruction.* Port Chester, NY: National Professional Resources, Inc.

Villa, R., J. Thousand, A. Nevin, and C. Malgeri. 1996. Instilling collaboration for inclusive schooling as a way of doing business in public education. *Remedial and Special Education 17:* 169–81.

Villa, R. A., J. S. Thousand, A. I. Nevin, and A. Liston. 2005. Successful inclusion practices in middle and secondary schools. *American Secondary Education Journal 33*(3): 33–50.

Villa, R. A., and J. Thousand. 2011. *RTI: Co-teaching & differentiated instruction.* Port Chester, NY: National Professional Resources, Inc.

Walther-Thomas, C. 1997. Co-teaching experiences: The benefits and problems that teachers and principals report over time. *Journal of Learning Disabilities 30:* 395–407.

Welch, M. 2000. Descriptive analysis of team teaching in two elementary classrooms: A formative experimental approach. *Remedial and Special Education 21:* 366–76.

Wilson, G. L., and Michaels, C. A. 2006. General and special education students' perceptions of co-teaching: Implications for secondary-level literacy instruction. *Reading & Writing Quarterly: Overcoming Learning Difficulties 22*(3): 205–25.

Zigmond, N. 2004. Research findings paint dark picture of co-teaching. *Inclusive Education Programs 11*(9): 1–3, 6.

Chapter 3: The Day-to-Day Workings of Co-Teaching Teams

Friend, M. 2008. *A handbook for creating and sustaining classroom partnerships in inclusive schools.* Port Chester, NY: National Professional Resources Inc.

■ PART II: THE FOUR APPROACHES TO CO-TEACHING

Chapter 4: The Supportive Co-Teaching Approach

Doyle, M. B. 2002. *The paraprofessional's guide to inclusive education: Working as a team.* 2nd ed. Baltimore: Paul H. Brookes.

Giangreco, M. F., S. Edelman, T. E. Luiselli, and S. Z. MacFarland. 1997. Helping or hovering? Effects of instructional assistant proximity on students with disabilities. *Exceptional Children 64*(1): 7–18.

Villa, R., and J. Thousand. 2002. One divided by two or more: Redefining the role of a cooperative education team. In *Creativity and collaborative learning: The practical guide to empowering students, teachers, and families,* 2nd ed., ed. J. S. Thousand, R. A. Villa, and A. I. Nevin, 303–24. Baltimore: Paul H. Brookes.

Chapter 5: The Parallel Co-Teaching Approach

Carson, R. 2002. *Silent spring.* 40th anniv. ed. Boston: Houghton Mifflin.

European Environment Agency (EEA). 2012. *Generation '92 video competition.* Retrieved June 3, 2012, from http://campus.ecology.com/2012/05/10/eea-video-competition/

Marzano, R., D. Pickering, and J. Pollock. 2001. *Classroom instruction that works: Research-based strategies for increasing student achievement.* Alexandria, VA: Association for Supervision and Curriculum Development.

Chapter 7: The Team-Teaching Co-Teaching Approach

Armstrong, T. 2009. *Multiple intelligences in the classroom.* 3rd ed. Alexandria, VA: Association for Supervision and Curriculum Development.

Hazel, J., J. Schumaker, J. Sherman, and J. Sheldon. 1995. *ASSET: A social skills program for adolescents.* Champaign, IL: Research Press.

Marzano, R., D. Pickering, and J. Pollock. 2001. *Classroom instruction that works: Research-based strategies for increasing student achievement.* Alexandria, VA: Association for Supervision and Curriculum Development.

Vygotsky, L. 1987. *The collected works of L. S. Vygotsky.* Trans. R. W. Rieber and A. S. Carton. New York: Plenum Press. (Orig. pub. 1934, 1960).

PART III: CHANGING ROLES AND RESPONSIBILITIES ■

Chapter 8: The Role of Paraprofessionals in Co-Teaching

Ashbaker, B., and J. Morgan. 2005. *Paraprofessionals in the classroom.* Boston: Allyn & Bacon.

Bueno Center for Multicultural Education. 1997. *7 modules for para-educators in culturally and linguistically diverse classrooms.* Boulder: University of Colorado, Bilingual Special Education Training of Trainers Institute.

Downing, J., D. Ryndak, and D. Clark. 2000. Paraeducators in inclusive classrooms. *Remedial and Special Education 21:* 171–81.

Doyle, M. B. 2002. *The paraprofessional's guide to inclusive education: Working as a team.* 2nd ed. Baltimore: Paul H. Brookes.

Etscheidt, S. 2005. Paraprofessional services for students with disabilities: A legal analysis of issues. *Research and Practice for Persons With Severe Disabilities 30:* 60–80.

Fisher, M., and S. Pleasants. 2011. Roles, responsibilities, and concerns of paraeducators: Findings from a statewide survey. *Remedial and Special Education 32:* 23–28.

French, N. K. 2003. *Managing paraeducators in your school: How to hire, train, and supervise non-certified staff.* Thousand Oaks, CA: Corwin.

Gerlach, K. 2006. *Let's team up: A checklist for para-educators, teachers, and principals.* Reprint. Washington, DC: National Education Association.

Giangreco, M., C. Smith, and E. Pinckney. 2006. Addressing the paraprofessional dilemma in an inclusive classroom: A program description. *Research and Practice for Persons With Severe Disabilities 31*(3): 215–29.

Giangreco, M. F., J. C. Suter, and M. B. Doyle. 2010. Paraprofessionals in inclusive schools: A review of recent research. *Journal of Educational and Psychological Consultation 20:* 41–57.

Liston, A., A. Nevin, and I. Malian. 2009. What do paraeducators in inclusive classrooms say about their work? *Teaching Exceptional Children Plus 5*(4): 2–17. Retrieved June 16, 2012, from http://journals.cec.sped.org/tecplus/vol5/iss5/art1/

Littleton, D. M. 1998. Preparing professionals as teachers for the urban classroom: A university/school collaborative model. *Action in Teacher Education 19*(4): 149–58.

Marks, S., C. Schrader, and M. Levine. 1999. Paraeducator experiences in inclusive settings: Helping, hovering, or holding their own? *Exceptional Children 65:* 315–28.

Morgan, J., and B. Ashbaker. 2001. Work more effectively with your paraeducator. *Intervention in School and Clinic 36:* 230–31.

Morgan, R., D. Forbush, and D. Avis. 2001. *Enhancing skills of paraeducators: A video-assisted program.* 2nd ed. (ESP 2) Logan: Utah State University, Technology, Research, and Instruction in Special Education.

Mueller, P. 2002. The paraeducator paradox. *Exceptional Parent 32*(9): 64–7.

Mueller, P., and F. Murphy. 2001. Determining when a student requires para-educator support. *Teaching Exceptional Children 33*(6): 22–7.

National Center for Education Statistics. 2000. *Non-professional staff in the schools and staffing survey (SASS) and common core of data (CCD).* Working Paper 2000–13. Washington, DC: U.S. Department of Education, Office of Education Research.

National Center for Educational Statistics. 2007, June. Description and employment criteria of instructional paraprofessionals. *Institute of Education Sciences Issue Brief,* pp. 1–3. Retrieved June 15, 2012, from http://nces.ed.gov/pubs2007/2007008.pdf

Nevin, A., E. Cramer, J. Voigt, and L. Salazar. 2007. *Instructional modifications, adaptations, and accommodations of co-teachers who loop: A case study.* Paper presented at the American Educational Research Association, Special Education Research Special Interest Group, Chicago.

Nevin, A. I., J. S. Thousand, and R. A. Villa. 2008. *A guide to co-teaching with paraeducators: Practical tips for K–12 educators.* Thousand Oaks, CA: Corwin.

Olshefski, T. 2006. *Survey of paraprofessionals on assignments post–NCLB. American Federation of Teachers.* Retrieved May 12, 2012, from http://www.nrcpara.org/paranews/survey-of-paraprofessionals-on-assignments-post-nclb

Perez, J., and J. Murdock. 1999. *Investigating the effects of a paraprofessional teaching sharing behaviors to young children with special needs in an inclusive kindergarten classroom.* Dissertation, University of New Orleans: AAT 9900965, *Dissertation Abstracts International-A* 59/08, p. 2928

Pickett, A. L., and K. Gerlach, eds. 2003. *Supervising paraeducators in school settings: A team approach.* 2nd ed. Austin, TX: PRO-ED.

Pickett, A. L., M. Likins, R. Morgan, K. Gerlach, and T. Wallace. 2007. *Paraeducators in schools: Strengthening the educational team.* Austin, TX: PRO-ED.

Piletic, C., R. Davis, and A. Aschemeier. 2005. Paraeducators in physical education. *Journal of Physical Education Recreation and Dance 76*(5): 47–55.

Radaszewski-Byrne, M. 1997. Issues in the development of guidelines for the preparation and use of speech-language paraprofessionals and their Sl supervisors working in education settings. *Journal of Children's Communication Development 18*(1): 5–21.

Riggs, C., and P. Mueller. 2001. Employment and utilization of paraeducators in inclusive settings. *Journal of Special Education 35*(1): 54–62.

Rogan, P., and M. Held. 1999. Paraprofessionals in job coach roles. *Journal of the Association for Persons with Severe Handicaps 24*(4): 273–80.

Rueda, R., and P. Monzo. 2002. Apprenticeship for teaching: Professional development issues surrounding the collaborative relationship between teachers and para-educators. *Teaching and Teacher Education 18:* 503–21.

Salazar, L., and A. Nevin. 2005. Co-teachers in an urban multicultural school. *Florida Educational Leadership 5*(2): 15–20.

Torrence-Mikulecky, M., and Baber, A. 2005. *Education Commission of the States policy brief: From highly qualified to highly competent paraprofessionals: How NCLB requirements can catalyze effective program and policy development—Guidelines from the ECS Paraprofessional expert panel.* Denver, CO: Education Commission of the States.

Villa, R., and J. Thousand. 2005. *Creating an inclusive school.* 2nd ed. Alexandria, VA: Association for Supervision and Curriculum Development.

Wenger, K. J., T. Lubbes, M. Lazo, I. Azcarraga, S. Sharp, and G. Ernst-Slavit. 2004. Hidden teachers, invisible students: Lessons learned from exemplary bilingual paraprofessionals in secondary schools. *Teacher Education Quarterly* 31(1): 89–111.

Young, B. 1997. An examination of paraprofessional involvement in supporting inclusion of students with autism. *Focus on Autism and Other Developmental Disabilities* 12(1): 31–38, 48.

Chapter 9: The Role of Students as Co-Teachers

Chisholm, I. 1995. Computer use in a multicultural classroom. *Journal of Research on Computing in Education* 28: 162–74.

Conn-Powers, C. 2002. Upper elementary mathematics for a student with gifts and talents. In *Creativity and collaborative learning: The practical guide to empowering students, teachers, and families,* 2nd ed., ed. J. Thousand, R. Villa, and A. Nevin, 333–39. Baltimore: Paul H. Brookes.

Countryman, L., and M. Schroeder. 1996. When students lead parent–teacher conferences. *Educational Leadership* 53(7): 64–8.

Echevarria, J., and A. Graves. 1998. *Sheltered content instruction: Teaching English language learners with diverse abilities.* Boston: Allyn & Bacon.

Faltis, C. 1993. Critical issues in the use of sheltered content teaching in high school bilingual programs. *Peabody Journal of Education* 69: 136–51.

Fuchs, D., L. Fuchs, P. Mathes, and E. Martinez. 2002. Preliminary evidence on the social standing of students with learning disabilities in PALS and non-PALS classrooms. *Learning Disabilities Research and Practice* 17: 205–15.

Fuchs, D., L. Fuchs, A. Thompson, S. Al Otaiba, K. Nyman, N. Yang, and E. Svenson. 2000. *Strengthening kindergartners' reading readiness in Title 1 and non-Title 1 schools.* Paper presented at the Pacific Coast Research Conference, La Jolla, CA.

Garcia, E. 2002. Using instructional conversations for content area learning. In *Student cultural diversity: Understanding and meeting the challenge,* 3rd ed., 392–93. New York: Houghton Mifflin.

———. 2005. *Teaching and learning in two languages.* New York: Teachers College Press.

Thomas, W. P., and V. P. Collier. 2001. *A national study of school effectiveness for language minority students' long-term academic achievement final report executive summary.* Berkeley, CA: Center for Research on Education, Diversity, and Excellence. http://crede.berkeley.edu/research/crede/research/llaa/1.1_es.html.

Gersten, R., and S. Baker. 2000. What we know about effective instructional practices for English-language learners. *Exceptional Children* 66: 454–70.

Graves, A. W., R. Gersten, and D. Haager. 2004. Literacy instruction in multiple-language first-grade classrooms: Linking student outcomes to observed instructional practice. *Learning Disabilities Research & Practice* 19: 262–72.

Harris, T. 1994. Christine's inclusion: An example of peers supporting one another. In *Creativity and collaborative learning: The practical guide to empowering students, teachers, and families,* 2nd ed., ed. R. Villa, J. Thousand, and A. Nevin, 293–301. Baltimore: Paul H. Brookes.

Hunter, M. 1988. *Motivation theory for teachers.* El Segundo, CA: Theory Into Practice.

Hunter, M. 1994. *Enhancing teaching.* New York: Macmillan College.

Hunter, R., and M. Hunter. 2006. *Madeline Hunter's mastery teaching: Increasing instructional effectiveness in elementary and secondary schools.* Thousand Oaks, CA: Corwin.

Johnson, D. W., and F. F. Johnson. 2005. *Joining together: Group theory and group skills.* 9th ed. Needham Heights, MA: Allyn & Bacon.

Johnson, D. W., and R. T. Johnson. 1989. *Cooperation and competition: Theory and research.* Edina, MN: Interaction Book Company.

———. 2000. Cooperative learning, values, and culturally plural classrooms. In *Classroom issues: Practice, pedagogy, and curriculum,* vol. 3, ed. M. Leicester, S. Modgill, and C. Modgill, 15–29. London: Falmer Press.

———. 2002. Ensuring diversity is positive: Cooperative community, constructive conflict, and civic values. In *Creativity and collaborative learning: The practical guide to empowering students, teachers, and families,* 2nd ed., ed. J. Thousand, R. Villa, and A. Nevin, 197–208. Baltimore: Paul H. Brookes.

Johnson, D., R. Johnson, and E. Holubec. 1998. *Circles of learning: Cooperation in the classroom.* 6th ed. Edina, MN: Interaction Book Company.

Kluth, P., R. Diaz-Greenberg, J. Thousand, and A. Nevin. 2002. Teaching for liberation: Promising practices from critical pedagogy. In *Creativity and collaborative learning: The practical guide to empowering students, teachers, and families,* 2nd ed., ed. J. Thousand, R. Villa, and A. Nevin, 71–84. Baltimore: Paul H. Brookes.

Kourea, L., G. Cartledge, and S. Musti-Rao. 2007. Improving the reading skills of urban elementary students through total class peer tutoring. *Remedial and Special Education 28:* 95–107.

LaPlant, L., and N. Zane. 2002. Partner learning systems. In *Creativity and collaborative learning: The practical guide to empowering students, teachers, and families,* 2nd ed., ed. J. Thousand, R. Villa, and A. Nevin, 271–83. Baltimore: Paul H. Brookes.

Palinscar, A., and A. Brown. 1984. Reciprocal teaching of comprehension: Fostering and monitoring activities. *Cognition and Instruction 1:* 117–75.

Villa, R., and J. Thousand. 2005. *Creating an inclusive school.* 2nd ed. Alexandria, VA: Association for Supervision and Curriculum Development.

Villa, R., J. Thousand, and A. Nevin. 2010. *Collaborating with students in instruction and decision making: The untapped resource.* Thousand Oaks, CA: Corwin.

Walter, T. 1998. *Amazing English!* New York: Addison-Wesley.

■ PART IV: ADMINISTRATIVE SUPPORT AND PROFESSIONAL DEVELOPMENT

Chapter 10: Training and Logistical Administrative Support For Co-Teaching

Bauwens, J., and P. Mueller. 2000. Maximizing the mindware of human resources. In *Restructuring for caring and effective education: Piecing the puzzle together,* ed. R. Villa and J. Thousand, 328–59. Baltimore: Paul H. Brookes.

Cook, L. 2004. *Co-teaching: Principles, practices, and pragmatics.* Paper presented at the New Mexico Public Education Department Quarterly Special Education Meeting, Albuquerque.

Council for Exceptional Children. 2009. *What every special educator must know: The international standards for the preparation and certification of special education teachers.* 6th ed. Arlington, VA: Author.

Council of Chief State School Officers. 2011. *Interstate Teacher Assessment and Support Consortium (InTASC) model core teaching standards: A resource for state dialogue.* Washington, DC: Author.

Cramer, E., A. Nevin, J. Thousand, and A. Liston. 2006. *Co-teaching in urban school districts to meet the needs of all teachers and learners: Implications for teacher education reform.* Paper presented at the annual meeting of the American Association of Colleges for Teacher Education, San Diego. (ERIC Document Reproduction Service No. ED491651)

Friend, M. 1996. *The power of two: Making a difference through co-teaching.* VHS. Port Chester, NY: National Professional Resources.

Hall, G. E., and S. M. Hord. 2001. *Implementing change: Patterns, principles, and potholes.* Needham Heights, MA: Allyn & Bacon.

Johnson, D. W., and R. Johnson. 1999. *Learning together and alone: Cooperative, competitive, and individualistic learning.* Needham Heights, MA: Allyn & Bacon.

Johnson, D. W., and R. T. Johnson. 2009. An educational psychology success story: Social interdependence theory and cooperative learning. *Educational Researcher* 38(5): 365–79.

McLaughlin, M. W. 1991. The Rand change agent study: 10 years later. In *Education policy implementation,* ed. A. R. Odden, 143–56. Albany: State University of New York Press.

Thousand, J., and R. Villa. 2000. Collaborative teams: A powerful tool in school restructuring. In *Restructuring for caring and effective education: Piecing the puzzle together,* ed. R. Villa and J. Thousand, 254–91. Baltimore: Paul H. Brookes.

Thousand, J. S., R. A. Villa, and A. I. Nevin. 2006. What special education administrators need to know about co-teaching. *In CASE 43*(6): 2–3, 5.

———. 2007a. *Differentiating instruction: Collaborative planning and teaching for universally designed learning.* Thousand Oaks, CA: Corwin.

———. 2007b. *Differentiating instruction: Collaboratively planning and teaching for universally designed learning: A multimedia kit for professional development.* Thousand Oaks, CA: Corwin.

Tomlinson, C. 1999. *The differentiated classroom: Responding to the needs of all learners.* Alexandria, VA. Association for Supervision and Curriculum Development.

Udvari-Solner, A., R. Villa, and J. Thousand. 2002. Access to the general education curriculum for all: The universal design process. In *Creativity and collaborative learning: The practical guide to empowering students, teachers, and families.* 2nd ed., ed. J. Thousand, R. Villa, and A. Nevin, 85–103. Baltimore: Paul H. Brookes.

Villa, R. 2002a. *Collaborative planning: Transforming theory into practice.* VHS. Port Chester, NY: National Professional Resources.

———. 2002b. *Collaborative teaching: The co-teaching model.* VHS. Port Chester, NY: National Professional Resources.

Villa, R., and J. Thousand. 2004. *Creating an inclusive school.* 2nd ed. Alexandria, VA: Association for Supervision and Curriculum Development.

Villa, R., J. Thousand, and A. Nevin. 2008. *Facilitator's guide to* A guide to co-teaching: Practical tips for facilitating student learning: *A multimedia kit for professional development.* Thousand Oaks, CA: Corwin.

———. 2010a. *Collaborating with students in instruction and decision making: The untapped resource.* Thousand Oaks, CA: Corwin.

———. 2010b. Multimedia kit for *Collaborating with students in instruction and decision making: The untapped resource.* Thousand Oaks, CA: Corwin.

Chapter 11: Co-Teaching in Teacher Preparation Clinical Practice

Bacharach, N., T. Washut Heck, and K. Dahlberg. 2010. Changing the face of student teaching through co-teaching. *Action in Teacher Education 32*(1): 3–14.

California Commission on Teacher Credentialing. 2008. *Appendix A of the CalTPA Candidate Handbook.* Sacramento, CA: Author.

Darling-Hammond, L., and J. Bransford, Eds. 2005. *Preparing teachers for a changing world: What teachers should learn and be able to do.* San Francisco: Jossey-Bass.

Ellis, J., and D. Bogle. 2008. November. *Placement—An unforeseen casualty of No Child Left Behind.* Paper presented at Southeastern Regional Association of Teacher Educators, Myrtle Beach, SC.

Larson, W. C., and A. J. Goebel. 2008. Putting theory into practice: A professional development school/university co-teaching program. *Journal of the Scholarship of Teaching and Learning 8*(2): 52–61.

McGrath, M. 2012, February 18. Co-teaching pilot program helps prepare teachers of the future. *Ventura County Star.* Retrieved from http://www.vcstar.com/news/2012/feb/18/co-teaching-pilot-program-helps-prepare-teachers/

Murawski, W., and L. Dieker. 2004. Tips and strategies for co-teaching at the secondary level. *Teaching Exceptional Children 36*(5): 53–8.

Murawski, W. W., and W. W. Lochner. 2011. Observing co-teaching: What to ask for, look for, and listen for. *Intervention in School and Clinic 46*(3): 174–83.

National Council for Accreditation of Teacher Education. 2010, November. *Transforming teacher education through clinical practice: A national strategy to prepare effective teachers—Report of the Blue Ribbon Panel on clinical preparation and partnerships for improved student learning.* Washington, DC: Author.

Nevin, A., J. Cohen, L. Salazar, and D. Marshall. 2007, February. *Student teacher perspectives on inclusive education.* Paper presentation at the 59th annual meeting of the American Association of Colleges of Teacher Education, New York. ED 495705

Stall, P., J. Thousand, E. Garza, J. Robledo, and J. Rich. 2012, October. *Preparing teachers to navigate complexity through co-teaching in clinical practice: A research and practice forum.* Paper presented at California Council on Teacher Education Fall Conference, San Diego, CA.

Stall, P., J. Thousand, E. Garza, J. Robledo, and J. Rich. 2013, February. *Enhancing district partnerships through co-teaching in clinical practice.* Paper presented at the 65th annual meeting of the American Association of Colleges of Teacher Education, Orlando, FL.

Swain, K. D., P. D. Nordness, and E. M. Leader-Janssen. 2012. Changes in preservice teacher attitudes toward inclusion. *Preventing School Failure 56*(2): 75–81.

Thousand, J. 2012. *Co-teaching to close the gap—Co-teaching to enhance teacher preparation clinical practice and close the achievement gap.* San Marcos, CA: CSU San Marcos, Distinguished Teacher in Residence Assigned Time Report.

Villa, R. A., J. S. Thousand, and A. I. Nevin. 2010. *Collaborating with students in instruction and decision making: The untapped resource.* Thousand Oaks, CA: Corwin.

Villa, R. A., and J. S. Thousand. 2011. *RTI: Co-teaching and differentiated instruction—The schoolhouse model.* Port Chester, NY: National Professional Resources, Inc.

Chapter 12: Meshing Planning With Co-Teaching

Raywid, M. A. 1993. Finding time for collaboration. *Educational Leadership 51*(1): 30–4.

Thousand, J., A. Liston, and A. Nevin. 2006. *Differentiating instruction in inclusive classrooms: Myth or reality? (A lesson plan and process for using principles of universal design).* Paper presented at the annual conference of Teacher Education Division, Council for Exceptional Children, San Diego, CA. (ERIC Document Reproduction Service No. ED493953)

Thousand, J., and R. Villa. 2000. Collaborative teams: A powerful tool in school restructuring. In *Restructuring for caring and effective education: Piecing the puzzle together,* ed. R. Villa and J. Thousand, 254–91. Baltimore: Paul H. Brookes.

Chapter 13: From Surviving to Thriving: Tips for Getting Along With Your Co-Teachers

Bradley, D., J. Pauley, and J. Pauley. 2006. *Effective classroom management: Six keys to success.* Lanham, MD: Rowman & Littlefield.

Brokenleg, M. 1998. Native wisdom on belonging. *Reclaiming Children and Youth* 7(3): 130–33.

Daunic, A., V. Correa, and M. Reyes-Blanes. 2004. Teacher preparation for culturally diverse classrooms: Performance-based assessment of beginning teachers. *Teacher Education and Special Education, 27:* 105–18.

Davis, J. 2008. *School enrollment in the United Statess: 2008—Population characteristics.* Washington DC: U.S. Census Bureau. Retrieved October 23, 2012, from http://www.census.gov/prod/2011pubs/p20–564.pdf

Glasser, W. 1999. *Choice theory: A new psychology of personal freedom.* New York: Perennial.

Gudwin, D., and M. Salazar-Wallace. 2009. *Mentoring and coaching: A lifeline for teachers in a multicultural setting.* Thousand Oaks, CA: Corwin.

Johnson, D., and R. Johnson. 1988. *Advanced cooperative learning.* Edina, MN: Interaction Book Company.

———. 1991. *Teaching children to be peacemakers.* Edina, MN: Interaction Book Company.

Kahler, T. 1982. *Process communication model: A contemporary model for organizational development.* Little Rock, AR: Kahler Communications.

Keefe, E. B., V. M. Moore, and F. R. Duff. 2004. The four "knows" of collaborative teaching. *Teaching Exceptional Children* 36(5): 36–42.

Nevin, A., K. Harris, and V. Correa. 2001. Collaborative consultation, school reform, and diversity among regular and special educators. In *Special education, multicultural education, and school reform: Components of a quality education for students with mild disabilities,* ed. C. A. Utley and F. E. Obiakor, 173–87. New York: Charles C. Thomas.

Paige, R. 2004. *A guide to education and No Child Left Behind.* Washington, DC: Department of Education, Office of the Secretary, Office of Public Affairs.

Pauley, J., D. Bradley, and J. Pauley. 2002. *Here's how to reach me: Matching instruction to personality types in your classroom.* Baltimore, MD: Paul H. Brookes.

Pauley, J. A., and J. F. Pauley. 2009. *Communication: The key to effective leadership.* Milwaukee: WI: AQS Quality Press.

Santamaria, L. 2009. Culturally responsive differentiated instruction: Narrowing gaps between best pedagogical practices benefiting all learners. *Teachers College Record* 111(1): 214–47.

Schrumpf, F., and G. Jansen. 2002. The role of students in resolving conflicts. In *Creativity and collaborative learning: The practical guide to empowering students, teachers, and families,* 2nd ed., ed. R. Villa, J. Thousand, and A. Nevin, 283–302. Baltimore: Paul H. Brookes.

Steinberg, S. (Ed.). 2009. *Diversity and multiculturalism A reader:* New York: Peter Lang.

U.S. Department of Education. 2001. *Archived information: Appendix A: Data tables.* http://www2.ed.gov/about/reports/annual/osep/2001/appendix-a-pt1.pdf.

Villa, R., J. Thousand, and A. Nevin. 1999. Eight habits of highly effective collaborators. *Missouri Educational Leadership* 9(2): 25–29.

Wenger, K., T. Lubbes, M. Lazo, I. Azcarraga, S. Sharp, and G. Ernst-Slavit. 2004. Hidden teachers, invisible students: Lessons learned from exemplary bilingual paraprofessionals in secondary schools. *Teacher Education Quarterly* 31(2); 89–111.

Chapter 14: Developing a Shared Voice Through Co-Teaching

Thousand, J. S., R. A. Villa, and A. I. Nevin. 2007. *Differentiating instruction: Collaborative planning and teaching for universally designed learning.* Thousand Oaks, CA: Corwin.

■ GLOSSARY

Gardner, H. 1983. *Frames of mind: The theory of multiple intelligences.* New York: Basic Books.

———. 1997. Are there additional intelligences? The case of naturalistic, spiritual, and existential intelligences. In *Education, information, and transformation,* ed. J. Kane, 135–52. Upper Saddle River, NJ: Prentice Hall.

Goode, T., and V. Jackson. 2003. *Getting started . . . and moving on . . . Planning, implementing and evaluating culturally & linguistically competent systems of care for children and youth needing mental health services and their families.* Washington, DC: National Center for Cultural Competence, Georgetown University Center for Child and Human Development.

Graner, P., M. Faggella-Luby, and N. Fritschmann. 2005. An overview of responsiveness to intervention: What practitioners ought to know. *Topics in Language Disorders 25*(2): 93–105.

Hall, T. 2002. Differentiated instruction. CAST: National Center on Accessing the General Curriculum: *Effective classroom practices report.* Retrieved August 26, 2006, http://www.cast.org/ncac/index.cfm?i=2876

Kahler, T. 1982. *Process communication model: A contemporary model for organizational development.* Little Rock, AR: Kahler Communications.

Pauley, J., D. Bradley, and J. Pauley. 2002. *Here's how to reach me: Matching instruction to personality types in your classroom.* Baltimore, MD: Paul H. Brookes.

Pauley, J. A., and J. Pauley. 2002. *Here's how to reach me: Matching instruction to personality types in your classroom.* Baltimore, MD: Paul H. Brookes.

Vygotsky, L. 1987. *The collected works of L. S. Vygotsky* (R. W. Rieber and A. S. Carton, Trans.). New York: Plenum Press. (Original Works Published 1934, 1960).

Wood, P. 2011, May 23. The core between the states. *Chronicle of Higher Education.* Retrieved June 15, 2012, from http://chronicle.com/blogs/innovations/the-core-between-the-states/29511

Photo Credits

Index